The *Star* for Beginners

Introductions to the Magnum Opus of Franz Rosenzweig

Edited by
Martin Brasser, Petar Bojanić
and Francesco Paolo Ciglia

]u[

ubiquity press
London

Ubiquity Press Ltd.
Unit 322–323
Whitechapel Technology Centre
75 Whitechapel Road
London E1 1DU
www.ubiquitypress.com

Text © Martin Brasser, Petar Bojanić and Francesco Paolo Ciglia 2021

First published 2021

Cover design by Mattin Delavar, Ubiquity Press

Print and digital versions typeset by Siliconchips Services Ltd.

ISBN (Paperback): 978-1-914481-08-6
ISBN (PDF): 978-1-914481-09-3
ISBN (EPUB): 978-1-914481-10-9
ISBN (Mobi): 978-1-914481-11-6

DOI: https://doi.org/10.5334/bco

This work is licensed under the Creative Commons Attribution 4.0 International License (unless stated otherwise within the content of the work). To view a copy of this license, visit http://creativecommons.org/licenses/by/4.0/ or send a letter to Creative Commons, 444 Castro Street, Suite 900, Mountain View, California, 94041, USA. This license allows for copying any part of the work for personal and commercial use, providing author attribution is clearly stated.

The full text of this book has been peer-reviewed to ensure high academic standards. For full review policies, see http://www.ubiquitypress.com/

Suggested citation:
Brasser, M., Bojanić, P. and Ciglia, F. P. (eds.) 2021. *The Star for Beginners: Introductions to the Magnum Opus of Franz Rosenzweig*. London: Ubiquity Press. DOI: https://doi.org/10.5334/bco. License: CC-BY

To read the free, open access version of this book online, visit https://doi.org/10.5334/bco or scan this QR code with your mobile device:

Wohinaus aber öffnen sich die Flügel des Tors? Du weißt es nicht?
INS LEBEN.
(Franz Rosenzweig, Stern der Erlösung 472)

Inhalt / Contents

Siglenverzeichnis / Abbreviations	vii
Einleitung / Introduction	**1**
Introduction I *Martin Brasser, Petar Bojanić, Francesco Paolo Ciglia*	3
Introduction II Viewing Rosenzweig from a Jewish Perspective. A Master of Return *Norbert Samuelson*	5
Kommentare / Commentaries	**7**
Erster Teil. Die Elemente oder die immerwährende Vorwelt / Part One. The Elements, or the Everlasting Fore-World	**9**
Première partie, introduction: De la possibilité de connaître le Tout *Gérard Bensussan*	11
Part One, Book One: God and his Being, or Metaphysics *Paolo Francesco Ciglia*	23
Erster Teil, zweites Buch: Die Welt und ihr Sinn oder Metalogik *Emanuele Pompetti*	41
Erster Teil, drittes Buch: Der Mensch und sein Selbst oder Metaethik *und* Übergang *Martin Brasser*	55
Zweiter Teil. Die Bahn oder die allzeiterneuerte Welt / Part Two. The Course, or the Always-Renewed World	**69**
Part Two, Introduction: The Renewal of the Miracle *Yehoyada Amir*	71
Part Two, Book One: Creation, or the Everlasting Ground of Things *Jules Simon*	83

Zweiter Teil, zweites Buch: Offenbarung oder die allzeiterneuerte
Geburt der Seele   99
Gesine Palmer

Zweiter Teil, drittes Buch: Erlösung oder die ewige Zukunft des
Reichs *und* Schwelle   113
Renate Schindler

**Dritter Teil. Die Gestalt oder die ewige Überwelt /
Part Three. The Structure, or the Eternal Over-World**   131

Part Three, Introduction: On the Possibility of Entreating
the Kingdom   133
Gabriela Caponigro

Part Three, Book One: The Fire or The Eternal Life   145
Petar Bojanić

Part Three, Book Two: The Rays or the Eternal Way   159
Ephraim Meir

Dritter Teil, drittes Buch: Der Stern oder die ewige
Wahrheit *und* Tor   167
Caspar Battegay

Autoren / Contributors   185

Der Prozess der Peer-Reviews / The Peer Review Process   191

Danksagung / Aknowledgments   193

Index   195

Siglenverzeichnis / Abbreviations

GS = *Gesammelte Schriften*, 4 volumes, Dordrecht / The Hague, 1976–1984

GS I (or GS 1) = *Briefe und Tagebücher*, 2 Bände, hg. von Rachel Rosenzweig und Edith Rosenzweig-Scheinmann, unter Mitwirkung von Bernhard Casper, The Hague 1979

GS II (or GS 2) = *Der Stern der Erlösung*, Hinweise und Verzeichnisse von Annemarie Mayer, 4. Auflage im Jahre der Schöpfung 536 mit einer Einführung von Reinhold Mayer, The Hague 1976

GS III (or GS 3) = *Zweistromland. Kleinere Schriften zu Glauben und Denken*, hg. von Reinhold und Annemarie Mayer, The Hague 1984

GS IV.1 (or GS 4.1) = *Sprachdenken [im Übersetzen]. Fünfundneunzig Hymnen und Gedichte: dt. und hebr. / Jehuda Halevi; mit einem Vorwort und mit Anmerkungen: Franz Rosenzweig – die sechzig Hymnen und Gedichte*, 3. Ausgabe hg. von Rafael N. Rosenzweig, The Hague 1983

GS IV.2 (or GS 4.2) = *Sprachdenken [im Übersetzen]. Arbeitspapiere zur Verdeutschung der Schrift*, hg. von Rachel Bat-Adam, The Hague 1984

SE = *Der Stern der Erlösung*, either cited by GS II or by the following edition: Bibliothek Suhrkamp, Bd 973, mit einer Einführung von Reinhold Mayer und einer Gedenkrede von Gershom Sholem, Frankfurt a.M., various editions since 1988 [online-version: https://freidok.uni-freiburg.de/fedora/objects/freidok:310/datastreams/FILE1/content]

[Digitalisat der ersten Auflage von 1921 hier: http://sammlungen.ub.uni-frank furt.de/freimann/content/titleinfo/596291]

HuS = *Hegel und der Staat*, München 1920 or edited in the series Suhrkamp Taschenbuch Wissenschaft no 1941 by Frank Lachmann, Berlin 2010

BGK = *Das Büchlein vom Gesunden und Kranken Menschenverstand*, hg. und eingeleitet von Nahum Glatzer, Frankfurt a.M. 1992

GB = *Die "Gritli"-Briefe – Briefe an Margrit Rosenstock-Huessy*, hg. von Inken Rühle und Reinhold Mayer, mit einem Vorwort von Raphael Rosenzweig, Tübingen 2002 [online-version: http://www.erhfund.org/the-gritli-letters-gritli -briefe/]

Zweistromland = *Zweistromland. Kleinere Schriften zu Religion und Philosophie*, hg. und mit einem Nachwort versehen von Gesine Palmer, Berlin 2001

SH = *Star of Redemption*, translated from the second edition of 1930 by William W. Hallo, London 1971

SG = *Star of Redemption*, in translation by Barbara E. Galli, Madison (Wis.) 2005

JL = *On Jewish Learning*, edited by N.N. Glatzer, 1955

CW = *Cultural Writings of Franz Rosenzweig*, edited and translated by Barbara E. Galli, with a Forward by Leora Batnitzky, Library of Jewish Philosophy, Syracuse N.Y. 2000

NT = *Franz Rosenzweig's The New Thinking*, edited by and translated from the German by Ulan Udoff and Barbara E. Galli, Syracuse N.Y. 1999

GMW = *God, Man, and the World: Lectures and Essays of Franz Rosenzweig*, edited and translated by Barbara E. Galli, Syracuse N.Y. 1998

USH = *Understanding the Sick and the Healthy: A View of World, Man, and God*, with a new introduction by Hilary Putnam, originally edited by N.N. Glatzer, New York 1953, and published in Cambridge (Mass.) 1999

PWT = *Philosophical and Theological Writings*, edited by Paul W. Franks and Michael L. Morgan, Indianapolis 2000

Further writings of Rosenzweig (which are not used in these commentaries):

Feldpostbriefe. Die Korrespondenz mit den Eltern (1914–1917), edited by Wolfgang Herzfeld, Freiburg Alber Verlag 2013

Franz Rosenzweigs Jugendschriften (1907–1914), edited by Wolfgang Herzfeld,

Teil 1 – Kant, Hamburg Verlag Dr. Kovac 2015

Teil II – Hegel, Hamburg Verlag Dr. Kovac 2015

Teil III – Schriften zu Geschichte und Kultur, Hamburg Verlag Dr. Kovac 2017

Einleitung / Introduction

Introduction I

Martin Brasser, Petar Bojanić and Francesco Paolo Ciglia

Unteroffizier Franz Rosenzweig began writing *Star of Redemption* toward the end of the First World War, on the Macedonian front, on August 22, 1918. Having contracted malaria shortly thereafter, he worked on his text in various hospitals, as the German army retreated in defeat. The thirty-year old Rosenzweig partially wrote the book in an army hospital in Belgrade, which he entered on September 25, 1918. Much later, on June 4–5, 2012, the same city hosted an International Conference, *Rosenzweig für Anfänger / Rosenzweig for Beginners* at the Institute for Philosophy and Social Theory, at which the majority of texts in this volume were initially presented. The book that came about in the midst of the First World War opposed above all abstract philosophy as such and classical German Idealism, but also served to deconstruct "Rosenzweig the philosopher" and create a "New Thinking," as well as a Jewish Philosophy.

On August 27, 1918 Rosenzweig writes to Gertrud Oppenheim:

> "(...) I am deeply involved in developing my letter (of November 1917) to Rudi (Rudolf Ehrenberg) into a book. It's going to be quite fantastic, entirely unpublishable, equally scandalous to "Christians, Jews, and heathens" – but I'll learn what I need to learn in the process, and that's enough. For the present... the introduction. I'll probably write to you again tomorrow. I just noticed that I am sending you this insolent announcement of my system on Hegel's birthday. It's a pity about him! Only Nietzsche (and Kant) pass muster!"

How to cite this book chapter:
Brasser, M., Bojanić, P. and Ciglia, F. P. 2021. Introduction I. In: Brasser, M., Bojanić, P. and Ciglia, F. P. (eds.) *The Star for Beginners: Introductions to the Magnum Opus of Franz Rosenzweig*. Pp. 3–4. London: Ubiquity Press. DOI: https://doi.org/10.5334/bco.a. License: CC-BY

This was a book written in dire circumstances, with the first two sections scrawled on army postcards. After Belgrade and Kassel, Rosenzweig continued writing it in Berlin where he completed it on February 16, 1919. Even though some friends and Christian cousins tried to convince him to publish it in some Christian publishing house, he refused resolutely, setting himself the fundamental task of preparing and publishing the text in Hebrew. A one-volume edition of *Der Stern der Erlösung* came out in 1921 from the Frankfurt publisher Verlag Kauffmann, with a three-volume second edition put out by Schocken, Berlin in 1930.

In 1976, Stern appeared in Rosenzweig's Gesammelte Schriften and since 1988 as a single edition in the Suhrkamp Library (11th edition 2018). A digital scan of this has been publicly available on the server of the University Library of Freiburg since 2002, and since 2009 the digital copy of the first edition from 1921 can be accessed via the University Library of Frankfurt am Main. Since 2014, a team of researchers has been working on the development of an online platform for collaboratively annotating the Star of Redemption in the spirit of the Digital Humanities. The prototype of this platform is already accessible and usable at https://www.annotatedstar.org.

These stages of the publication history show: Rosenzweig's assessment that the Star could not be published was – fortunately – a touch too skeptical. Behind Rosenzweig's assessment was probably the fear that the book would not find its readers because its thoughts and arguments were so difficult to grasp and comprehend. In any case, shortly after the publication of Stern, Rosenzweig was clearly more optimistic about the mark it would leave. In January 1923, he wrote in a letter to Rudolf Hallo: "Our work will be honored to us by Germany at most posthumously..." (GS I, 887). As far as the reception of the Star of Redemption is concerned, this assessment has indeed proved to be correct. After an initially hesitant reception, the Star is still today, and today perhaps more than ever, intensively read, discussed, received, critically questioned, and thought about further. What has remained is that Rosenzweig's argumentation is demanding and difficult – for professionals in philosophy and theology as well as for everyone who simply out of interest in religion and faith wants to find inspiration in the Star of Redemption.

The following introductions are intended for this interest. Each book of the Star of Redemption is treated individually and its argumentation is reconstructed step by step. The authors elaborate the central patterns of argumentation on which Rosenzweig's train of thought is built. The introductions allow those who wish to read The Star of Redemption to see the "big picture" in each chapter. On this basis, reading "en detail" can then bring further inspiration.

The editors
Martin Brasser, Petar Bojanić, Francesco Paolo Ciglia

Introduction II: Viewing Rosenzweig from a Jewish Perspective. A Master of Return

Norbert Samuelson

In many respects Franz Rosenzweig is the antithesis of Baruch Spinoza. First, these two philosophers live at different ends of the so-called "modern" age of Jewish philosophy. Spinoza, trained in pre-modern Jewish texts, advocates all of the major values of enlightenment Humanism. The key topics of Jewish belief are reconstructed in the light of Cartesian values in sharp criticism of his inherited Maimonidean interpretations of rabbinic philosophy. Spinoza is in every sense of the phrase the first Jewish modern philosophy. His very heterodoxy is inherently modern. In contrast, Rosenzweig, trained as a modern German intellectual in the most modern and German of philosophers, George Wilhelm Friedrich Hegel, turns against that tradition to devote his life to recapturing traditional Jewish values. He does so both in his writings, especially in his magnum opus, *The Star of Redemption*, a word painting of all of human history which functions for him as a prolegomena for the direction of his life, viz. to being a teacher of Jewish adults in a school (the Lehrhaus) whose most fundamental commitment was to bring back Jews from the "enlightenment" (Aufklärung) of the newly emerged German civilization of a post-enlightenment, rooted-in-rabbinic-tradition

---

How to cite this book chapter:
Samuelson, N. 2021. Introduction II: Viewing Rosenzweig from a Jewish Perspective. A Master of Return. In: Brasser, M., Bojanić, P. and Ciglia, F. P. (eds.) The Star *for Beginners: Introductions to the Magnum Opus of Franz Rosenzweig*. Pp. 5–6. London: Ubiquity Press. DOI: https://doi.org/10.5334/bco.b. License: CC-BY

Jewish civilization. As Emil Fackenheim said[1], the new modern world gave Jews, at least intellectually, the option of living as a modern or as a Jew. Spinoza showed these Jews how they could become human, while Rosenzweig showed these humans how they could become once again Jews. Together, Spinoza and Rosenzweig, mark the bookends of modern Jewish civilization, from the Jews who learn to be modern to the moderns who learn how to be Jewish.[2]

Second, the directions of their intellectual and spiritual lives are opposed. Spinoza begins his youthful education at home in his synagogue in Amsterdam as a spiritually committed Jew, who learns the Hebrew Scriptures as well as rabbinics, medieval Jewish philosophy, and Kabbalah.[3] But he also begins to learn modern Western European philosophy and science, not least of all Descartes and Hobbes. In the course of these studies Spinoza is transformed spiritually. It is not that he ever chooses to become "spiritual". Rather what changes is the direction that the spirituality takes, as he grows from a quiet youth absorbed with his community and teachers in rabbinic texts that claim to express the will of God into a quiet adult, absorbed with his friends in the new sciences (especially optics) and their related works in modern philosophy.

Rosenzweig moves in the opposite direction. His light is at first the light of Hegelian reason, but with time, thought, and conversations with his circle of extended family friends, he moves into a new spiritual light of revelation. His magnum opus, *The Star of Redemption*, is literally a vision of everything, and as such it appears to be an excessively objective, universalistic, picture. But his universe is a universe that is constantly in motion, and that motion – from its beginning to its end – maps out his own personal religious-philosophical movement from the history of German philosophy (from Plato through Aristotle, the scholastics, to Hegel and beyond to at least Nietzsche) into a recovery of rabbinic faith (from the Hebrew Scriptures through at least Moses Maimonides, Judah Halevi, and, most importantly, Hermann Cohen).

---

[1] In Emil Fackenheim, To Mend the World: Foundations of Future Jewish Thought. Part II, The Problematics of Contemporary Jewish Thought: From Spinoza Beyond Rosenzweig, New York 1982, 31–101.

[2] See Norbert Samuelson, Jewish Philosophy: An Historical Introduction, London and New York 2003; Revelation and the God of Israel, Cambridge 2002; An Introduction to Modern Jewish Philosophy, Albany 1989.

[3] Little research has been done on what the youthful Spinoza read and studied as a Jew. The best work remains Harry A. Wolfson's *The Philosophy of Spinoza: Unfolding the Latent Processes of His Reasoning* (Cambridge, MA, 1934). Wolfson constructs a hypothesis of what Spinoza would have needed to know in Jewish philosophy at least to believe what he wrote he believed. Whatever Wolfson says, it has to at least be modified by what Yermiyahu Yovel, in *Spinoza and Other Heretics* (Princeton, 1989), has shown about the heretical nature of Spinoza's Jewish education, for he learned his rabbinic philosophical wisdom through the lenses of his Spanish born, "converso" teachers whose ideas of what Jewish tradition taught was anything but what any Ashkenazi (European) rabbinic philosophers would call "orthodox".

Kommentare / Commentaries

Erster Teil. Die Elemente Oder Die Immerwährende Vorwelt

/

Part One. The Elements, Or The Everlasting Fore-World

Première partie, introduction: De la possibilité de connaître le Tout

Gérard Bensussan

Le commentaire de cette l'*Einleitung* du *Stern*, vingt pages dans l'édition de référence[4], fera ici l'objet d'une lecture « carrée ». « Carrée » signifie exactement cadrée entre *les quatre coins* que l'on peut discerner dans ce texte.

Les deux premiers sont opératifs (car ils commandent le Bris) :

–le Tout comme mensonge ;
–l'angoisse de mort comme vérité.

Les deux derniers sont constructifs (car ils commandent l'horizon de la Pensée Nouvelle) :

–la métaphore de la fresque et du tableau ;
–le maintien (*Bewahrung*) et l'avération (*Bewährung*).

Notre commentaire les emmêlera afin de restituer le tissu singulier et précis de l'*Einleitung*.

---

[4] GS II.

1. Le Tout comme mensonge[5]

Principe de départ et salubrité de la pensée : il convient de ne pas « être dupe » de la philosophie (S.4), selon une expression d'Emmanuel Levinas, et, surtout, de « son idée du Tout » dont la brume bleue et métaphysique enveloppe le terrestre, l'immanent, le matériel. Contre le « coucouville-les-nuées » (Aristophane) et les vapeurs de la philosophie, Rosenzweig s'affirme sans hésiter « matérialiste »[6] et associe son matérialisme à la révélation: « la révélation sauve la matière de la décomposition (*Zersetzung*) que lui impose l'idéalisme autant que le paganisme, elle lui redonne ses droits contre l'esprit, en-dedans de l'esprit, à l'âme contre l'esprit, et encore au temps contre l'atemporalité, à l'espace contre le concept, etc. [....] A propos de la « chair » : quelle force d'*effectivité* par rapport à Platon ! »[7]. Ce *matérialisme de la révélation* se déploie dès l'entrée en scène de la philosophie dans les premières pages du *Stern* selon un argument implacable et lapidaire. Premièrement, il convient de sérieusement méditer le statut traditionnel de « pensée de la connaissance une et universelle du Tout » de la philosophie (*das eine und allgemeine Erkennen des All*, 5) –tel est d'ailleurs le titre de l'*Einleitung* dans son ensemble, « *Über die Möglichkeit, das All zu erkennen* ». Cette tradition prévaut de Thalès ou Parménide à Hegel : le Tout sera déterminé en tant qu'il se comprend lui-même « sans reste » (*restlos*, 6). C'est évidemment Hegel, en tant qu'il achève et accomplit ce statut gnoséologique, qu'il s'agit ici de pleinement com-prendre pour mieux le déstructurer. Selon lui, l'autoprésentation de la pensée comme pensée du Tout s'incluant elle-même dans son automouvement systématisé va jusqu'à inclure la Révélation, en tant que représentation, dans le Tout de l'automouvement du concept. C'est cette circularité qui emporte la conclusion selon laquelle il faut tenir ce Tout pour un « mensonge », comme le mensonge de tous les mensonges (*Lüge, Lügen*, 5).

Pourquoi? Le présupposé réductible à la vieille proposition parménidienne, « être et penser, c'est le même », a l'avantage de défaire d'emblée toute contre-proposition au nom de l'impossibilité pour le « sujet Tout » (*Subjekt Alles*, 13) de ne pas recevoir un prédicat parfaitement univoque (*ein eindeutiges Prädikat*, 13). : « une révolte contre la totalité du monde signifierait une négation de l'unité de la pensée » (*ein Aufstand gegen die Allheit der Welt (bedeutet) zugleich eine Leugnung der Einheit des Denkens*, 13). Autour de cet argument-massue, le gant est jeté à l'honorable confrérie des enfants de Parménide, de l'Ionie à Iéna (13). C'est en quelque sorte l'infalsibilité du présupposé qui en signale le « mensonge ». Au fond, le vrai, c'est bel et bien le Tout. Et ce constat (qui emporte un *Aufstand* !) est consacré et définitivement sanctionné par Hegel, lequel montre que le Tout, c'est son mouvement même, le Tout qui ne cesse jamais de se totaliser. L'*Einleitung* comporte une petite esquisse d'histoire

---

[5] Ibid., 5. Dans la suite, la pagination du *Stern* est intégrée au texte.
[6] « Ich als Materialist », in GS I, 843.
[7] GS I, 559.

de la philosophie qui aboutit à la philosophie de « notre temps » (*unsere Zeit*, 13). Cette philosophie de notre temps, Rosenzweig l'appelle, ailleurs, dans une lettre du 5 septembre 1916 à E. Rosenstock [8], philosophie de la « forme du monde », c'est-à-dire de la contingence pure et simple, du *nun einmal so sein* du monde. Le mensonge, c'est donc d'abord l'*Unwahr* du Tout qui annule cette contingence et se constitue en piège logique : la pensée doit prendre garde à ne pas s'y laisser enfermer si elle veut demeurer ce que Rosenzweig nomme notre « patrie » (*Heimat*, 15). Il y faut l'invention d'une figure concurrente du Tout omni-englobant (*allumschliessend*, 14). Cette figure, que Rosenzweig appelle dans l'*Einleitung* le Tout excluant (*ausschliessend*, 14), permettrait de laisser jouer l'imbrication des multiplicités Dieu Monde Homme pour déjouer l'engrenage fatal du Tout. Il ne s'agit pas d'une autre figure du Tout, d'un autre Tout, mais véritablement d'un infini non clos, d'une unicité expressive où s'articulent infiniment des multiplicités qu'on peut bien appeler des « touts », comme les tableaux ou les images de notre pensée, inégaux, discontinus, figurés, fragmentés, disposés sur un mur nu, indéterminé et matériel, où ils seraient suspendus.

2. La fresque et le tableau (14)

Pour Rosenzweig, tout se serait passé dans l'histoire de la métaphysique, de l'Ionie à Iéna, comme si le mur avait toujours été peint à fresques (*al fresco*). L'être (le mur) et la pensée (l'image, le tableau : suspendus ? dessinés ?) font Un, au sens le plus fort. On ne pourrait même pas les distinguer. Tel est le tout incluant, inclusif (*ein allumschliessendes All*, 14) : en fait *tout un univers*. On pourrait même dire qu'on a à faire, avec l'idéalisme, en fait d'univers, à un véritable *trompe-l'œil*. On connaît l'anecdote rapportée par Pline l'Ancien : Zeuxis avait peint des raisins tellement parfaits que des oiseaux, trompés par une exécution si fidèle, se seraient jetés sur eux pour les consommer. Voilà bien l'idéalisme : il nous donne l'illusion de l'unité, illusion bienfaisante, consolante, esthétiquement aussi gratifiante qu'une belle fresque ou qu'un magnifique trompe-l'œil. Et cette jouissance ne cesse nullement avec le savoir de l'illusion comme illusion. Peut-être même s'accroît-elle encore par ce biais pervers.

Telle a longtemps été la situation historique de la pensée en Occident. Désormais au contraire, nous dit Rosenzweig, il faut tenir l'image, le tableau suspendu au mur, c'est-à-dire tel ou tel tableau, telle ou telle image, donc une singularité, pour un « tout excluant », une unicité incluse (*ein eingeschlossenes Eins*, 14). Ceci requiert que soit pensé un rapport multiversel entre un support et une multiplicité infinie en droit. La pensée (le tableau dans la métaphore rosenzweigienne) n'est pas le moins du monde niée ou méprisée. Au contraire, elle est exhaussée dans sa singularité, dans le « point de vue » qu'elle propose dans les modes de philosopher « après Hegel » (117). Cette expression, le « point de

---

[8] GS I, 222.

vue », les « philosophes du point de vue », convient particulièrement et elle entre en congruence avec la métaphore de la fresque et de l'image. Un tableau ouvre une vue, il détache une vision dans le mur lui-même, à même son uniformité. Ce qui s'engage nécessairement dans la distinction entre le mur et l'image qui y est accrochée (et qu'on peut décrocher), c'est l'exploration du rapport entre une unité et une multiplicité, entre une unité elle-même disséminée (ou cassée en trois « unités » Dieu Monde Homme) et une infinité de « patries », c'est-à-dire d'images à chaque fois uniques et valant pour elles-mêmes de mille façons. Il s'agit donc, et tel est l'effet de la métaphore de la fresque et du tableau, de travailler à dégager les pensées ou les œuvres de toute totalisation, de toute universalisation, de toute contextualisation –pour les restituer à leur unicité inclusive et donc, par là même, exclusive.

Il y a toujours un au-delà du tableau : c'est le mur. Mais cet au-delà n'en supprime nullement l'unicité. Il en forme bien plutôt la condition. Les rapports entre les deux, le mur et les images, relèvent alors d'une attention philosophique continue à la multiplicité inenglobable, aux restes de la totalisation du tout, à la non-identité originaire sur laquelle Rosenzweig insiste beaucoup dans ces pages (*eine innere Nichtidentität*, 14).

Au piège *logique* du Tout, soit à la confusion (*Verwechslung*, 17) entre le mur et le tableau qui est à « craindre » (*fürchten*), à son caractère de mensonge en trompe l'oeil, s'ajoute une autre détermination, un autre aspect du mensonge. Le mensonge du Tout est également, et même foncièrement, mensonger du point de vue moral, ou, beaucoup plus précisément, *du point de vue de l'existence*. Le Tout est mensonger parce qu'il dénie la finitude de l'existence, l'angoisse de mort des sujets mortels. Dans le Tout, rien ne meurt, un Tout, ça ne meurt pas (*ein All würde nicht sterben und im All stürbe nichts*, 4), c'est sa fonction la plus évidente, sa force d'illusion vitale. Le trompe-l'œil est aussi un trompe-la-mort. Il y a une sorte de jeu redoutable et funeste entre le Tout et le Rien. Le tout « apaise » (*beruhigt*) et le rien est « paresseux » (*träge*)[9]. A la connaissance universelle du Tout et du Néant universels, Rosenzweig n'a cessé d'opposer une véritable philosophie du Quelque-Chose, non seulement dans les passages bien connus de l'*Etoile*, mais aussi dans toutes sortes de notations dont fourmille en particulier sa *Correspondance*, par exemple à propos de choses très empiriques et contingentes, le respect des *mitzvot* ou encore l'observance du *chabbat*[10]. Quelque chose, faire quelque chose, est toujours préférable à la ruineuse alternative du tout ou rien, à condition de ne pas négliger son absoluité : le quelque-chose est radicalement distinct d'un quelconque « juste-milieu ».

---

[9] Lettre à R. Hallo du 27 mars 1922, GS I, 763.
[10] Ibid., 886. Rosenzweig conseille à Hallo, qui se demande s'il doit et ce qu'il doit faire pour observer le *chabbat*, d'inviter au moins quelques amis le vendredi soir, ce qui serait déjà *quelque chose*.

3. L'angoisse de mort comme « vérité »

Le quelque-chose qui fait exception au Tout et au Rien, c'est le quelque-chose qui *meurt*. C'est par sa mort, qui n'est pas Rien, qui enlève Tout, que le sujet existant, le *Dasein* créé est ce qu'il est. Son quelque chose d'irréductible, c'est sa peur de la mort. Cela, la philosophie, l'idéalisme, le nie. Et la voie royale de cette négation, c'est le Tout. Il y a bien sûr un bénéfice secondaire de cette crainte niée, de cette angoisse subsumée dans une totalité où elle prend « place » (comme si la mort et la peur de la mort pouvaient se tenir à une place à côté d'une autre place !). Avant de statuer sur ce bénéfice secondaire, à savoir l'*Erkennen*, il faut s'arrêter sur ce qu'on pourrait appeler *l'effet de vérité* de la mort, premier mot de l'arc qui se clôt « sur la vie », à la toute fin de l'œuvre, via « l'amour », arc métaphysique ou contre-métaphysique de la mort et de l'amour, où s'entrevoit peut-être une réminiscence de Schopenhauer –pour des conclusions radicalement opposées à celle du *Welt als Wille und Vorstellung*. Cet effet de vérité est d'abord un effet de choc. Celui-ci, très notable dans les premières pages, est sans doute calculé, selon une rhétorique, c'est-à-dire une stratégie discursive, qui peut faire penser au *Sermon sur la mort* de Bossuet sous la rubrique « ouvrir un tombeau ». Ajoutons que la comparaison s'arrête là. Pour Bossuet en effet, l'homme, « en tant qu'il passe », est « méprisable » et, à ce titre, l'auteur du *Sermon sur la mort* fait partie de l'honorable confrérie de ceux, philosophes d'une part, théologiens de l'autre, qui distillent leur brume bleue, leur opium aux noms divers : Dieu ou bien le Tout, ou encore l'Esprit, c'est du pareil au même, soit ce que Schopenhauer nomme, au complément 41 du *Welt als Wille und Vorstellung* un puissant « antidote contre la certitude de la mort ». Contrairement à Bossuet, donc, pour Rosenzweig, « l'estimable », c'est l'existence, soit précisément l'homme « en tant qu'il passe » et trépasse.

L'*Etoile de la rédemption* s'ouvre donc sur un effet de vérité prémédité, un choc mis en scène, une dramaturgie qui voit s'affronter deux protagonistes. D'un côté le Je vivant, irréductible, inconvertible en quoi que ce soit, vivant-contre jusqu'à ce qu'il meurt, terrifié, hurlant d'angoisse Je Je Je, tout entier corps. De l'autre la Philosophie, portraiturée en pied dans une sorte d'allégorie : une grande consolatrice, compatissante mais menteuse, sourire vide, air béat, indifférente et ayant l'air de se moquer, index pointé vers un au-delà du champ de bataille où le Je n'a qu'une peur, celle d'être réduit à un ça (*nur ein Es*, 3). Ce qui suscite l'angoisse du Je, c'est qu'il se voit en ça, en troisième personne, en cadavre. Une brève remarque ici : pour comprendre jusqu'au bout et dans leur « logique » propre ces lignes qui ne sont pas le fin mot de l'*Etoile* sur la mort, il faudrait pouvoir s'ouvrir déjà sur la révélation comme cette instance où la créature advient à son statut parlé de Je. La mort remet en question la révélation elle-même, en quelque sorte, en revenant en amont de la création, elle est une décréation retotalisante (304), tout comme l'existence est une révélation détotalisante.

La Philosophie, dans l'allégorie où elle se pose dans les premières pages de l'*Etoile*, nous sermonne et nous assure que la mort n'est rien. Or la mort n'est pas rien, elle n'est pas ce rien dont on ne peut rien savoir, ce rien qui ne serait qu'un rien du savoir, justement (pour « l'idéalisme », bien sûr, le rien du savoir, c'est : *rien du tout*). Or la mort n'est pas du côté du néant ainsi déterminé, elle est bien quelque chose (5). Le grand présupposé de l'idéalisme (cette question du présupposé, du *dunkle Voraussetzung* (5), est absolument centrale), c'est que : 1. seul le pensable peut s'articuler en totalité ; 2. seul le tout est pensable dans la mesure où la multiplicité qu'il englobe totalement peut se réduire à l'Un. Ceci, que Rosenzweig pointe comme le « grand présupposé », constitue le geste même, si l'on peut dire, de la pensée idéaliste, laquelle commence par *réduire* le multiple afin de le *fonder* ensuite en unitotalité. Hegel, le véritable penseur du « Tout où rien ne meurt », est évidemment le principal incriminé, sur ce point du « rien », de l'« ineffectif » de la mort : « *Der Tod, wenn wir jene Unwirklichkeit so nennen wollen, ist das Furchtbarste, und das Tote fest zu halten, was die grösste Kraft erfordert. [...] Aber nicht das Leben, das sich vor dem Tode scheut und von der Verwüstung rein bewahrt, sondern das ihn erträgt, und in ihm erhält, ist das Leben des Geistes* »[11]. Hegel pense le deuil et la douleur de la conscience comme une mort qui vient vivifier l'Esprit, la vie de l'Esprit. Pour lui, la mort est une extase négative: en se niant dans la différence, l'Esprit nie la différence en soi-même et la pose pour soi. La vie est alors le résultat substantiel de la négation surmontée, en-soi-pour-soi, et l'hégélianisme une sorte de stoïcisme christianisé où l'Esprit inscrit sa transcendance dans les plis de l'immanence. Ceci correspond exactement à la fonction du spéculatif telle que la détermine Rosenzweig –fonction de « protection » face à la mort (*Schutz*, 16), de déni et de forclusion ou encore, selon le mot de Jacques Derrida dans *Glas*, d'« amortissement » de la mort.

Seul le suicide pourrait à l'extrême rigueur constituer la forme sous laquelle la philosophie serait éventuellement à même d'envisager la mort. L'allusion au suicide, prudente, se trouve à la page 4 où la fameuse nuit de Leipzig de juillet 1913, la nuit de la tentation du suicide, est évoquée, via un mot (*Phiole*) emprunté à un vers du premier Faust: « *Ich grüsse dich, du einzige Phiole ! / Die ich mit Andacht nun herunterhole* »[12]. Un an avant le début de la rédaction du *Stern*, le 13 août 1917, Rosenzweig revient encore sur cette nuit du suicide évité, dans une lettre à Eugen Rosenstock : « *im übrigen war ich einfach auf den Mund geschlagen, noch viel zu nahe jenem völligen vis-a-vis du rien mit dem ich an jenem Morgen nach der Nacht in mein Zimmer gekommen war und meinen Browning ‹6,35› aus der Schreibtischschublade nahm* »[13]. Dans les premières pages du *Stern*, le « vis-à-vis du rien » est ainsi remémoré, douloureusement,

---

[11] G.W.F. Hegel, Phänomenologie des Geistes, Hamburg 2006, 26.
[12] Johann Wolfgang von Goethe, Faust. Der Tragödie erster Teil [1829], Hg. Albert Schöne, Frankfurt a.M., 43.
[13] GB, 22.

au détour d'un développement sur l'angoisse de mort du combattant dans les tranchées du front –le « Browning 6.35 » ayant cédé la place à la fiole de poison.

Même si elle n'est pas sans importance, la question du suicide doit être ici mise de côté. Car ce qui se joue dans ces pages, c'est tout autre chose. Pour Rosenzweig, si l'Esprit peut regarder la mort en face, si la vie de l'Esprit se nourrit de son face à face avec la mort, comme l'écrit Hegel, alors c'est que cette mort est une *pseudo-mort*, un mensonge figuré et dissimulé sous les innombrables formes du Spéculatif : aliénation, scission, devenir-autre de l'Esprit, négativité. Pour Hegel, la mort, le mort, c'est la séparation, c'est le séparé. Pour Rosenzweig, au contraire, la mort c'est l'unité ultime, la retotalisation finale dans le cadavre. Ce que Rosenzweig détermine dans l'*Einleitung* comme Je (*Ich*), c'est l'anti-Esprit, si on peut ainsi dire, à savoir l'irréductible, l'inenglobable, l'inconvertible, brut et sauvage, sans devenir-autre ni *Aufhebung*. On songera ici à Kierkegaard qui disait : le système hégélien, dans l'auto-engendrement de sa vérité, peut parfaitement *tout* embrasser, *tout* totaliser, *sauf Moi* dès lors que je m'y refuse. Dans le paragraphe intitulé *Kierkegaard* (8), Rosenzweig se réapproprie la sentence afin de situer le sens du cri de la créature saisie d'effroi qui ouvre ces premières pages, tout en inaugurant la perspective, issue de l'angoisse de mort, d'une véritable métaphysique du nom propre : « *denn mochte auch alles an ihm /dem Bewusstsein/ ins Allgemeine zu überstezen sein –die Behaftetheit mit Vor- und Zunamen, das Eigene…blieb übrig, und gerade auf dies Eigene kam es* » (8).

Une dernière précision résulte clairement de ce qui précède : ce n'est pas *à la mort même* que le Je doit faire face, c'est à l'*angoisse* de mort. Dans le premier cas, l'alternative oscillerait entre le suicide et la spéculation ; dans le second cas, c'est de l'*existence* qu'il y va. Rosenzweig considère l'angoisse comme une sorte de stimulus de pensée, en tant qu'elle nous place devant le tout de l'être, au sens heideggérien, devant le tout de l'existence. C'est à elle qu'il convient de faire face et non à la mort elle-même. Il *déplace* donc *le face à face réclamé par Hegel*. « *Der Mensch soll die Angst des Irdischen nicht von sich werfen ; er soll in der Furcht des Todes – bleiben* » (4). En effet, cette angoisse de mort est à sa façon, très singulière, une source de connaissance qui permet de rester dans la vie tout en sachant que cette dernière est marquée par la mort.

Il n'y a donc pas chez Rosenzweig de « pensée de la mort ». Le 26 novembre 1918, il écrit à Margrit Rosenstock: « *Meinst du, ich hätte wohl ein klares Wort über den Tod geschrieben. Ich weiss es selbst nicht; er kommt immer wieder vor, immer wieder anders, aber nirgends mit endgültiger Klarheit* »[14]. Affirmation d'un non-savoir indépassable, non-savoir d'un Quelque-chose d'irréductible – là où le geste spéculatif par excellence consisterait à faire s'égaliser le savoir et le quelque-chose, d'une part, et le non-savoir et le néant d'autre part. Cette mise en non-correspondance de l'idéalisme avec soi est le stimulus de la destruction de la « philosophie » engagée dans la première partie du Stern, *in philosophos*. Elle

---

[14] GB, 200.

lui fournit son commencement, ce qu'on voit très bien dès la première phrase de l'*Einleitung*, laquelle connecte d'emblée deux mots, *Tod* et *All*, afin de s'acheminer à grande allure vers la description de la faillite de l'idéalisme unitotalisant. Dans une autre lettre, toujours adressée à Gritli, Rosenzweig écrit : « *Der Tod ist ja überhaupt das Feste im Leben* »[15]. La mort est tout à la fois constante, *fest*, et protéiforme. Elle est « quelque-chose » de constant parce que chacun vit avec cette certitude, de façon « authentique » ou pas n'a guère d'importance ici. Cependant, elle n'est pas réductible à une forme ou à une interprétation unique. Son statut n'est pas définissable pour tous, une fois pour toutes. Si tel était le cas, cela impliquerait d'une certaine manière qu'il est possible de l'apprivoiser, voire de se l'approprier, d'« apprendre à mourir » selon l'adage, ce qui est tout le contraire de ce que nous dit Rosenzweig.

Il y a donc, comme explique Schopenhauer dans le complément 41 déjà cité du *Welt als Wille und Vorstellung*, une relation consubstantielle, co-originaire, entre la pensée, la raison, la philosophie et la conscience de notre statut mortel : « la connaissance lutte contre la crainte de la mort ». Le déni ou l'amortissement de ce quelque chose anime et donne son élan à l'idéalisme spéculatif (mais aussi aux religions) qui, sous couvert de regarder la mort droit dans les yeux, la réduit à rien, à un néant dont il convient de sortir par la voie de l'être, comme au début de la *Grande Logique* hégélienne. L'*Einleitung* promet un autre chemin, celui de « la révolution post-hégélienne de la philosophie » (18), scandé et balisé par les trois noms mentionnés, Schopenhauer, Kierkegaard, Nietzsche, auxquels il faut ajouter le dernier Schelling. C'est bien ce chemin que Rosenzweig entend à son tour emprunter dans le *Stern* –mais à sa façon à lui.

Quelle est cette façon ? Elle consiste à prendre au sérieux, non point tant la mort, car celle-ci n'apporte pas de « clarté définitive », que l'angoisse de la mort qui, elle, dit la vérité du Je fini. Quel en est l'effet le plus immédiat ? La réaffirmation d'un cri, le cri du Je vivant. Quel en est la conséquence intra-philosophique ? La détotalisation, la destruction, le bris de la totalité comme irrigués par les « bras de mort » qui s'y avancent. C'est à partir de ce bris que se dégagent comme d'eux-mêmes les « éléments » –et la philosophie élémentaire esquissée dans la première partie du *Stern*.

Le bénéfice secondaire de la « crainte de la mort » et de ses avatars idéalistes, c'est la connaissance du Tout. Pour Rosenzweig, c'est déjà quelque chose, cet *Erkennen*. Ni plus ni moins que le terme hégélien de l'histoire de la philosophie –une sorte de fin de la philosophie. Cette connaissance terminale, considérée depuis « la révolution post-hégélienne de la philosophie » ou depuis cette philosophie pour « notre temps » qu'est la « philosophie du point de vue », ne peut apparaître que biaisée, tronquée. C'est le premier volet du refus d'obtempérer (*Gefolgschaft versagen*, 22) à la philosophie du Tout, le second pouvant être rapporté au Cri. Articulé en deux pans, comme si le mensonge pouvait se décrire

---

[15] Lettre du 18 avril 1918, GB, 77.

selon deux volets, logique et existentiel, il y a donc dans les vingt premières pages de l'*Etoile*, un refus très radical de tout Tout, pour ainsi dire. Refus gnoséologique et en fin de compte philosophique. Refus moral aussi –non pas en un sens axiologique, comme si l'on pourrait dériver ce refus du Tout de la raison pratique elle-même ou du Sujet transcendantal, à partir de quoi on déduirait des valeurs. Le Tout fait l'objet d'un refus et d'un bris, parce que le mensonge qu'il autorise est un vice existentiel, un mensonge du point de vue de l'existence, une inhumanité qui redouble une fausseté cognitive. *L'Etoile commence où finit la philosophie et ses systèmes.*

4. Le maintien (*Bewahrung*) et l'avération (*Bewährung*)

L'*Einleitung* met en place des axes méthodologiques et des procédures expérimentales qui président à la déconstruction élémentale mise en œuvre dans la première partie. Quatre outils sont expressément mentionnés par Rosenzweig, le Néant, le Oui, le Non, le Et. Ils servent à disposer deux grandes transversales épistémologiques, commandées l'une par le temps, l'autre par la parole, la seconde absorbant en quelque sorte la première.

Le premier rappel anti-idéaliste, c'est la différence entre le résultat et le commencement, appuyée sur les métaphores de la *valise* dans le *Stern* (125) et du *programme de théâtre* dans *Das neue Denken*[16] : ce qui est présent dans la pensée, c'est-à-dire dans le temps du concept (dont Hegel assurait qu'il se donnait comme une sorte de maintenant éternel), n'est que le résultat d'un passé dans le réel. Et ce qui est résultat doit être ce qui met en branle la pensée, son re-commencement en quelque sorte après le bris du tout. Dieu-Monde-Homme, obtenu par la détotalisation de l'unitotalité, se tiendra aussi bien au principe de la nouvelle pensée en tant que « réponse à la vieille question philosophique de la quoddité »[17]. Le *Stern* se donne pour tâche d'en construire les « éléments » en en déconstruisant la structure : les trois monismes, les trois substances, les trois points, etc. On comprend pourquoi Rosenzweig a pu donner à ses lecteurs le conseil (à ne pas suivre aveuglément !) de passer très vite sur la première partie : le bris, les trois substances fixes, la ré-initialisation de la pensée, les figures du « tout » (excluante, incluante), etc. –toutes choses qui en passent par la temporalisation du connaître. Or tout commence après le « commencement » du *Stern*, après le prémonde, dans le monde, lorsqu'il s'agit de « révéler » pourquoi cette structure élémentale elle-même, issue du bris du tout, pro-vient d'une expérience, d'une épreuve, d'un *Erlebnis*. En effet, dans la première partie, on est toujours dans la pensée, fût-elle « nouvelle », on est toujours dans le prémonde, mais plus du tout de la même façon : ce prémonde ne se prend pas pour le monde!

---

[16] GS III, 147.
[17] Ibid., 148.

A ce rappel de la « philosophie » au temps et par le temps s'adjoint pour le surdéterminer une distinction fondamentale qui se trouve à la page 16 : « *Die Wahrheit bewährt nicht die Wirklichkeit, sondern die Wirklichkeit bewahrt die Wahrheit. Das Wesen der Welt ist diese Bewahrung (nicht Bewährung) der Wahrheit* ». Il convient donc pour *einen gesunden Menschenverstand* de ne jamais confondre la preuve et la garde, la vérité et l'effectivité –le mur et l'image. Tels sont les enjeux portés par « *die Methode, die in der Vorsilbe « meta » bezeichnet ist* » (21). La méthode méta permet en effet de comprendre (et ceci, de provenance schellingienne, est essentiel pour lire le *Stern*) que c'est bel et bien l'effectivité qui permet la garde de l'essence de la vérité. La raison, le concept sont supportés par l'effectivité qui en assure le maintien en quelque sorte. La maintenance du vrai s'effectue par ce qui est plus vaste que le vrai, comme le mur pour le tableau qui y est suspendu. La « nouvelle pensée » doit inventer un nouveau type d'exercice « philosophique », une nouvelle méthode qui ne reconduise plus la *Wirklichkeit* à son *essence* par réduction et fondation – mais qui en discernera la vérité dans la *parole* en tant qu'antonyme du concept. Ce *Sprachdenken* procède d'une défection de l'être. Tel est le sens de la formule de *Das neue Denken* : « *das Wirkliche 'ist' nicht* »[18]. Ce qui, évidemment, ne veut pas dire : l'effectif n'existe pas, mais il n'est rien d'étant, il échappe à toute essence, à toute quiddité. « L'effectif n'est pas » signifie dire que *l'être n'est pas effectif*. Le principe énoncé à la page 16 du *Stern* croise évidemment la monstration de *Das neue Denken*. On peut d'ailleurs considérer que la révélation est une façon de produire une réversion de l'être en effectivité, du *ist* (la *Ist-frage* comme question de la philosophie pérenne) en *wirkt* (la *Wirklichkeit* comme garde et maintien).

L'impératif, dans notre *Einleitung*, est de sortir de la feinte logique et du leurre existentiel du « Tout » total, ce piège à deux mâchoires. Rosenzweig y engage une démarche spécifique qui permettra de « détricoter » la totalité spéculative (19). Au terme du Bris qui s'opère au long des chapitres de la première partie, on obtiendra *quelque chose de positif*, comme si cet envol hors du néant-et-du-tout permettait d'accéder à un autre genre de connaissance que la connaissance une et universelle, à la fois plus fragile, car le tout est le non-vrai, et plus assurée, puisque le vrai est le non-tout. Après le Bris, nous aurons donc entre les mains des « parties », des morceaux, des éléments, le Dieu mythique, le Monde plastique, l'Homme tragique –qui nous apparaîtront alors comme des « pures *hypothèses* » (91) et comme *des touts*. Mais ces touts hypothétiques ne se retotaliseront plus car ils ne sont pas des Touts, même s'ils peuvent bien en avoir l'apparence « moniste ». Le Tout est brisé, non seulement en trois – mais en une multiplicité miroitante de facticités (95). Le Bris donne lieu à un emboîtement de bris, à une élémentarisation continuée des éléments. En effet, chacun de ces éléments, chaque quelque-chose a l'ambition récurrente de se reconstituer en Tout, en une « *Riesenform* » (95) gigantesque et monstrueuse. A

---

[18] GS III, 148.

partir de là, le geste philosophique quasi-idiosyncrasique de Rosenzweig dans le *Stern* consistera *à toujours multiplier ce qui se donne dans l'unicité d'une forme stable tenue en suspicion, à soustraire l'Un, à diviser le Tout*. L'*hubris* du Tout et de la totalisation fait du *bris* une tâche sans terme, et du « philosopher après Hegel » un ouvrage incessant plus qu'un programme accompli. Ce qui donc restera après le bris, après chaque bris, ce sera de la relation, de la circulation, de la liaison et de la reliaison, une diachronie qui n'est rien d'autre que la temporalité du sujet existant. Du fragile et du brisé –mais cette fragilité détient désormais une force singulière, la force de l'ouvert, l'ouverture par et dans la langue. Car les éléments du Tout ont toujours déjà vocation à se mettre à parler (121), leurs contenus étant autrement inassemblables (154). Cet assemblage par la parole (et par le temps et par l'autre, comme le rappellera *Das neue Denken*) ne pourra plus jamais relever d'une totalisation. Le contenu des éléments est absolument hors d'état de s'assembler en totalité car, dans leur surgissement, les éléments retiennent encore des contenus qui ne peuvent entrer en action que dans d'autres directions (« *der ganze Inhalt der Elemente kann gar nicht in einem einzelnen Begriff zusammentreten* », 154).

Le mensonge brisé, demeurent ainsi des morceaux d'existence, du temps, des temps (Création, Révélation, Rédemption), des langues, des langues silencieuses et des langues sonores. Là, l'*Einleitung* s'ouvre vers l'ensemble des trois parties qui composent le *Stern*, comme un fleuve se jette dans une mer incertaine.

lectures supplémentaires

Bertolino, L., *Das Nichts und die Philosophie. Rosenzweig zwischen Idealismus und einer Hermeneutik der religiösen Erfahrung*, in: Wolfdietrich Schmied/Kowarzik (Hg.), Franz Rosenzweigs »neues Denken«. Internationaler Kongreß Kassel 2004, 2 Bde, Karl Alber, Freiburg/München, 2006, Bd. I: Selbstbegrenzendes Denken – in philosophos, 111–125 [https://philarchive.org/archive/BERDNU]

Pollock, B. (2009). *Franz Rosenzweig and the systematic task of philosophy*. Cambridge University Press.

Part One, Book One: God and his Being, or Metaphysics

Francesco Paolo Ciglia

The present contribution sets out to critically explore some very specific, yet notably relevant aspects of Rosenzweig's reflection about *the theological question*. To reach this end, this same contribution will provide a *first* and *elementary* introduction to the reading of a particular section of the thinker's philosophical masterpiece, *The Star of Redemption*[19], in which are cast the basic foundations of the complex, and much more ample reflection on the subject, which will be later articulated throughout the entire course of the work. The section in question is represented by Book One of Part One of *Star* (henceforth, *Star* I.1)[20].

Before beginning our exploration, it seems important to underline the absolutely undeniable fact that the thinker's philosophical masterpiece presents

---

[19] F. Rosenzweig, Der Stern der Erlösung, Frankfurt a.M. 1921; 2nd ed., ibid., 1930; 3rd ed., Heidelberg 1954; 4th ed. in: F. Rosenzweig, Der Mensch und sein Werk. Gesammelte Schriften, 2. Abteilung: Der Stern der Erlösung, Haag 1976; 5th ed., Frankfurt a.M. 1988. Our citations of the work, mentioned hereafter as: GS II, followed by the page number, will be taken from the 4th ed., just cited.

[20] GS II, 25–43.

How to cite this book chapter:
Ciglia, F. P. 2021. Part One, Book One: God and his Being, or Metaphysics. In: Brasser, M., Bojanić, P. and Ciglia, F. P. (eds.) *The Star for Beginners: Introductions to the Magnum Opus of Franz Rosenzweig*. Pp. 23–40. London: Ubiquity Press. DOI: https://doi.org/10.5334/bco.d. License: CC-BY

itself to an interpretative approach as a philosophical work of extreme difficulty. It, at times, appears even obscure and enigmatic, and certainly not only to those who approach it for the first time! The difficulty that marks the entire work appears to grow, if that is possible, in a particular way, one would say to its highest degree, through the course of *Part One*. This notice does not in any way aim to discourage the reader who intends to face the work as a beginner; on the contrary it is an encouragement to bravely face a true *interpretative challenge*, the undertaking of which will not fail to amply repay the profuse efforts it requires.

1. The context

Our analysis begins with a very rapid contextualization of *Star I.1*, within the work's overall economy.

The *Star* is subdivided in three basic *Parts*, each of which contains three large sections of text, which the thinker denominates *Books*. Each Part of the *Star* is accompanied by an introductory text and a conclusive text, the latter, for the first two Books, has the function of mediating the transition to the following Part; while for Book Three, it serves as the closure of the entire speculative itinerary traveled throughout the course of the work.

The work's three main parts seek to peruse the three fundamental dimensions which, according to the thinker, constitute the plot of all reality. The dimensions in question, which are *based*, in some way in succession, each on the preceding one, are called by the thinker respectively: "everlasting primordial world"[21], "ever renewed world"[22], and "eternal over-world"[23] [*immerwährende Vorwelt, allzeiterneurte Welt, ewige* Überwelt].

The work's central part – the Second Part, which deals with the "ever renewed world"- enjoys a marked preeminence with respect to the other two parts. It searches the horizon within which our common daily human existence takes place inside the world. This preeminence cannot astound, if one considers the fact that Rosenzweig's meditation understands itself in terms of *erfahrende Philosophie* – literally, "experiential philosophy" – that is, in terms of a "militant" philosophy working at the front lines in the elaboration of a critical reflection of the concrete existence of man within the world[24].

---

[21] Ibid., 1–100.
[22] Ibid., 101–292.
[23] Ibid., 293–472.
[24] Franz Rosenzweig, Das neue Denken. Einige nachträgliche Bemerkungen zum *Stern der Erlösung*, initially published in "Der Morgen", October 1925, it appeared in various collections, before coming together in: F. Rosenzweig, Der Mensch und sein Werk. Gesammelte Schriften, 3. Abteilung: Zweistromland. Kleinere Schriften zu Glauben und Denken, Dordrecht/

The Third Part of the work – which is "about the eternal over-world" – thematizes that particular ontological dimension toward which a complex framework of relational dynamisms, which fully permeate and deeply penetrate the actual makeup of the world we daily experience, appears to be intentionally and spasmodically projected. These dynamisms prefigure, and in a certain sense also *prophesy* in an allusive manner, and in the form of "already" but "not yet", a *complete* and *total fulfillment* of the world of our daily experience – an *eschatological* fulfillment. Employing a term which comes from the biblical tradition, the thinker names this fulfillment "redemption". It represents the primary object of teleological dynamism – or of the *speculative hope* – which takes flesh in the entire work, and is significantly reflected even in its very title.

Part One of the *Star* – the part containing the Book which is of interest to us in this essay – attempts to bring to the light a dimension of reality that is normally invisible and therefore not accessible from the perspective of our most common and daily existence within the world. In this dimension, which can only be reconstructed in an indirect way through – so to speak – circumstantial procedures, lie the *primordial* or *elementary foundations* upon which our existence within the world rests. This "primordial-worldly" dimension is much poorer, far rougher, and more abstract than the worldly sphere within which we normally live, yet it constitutes the *necessary condition – the condition of possibility* or *conditio sine qua non* – of the worldly sphere in question. However, it cannot represent the worldly sphere's *sufficient condition*. There subsists, between "primordial-world" and "world", an ontological gap that is unfillable, and therefore absolutely inexplicable at the level of pure thought.

The primordial or elementary foundations – the "primordial-worldly" foundations – of the world dimension within which we normally live are represented, according to Rosenzweig, by the three classical figures of the *mythical God*, the *plastic world*[25] and the *tragic man*, which were brought to light with an exceptional clarity in the literary and religious culture of Ancient Greece. These same figures, after having undergone complex reworking in a speculative key, will constitute the privileged objects of the three fundamental metaphysical sciences, which are: rational theology, rational cosmology and

---

Boston/Lancaster 1984, 139–161. The essay, hereafter mentioned as GS III, followed by the page number, will be be cited according to the 1984 edition. The self-understanding of Rosenzweig's thought in terms of "*erfahrende Philosophie*" recurs in GS III, 144.

[25] The "plastic world", evoked here, is explored in the First Part of the *Star*, and must not be mistaken for the "ever renewed world" which constitutes the object of the work's Second Part. In the first case, it is one of the three constitutive elements of the "primordial-world" – elements which are specific and well circumscribed. In the second case, it is much broader dimension of reality, that in which (as we have said) our daily life is immersed in the world.

rational psychology. The sciences in question will represent, in the end, the load-bearing structure of the entire Western onto-theological tradition.

2. The theme

The three Books which compose Part One of the *Star* are dedicated to the three fundamental speculative figures that constitute the "primordial-world", that is to say, in order: to *God*[26], to the *world*[27] and to *man*[28]. The three figures in question, in their peculiar primordial-worldly conformation, are understood by the thinker as "elements" [*Elemente*][29]. It is important to underline the fact that this definition does not exhaust the peculiar richness and the overall and ultimate meaning of the figures just evoked.

Even if their pre-worldly conformation is undoubtedly and indispensably presumed, the divine, worldly, and human horizons as they appear and are experienced within what the thinker names "ever renewed world" – that is, as we know, within the most common daily experience of man within the world – transcend it, and radically transfigure it.

The Book of Rosenzweig's masterpiece which we are to examine – that is *Star I.1* – bears an extremely meaningful title which immediately unveils the *object* it seeks to portray and the modalities, strongly ambiguous or even misleading as they may be, which it proposes to adopt from the beginning. The title sounds much like this: *God and his Being or metaphysics* [*Gott und sein Sein oder Metaphysik*][30].

In order to begin treating the Book in question, I would like to preliminarily propose some brief reflections, first of all, about its *strategic placement* within, not only Part One of the *Star*, but also of the entire work; secondly I'd like to reflect on the overall *speculative layout* of the subject, as it seems to transpire from the title.

2.1 Strategic placement

Rosenzweig's choice of placing the philosophical question about the "elemental God" in *Star I.1*, and consequently at the *very opening* – at the *incipit* – of the *entire work* cannot be the product of chance. This same choice could not but produce, *in fact* – and thus, even *beyond* the thinker's *explicit intentions* – general speculative effects of enormous bearing for the entire work. One

---

[26] See GS II, 25–43.
[27] Ibid., 44–66.
[28] Ibid., 67–90.
[29] Ibid., 1.
[30] Ibid., 25.

could sustain instead that the thinker's explicit intentions, with reference to this choice, and the speculative effects which it in fact produces on the entire work, intertwine in a truly singular dialectic. In an important programmatic text from 1925[31], the thinker in fact peremptorily denies that the placement of the philosophical question about the "elemental" God in *Star I.1* expresses the intention of clearly favoring that question over the meditations on other issues, which are respectively, cosmological and anthropological, and which will be treated in *Star I.2* and *Star I.3*. The thinker declares, in the same sense, that *Star I* could just as well have begun, with the cosmological question as with the anthropological question[32]. In fact, at least in *Star I*, the thinker intends to pursue a very particular speculative strategy, which tends to value and exalt to the highest degree the *absolutely equal worth* of the three "*elements*", together with their *irreducible difference*, and their absolute reciprocal *independence*.

However, the subsequent developments of the theological question throughout the work in fact create radically different speculative dynamics. In *Star II*, for example, out of the three relational events that constitute the object of its three Books – that is to say, *creation*[33], *revelation*[34] and *redemption*[35]–, two – *creation* and *revelation* – find their primordial motivation and their absolute point of origin precisely in God. *Star III.3*, which is the last Book of the entire work[36], culminates in a passionate meditation on God, intended as conclusive and definitive "eternal truth". The brief text entitled *Door* or *Gate* [*Tor*][37], which concludes the work after *Star III.3*, finally stops with a sort of muted contemplation of God's very face.

Therefore the theological question, even if presented through radically different modalities, opens and closes the entire Rosenzweigian work. Thus it seems to delineate a sort of powerful *speculative inclusion* – a genuinely *theological* inclusion – which, in embracing the entire philosophical itinerary covered by the *Star*, cannot but shed a singular light on it, a light of absolutely unequivocal meaning.

2.2 Speculative setup

The *title* given to *Star I.1* by the author, generates absolutely misleading impressions, even in the most common of readers endowed with a discreet philosophical background. The short circuit which the title in question establishes

---

[31] The already cited *Das neue Denken*.
[32] GS III, 148.
[33] GS II, 124–173.
[34] Ibid., 174–228.
[35] Ibid., 229–282.
[36] Ibid., 423–464.
[37] Ibid., 465–472.

between the *question of God*, the *question of being* – or *ontology* – and metaphysics, seems to refer to the well-known – and classical – Aristotelian theorization. Aristotle's *first philosophy*, later named "metaphysics", is centered, as is well known, in a privileged way on the *question of being* and the founding structures of the latter, amongst which the *substance* or *ousia* stands out because of its importance. Among the innumerable substances that populate the physical and metaphysical universe explored by Aristotle, the *divine substance* stands out because of its absolute excellence. Aristotelian metaphysics as a whole appears to find its arrival point and highest apex in theology[38].

In its reuse of terminology consecrated by the classical tradition, Rosenzweig's treatment of the "elemental" God appears to violently introduce – to utilize a well-known New Testament metaphor – some "absolutely new wine" in "old wineskins". These last ones, as we shall see together, will explode under the bursting action of the Rosenzweigian theological reflection's new wine, yielding results of rare and extreme originality.

3. One God, two faces

The meditation on God, grasped as "element" of the "primordial world" described by Rosenzweig in *Star I.1*, unfolds along the tracks of a very precise *methodological itinerary*. The starting point of such an itinerary is represented by a very special, and somewhat paradoxical, understanding of the "element" God. The "element" in question is assigned two configurations which seem contradictory but are in reality very closely connected by the underground logic of deep solidarity. In fact they are two different, yet complementary, faces of the same medal. Let us begin to examine them right away.

3.1 God as "nothing [*Nichts*]"

At first sight the beginning of Rosenzweig's meditation on the "elemental" God seems inspired by the classical tradition of "*negative theology*"– yet here too, it is a only a misleading impression. From the very outset of his theological meditation, the thinker hastens to say: "We know nothing about God"[39]. In front of the human reason's approach, God presents himself as *nothing*, at least at first, according to Rosenzweig. Therefore philosophical meditation about God cannot begin if not from a radical *non-knowledge* about God. In what terms exactly must the nothing of God be understood? Two essential clarifications are to be offered on this matter.

---

[38] Aristotle, *Metaphysics*, VI (E) 1, 1026 a 15–20, XI (K) 7, 1064 b 3, and XII (L) 7, 1072 a 19 – 1073 b 3.
[39] GS II, 25.

3.1.1 The divine nothing as a problem

The nothing found by human reason in the moment in which it questions itself about God is not banally a *nothingness*, but rather it is *something*; it could well be said, it is something which *makes one think*. It is not an absolute void, the void of pure and simple absence or non-existence. One could perhaps say, metaphorically speaking, that the divine nothing is akin to a sort of extremely dense and compact, obscure cloud, which hides in its depths something that is inaccessible, at least initially. The divine nothing is therefore a nothing that is full, loaded, or rather, overloaded, with content. It is the nothing of God's *hiddenness* or *veiledness* in the eyes of human reason. On the other hand, the same thinker explicitly points out that to begin the meditation about God considering his nothing is no different than saying that for us – at least initially –, God cannot be other than a *problem*[40]. The nothing which reason stumbles upon in its search for God would then coincide with the extreme, absolute, *problematicity* of his intentional objective.

3.1.2 Determinate nothing

Not-knowing about God, the nothing which human reason stumbles upon in its approach to the theological question, must not be understood to be, in Rosenzweig' s perspective, a –general or generic – universal nothing; that is to say an all-embracing or total nothing. The nothing of the knowledge about God is not *the* full-court nothing or *überhaupt*, but, on the contrary, it is *a* nothing, that is, an absolutely *determined* and *circumscribed* nothing. It is precisely the type of nothing which the human reason faces when it walks down a specific research path, that is to say a path that should lead to God. It is the nothing *of* God or of human knowledge *about* God. Here the objective genitive of the nothing *of* God appears marked and enlivened by an *intentional dynamism* and by a global orientation that are absolutely unequivocable. The nothing *of* God indicates a very precise *direction of movement* that points towards the obscure cloud of the knowledge *about* God.

3.2 God as factuality [*Tatsächlichkeit*]

Let us now pass to the second configuration; it is different, yet complementary to the first Rosenzweigian understanding of the "elemental" God. Comparing both faces of the same medal, of which we spoke earlier, cannot avoid producing surprise and disconcert; it cannot but generate an authentic paradox. Besides the understanding of God in terms of *problematicity*, in terms of a "*nothing*" which human rationality seeks to grasp, the thinker is not afraid to – quite

---

[40] Ibid., 27.

brusquely – present an understanding of God in terms of an absolutely *obvious* and *immediate fact*. The same God who, in the eyes of human reason, is enveloped by an obscure and impenetrable cloud represents, *contemporaneously*, for reason itself, a sort of irreducible *positum*, that is to say: an imprescindable and undeniable *factuality*. Human reason is neither capable of *producing* nor *building* this *positum* by itself and with its own formidable resources; nor, one could well say eyeing the latest developments of post-modern debate, is reason capable to *deconstruct* the *positum* through speculative *procedures*, be they more or less sophisticated. In the previously cited text from 1925, the thinker affirms that we know equally *little* and *much, nothing* and *everything* about God – and about the two other "elements", which are the world and man. This "knowing much" or "knowing everything" about God and about the other elements reaches man, according to the thinker, through a source radically different from pure philosophical thought. He intends to refer to *"anschauliches Wissen der Erfahrung"*, or *intuitive knowledge* – which is absolutely clear, absolutely evident – *from experience*, from which philosophical thought cannot and absolutely must not prescind, but with which a deep, or better yet *constitutive*, interrelation, must be constantly maintained – even when there are contrasts and conflict. In the end, the contrast and conflict will reveal themselves to be particularly fecund.

In an important part of the *Star*, which is outside the Book we are now analyzing, Rosenzweig designates the "elemental" God – but also equally, the other two "elements" – with the high-risk – yet nonetheless highly significant – expression of *"irrational* object". The thinker prudently placed the adjective "irrational" between quotation marks. The expression's context makes clear, beyond any shadow of doubt, that the term "irrational" must not be interpreted literally here, as if it meant "non-rational", "opposed" or "contrary" to reason. Otherwise the quotation marks would not have been necessary at all. "Irrational" here undoubtedly stands for "meta-rational" or "trans-rational". The "elemental" God is neither a product of reason nor appears to be exhaustively graspable through reason's resources. The "elemental" God, in a certain sense, imposes or proposes himself to reason, which has the task of grasping him, focusing on him, critically *problematizing* him and exploring him up to the point allowed by reason's constitutive limits.

The ambiguity of an "elemental" God, who constitutively oscillates *between problematicity* and *obviousness*, between *nullity* and *immediate factuality*, represents a real provocation which human reason cannot escape. The provocation shows itself to be a real *challenge* as it is contextualized within the same historical and problematic horizon in which the dark, grave and terrible Nietzschean announcement – "God is dead" – resounded with strength. It was an announcement which Rosenzweig knew very well and one he demonstrably considered with extreme seriousness within his philosophical masterpiece. It could be said, not without a bit of irony, that God, even when dead, continues to make problems for human reason – or to be a problem for it. Perhaps this same God gives us problems and constitutes a problem more if dead than alive.

3.3 Deus absconditus sed tamen non ignotus

The profound ambiguity of the Rosenzweigian "elemental" God could be enlightened, in an extremely synthesized manner, by two historical examples, which I analyze here with the greatest freedom, and therefore without any philological preoccupation.

The first example could be given by the *docta ignorantia*, a concept known to have been developed by Nicholas of Cusa[41]. This reference must necessarily be accompanied by an essential clarification. The *docta ignorantia* of which we speak, in contrast to the Cusanian understanding, which Rosenzweig polemically evoked in *Star I.1*[42], only constitutes a starting point for our thinker – and not an endpoint– in a discourse about God that intends to go *much further*. In the Rosenzweigian perspective, the *docta ignorantia* wishes to become, ever *wiser*, and ever less *ignorant*.

The second example could be represented by the well known Augustinian expression that expresses the complexity of the human being's relationship with the difficult question of time. Augustine poses the question: "*quid enim est tempus?*", that is: "what in fact is time?" He answers: "*Si nemo ex me quaerat, scio; si quaerenti explicare velim, nescio*", that is: «If no-one ask me, I know; if I wish to explain it to him who asks, I know not"[43]. The first part of the Augustinian statement lends itself as a good example of the second face of the medal of the Rosenzweigian understanding of the "elemental" God. God, as philosophically problematic and inexplicable as he may be, presents himself as absolute factuality, as *positive givenness*, which is always newly offered to us by the intuitive knowledge of concrete experience. This God is present, in some way, *immediately* and *unreflectively*, within or before human reason. The God who springs forth from Rosenzweig's considerations presents himself then as a hidden, but not completely unknown, God: *Deus absconditus sed tamen non ignotus*.

4. Toward positive theology

In Rosenzweig's view nonetheless, the configuration of the "elemental" God in the modalities we have just examined, does not represent the *arrival point* of

---

[41] Nicholas of Cusa, *De docta ignorantia* [1440]. The expression that is of interest to us is already found in the work's *Capitulum I, Liber Primus*, in addition to the title and throughout the course of the work.
[42] GS II, 25.
[43] Augustine of Hippo, *Confessiones*, XI, XIV, 17.

his meditation on this theme. On the contrary, negative – and factual – theology together represent the *starting point* of a much more ambitious research itinerary that wishes to go much further. In the end, the thinker in fact aims to achieve some form of *positive knowledge* about God; this knowledge is, at least initially, only "elemental". How then can one exit from the *nothing of knowledge* or from *non-knowledge* about God, how can it be left behind?

4.1 Two paths of research

Exiting, and therefore, even if at the embryonic or "elemental" stage, acquiring some form of *positive knowledge* about God, can happen according to Rosenzweig, along the road of *two* well defined paths of research. They present themselves as, and in fact *are*, profoundly different one from the other – frankly they are *opposites*. The figure of the divine which the thinker wants to delineate in *Star I.1* gushes forth from their *combined* and *synergetic* action.

The first of these two paths follows the sign marked *yes, affirmation, position* or *positivity*. The second path, in an opposite manner, develops along the way of *no*, of *negation* or *negativity*. For the thinker however, within this specific theorization, positivity and negativity do not acquire, in any way, *evaluative* meaning, but rather are intended in a strictly *descriptive* sense. Both research paths start out from the originary and initial *non-knowledge* or *nothing* of God. Precisely for this reason, they present and continue to maintain a very close relationship – more properly said a *constitutive relationship* – with this same nothing or non-knowledge. In the thinker's characteristic philosophical terminology, the first path presents itself – and is designated as – that of "the affirmation of the not nothing [*Bejahung des Nichtnichts*]", the second path instead is "negation of the nothing [*Verneinung des Nichts*]"[44].

4.2 A polar theology

The terminology used by Rosenzweig at this point, and above all the philosophical conceptuality that appears to be underpinning this same terminology, doubtlessly present themselves as being particularly difficult to comprehend; let us say that they are frankly abstruse. They come from a plot of very precise historic-speculative referents, which it is clearly not possible to suitably examine in depth here. For this reason we would like to suggest an overall interpretive hypothesis, which we are glad to submit to an open critical analysis.

To storm the conceptual fortress erected by the thinker here before the eyes of his unfortunate readers, I would like to formulate two preliminary questions which aim to introduce my interpretive hypothesis and make it understandable.

---

[44] GS II, 26.

Let us begin by asking: According to the thinker, *why* is it necessary to follow *two* research paths, and not *only one*, to pass from the obscure horizon of the *non-knowledge* of God to a form of *positive knowledge* about him?

Let us immediately add a second question to the first: *why* are the two paths placed under the signs of two reciprocally *opposite polarities*?

In order to answer these questions it is necessary to articulate some general considerations from which will emerge the characteristic speculative profile which the thinker intends to attribute to his conception of the "elemental" divine.

With reference to the first question which we have just now stated one must note that the peculiar figure of the "elemental" God, which Rosenzweig wishes to propose, does not take up the physiognomy of a flatly unidimensional, absolutely rigid, compact and homogeneous, monolithic ontological boulder. Quite on the contrary, the thinker has in mind a multidimensional, full-circle and richly articulated vision of the divine. A single way of access to the divine in question would not be capable to adequately grasp its constitutive complexity. Each of the two research paths for a positive knowledge of Rosenzweig's "elemental" God will then have the task of enlightening a different aspect of the God in question.

In reference to the second question it seems important to mention that the very figure of the divine which Rosenzweig wishes to clarify, does not present itself as a fundamentally *static* reality – one that is, so to speak, perennially *coincident with itself*. Rosenzweig's "elemental" God will soon reveal himself to be pervaded by an unstoppable disquietude – a *vital* disquietude. He will present himself as a sort of *force field*, perennially inhabited and agitated by two opposite and synergetic polarities, which are in acute and irreducible *tension*. Precisely for this reason the two ways of research that unlock the access to the figure of Rosenzweig's "elemental" God acquire a different polar disposition – they are reciprocally opposite. Each one of them will reach one of the two different dynamic poles that constitute the figure of the "elemental" God.

4.3 Affirmation of the not-nothing

As we have said earlier, the "affirmation of the not-nothing" represents the first way out of the *nothing of God*, or the *non-knowledge* about God. The Rosenzweigian expression appears to be quite contorted and convoluted, and thus precisely undecipherable. What does he wish to indicate? Why the *double negative* – not-nothing! – if the reciprocal negative elision of its constitutive elements ends up as an *affirmation*? Isn't the "not-nothing", which *establishes itself* along the first way out of the divine nothing, "something"?

In fact the thinker uses the expression "something" in his text to explain the meaning of the not-nothing which is affirmed along the first way out of non-knowledge of the "elemental". Nonetheless, he uses the expression very cautiously, in our text[45], it is found in some cases between quotation marks, and is constantly accompanied by the denunciation of its substantial inadequacy to describe exactly what the thinker has in mind.

To explain the deep motivations of the extreme reluctance with which the thinker uses the term "something" to suggest the idea of "not-nothing", one could hypothesize that the same term must have appeared to him as if overburdened by disturbing reverberations, produced, inevitably, by the term's timeless usage in the context of the philosophical tradition. The term "something [*Etwas*]" cannot avoid evoking, in the mind of the well-educated reader, the idea of the Greek *tode ti*, or of *quid* and *quidditas*, which emerge from the semantic horizon of the Latin language. These terms irresistibly evoke the idea of an *absolutely determined and exactly circumscribed essence*. This idea appears to be too narrow and much too well defined for what the thinker has in mind. On the other hand, the "not nothing" in its inelegant use of the double negative, holds the advantage of presenting itself as being much broader, much more undefined, undetermined and all-embracing than "something"[46]. Thus, the first way out from the nothing of God, affirms something *positive*, yet its positivity is absolutely *open and boundless*. In conclusion this way affirms an *essence*, yet one that is absolutely not *de-fined* or *de-termined*. What this *undefined and undetermined essence* could mean in reference to God will be examined shortly.

4.4 Negation of the nothing

The "negation of nothing" represents the second way out from the *nothing of God* or from the *non-knowledge* about him. It is evidently a totally different research itinerary than the first. The path of "no", "negation" or "negativity" immediately presents itself as being much more traumatic than the "yes" path. The "negation of nothing" as such must mark a *cut*, a *break* or a violent *tear* from the nothing which it detaches itself from. Where does such a negation lead to exactly? Calling to mind an age-old principle of the philosophical tradition, according to which "*omnis determinatio est negatio*", the thinker is able to present negation as *de-finition*, and thus as the *position of a finite being*, as in *de-limitation*, and *de-termination*. However these are unlike the – absolutely *static* and tranquil – *definition*, or *delimitation* or *determination*, which traditional logic places before our eyes. In fact they are the fruit of a dynamic process of detachment from the nothing, thus the "negation of the nothing" presents itself

---

[45] GS II, 26.

[46] At a certain point in the text (GS II, 26), the thinker substitutes the term "*Etwas* ["*something*"]" for the much more archaic and unused expression "*Ichts*", which in modern German, both in Rosenzweig's time and ours, figures almost exclusively as a component of the negative term "*Nichts* [contraction of *Nicht-Ichts*, that is "not-something", "nothing"]".

as an *event* [*Ereignis*]⁴⁷, a term which the thinker used and which has extremely dense meaning, as well as a rich future in the philosophical debate of the second half of the 20th century. The same negation of the nothing is taken as an *act* or *action* [*Tat*]⁴⁸. *Acting* means decidedly breaking with a series of rejected and not experienced *possibilities*, it means *de-ciding*, which according to the word's Latin etymology means to cut off, or according to the etymology of the German verb *sich ent-scheiden*, to separate or divide. Here too we must ask ourselves what this *determinate* and *determinating act* means with respect to God.

4.5 Ontological profile of the "elemental" God

The way of the "affirmation of the not-nothing" opens before our eyes an *essence* with a peculiar profile, a thought-of essence, which goes against a certain tradition of thought *undefined* and *undetermined*. Instead, the way of the "negation of the nothing" presents to us, an *event*, or an *act*, which are understood as *decision* and *choice*, and *exclude* all other possibilities. These two ways will always be treaded anew by the thinker, evidently with different contents, in his later search for the "elemental" figures of the world and of man, in *Star I.2* and in *Star I.3*. If they are applied to the "elemental" God, what configuration will they give us of him?

4.5.1 Divine nature

The affirmation of the "not-nothing", applied to the research of positive knowledge about the elemental God, is metaphorically revisited by the thinker and described as the tranquil flow of a spring that spreads out into an ocean that is in-finite, un-limited, all-embracing and un-circumscribable. It is a perennially peaceful ocean, it is absolutely still, its depths unfathomable and inexhaustible. The metaphor seeks to evoke the infinite *essence* of God, his peculiar *nature*, his *physis*. Such an essence is placed under the sign marked "yes", *affirmation, position* or *positivity*. This same essence articulates the *positive dynamic polarity* that profoundly constitutes and distinguishes the figure of the "elemental God".

According to the thinker logic-algebraic symbology is best suited to express the primordial world's configuration – God's *nature* is marked, in its naked simplicity, by the letter A. The letter A is not preceded by other letters, it is the first one in the series.

Rosenzweig's choice of establishing a *second* way of access to the figure of the "elemental" God, as if *first* way were insufficient by itself, opens a relevant speculative problem, which must be faced and resolved. This same choice unveils and enlightens on one hand the deep theoretic intention present in

---

[47] GS II, 26.
[48] Ibid.

Rosenzweig's theorization of the "elemental" God, and on the other hand, its extraordinary and surprising originality.

Exploring the way of the "affirmation of the nothing" in reference to the "elemental" God and this way's arrival point at the essence or infinite nature of God immediately generate an underlying question. What could there ever be within the figure of the elemental God, *beyond* his infinite *essence* and *nature*? Perhaps God does not exhaust himself *entirely* in his own infinite essence?

The predisposition of a *second way of access* to the figure of the "elemental" God gives room to the doubt that this God may *not exhaust himself at all* in his essence, infinite as it is. Within this same God's figure there must then be something *other* than or *different* from his essence.

4.5.2 Divine liberty

The "negation of nothing", applied to the research of positive knowledge about the "elemental" God, is also metaphorically revisited by the thinker; this time it is seen as the impetuous breaking forth of a jet of water from the dark pond of the divine nothing, or as a hurricane that, from the outside, falls upon the infinite and still ocean of the divine essence. Yet in this case the metaphor's intention appears to be much more problematic than the objective of the metaphor that described the Rosenzweigian understanding of the divine nature. What de-finition, intended as *position of a finite* being, what de-limitation, what de-termination could ever be produced within the infinite ocean of divine life; furthermore, at whose or what's hand? If all the previous question's terms were given a *dynamic, kinetic* and *procedural* meaning, what *event* or what act could ever take place within this same infinite ocean? Rosenzweig's answer to these questions is extremely simple yet equally surprising. The only processes of de-finition/de-limitation/de-termination which are possible within the infinite ocean of the divine life are thinkable only and exclusively as the product of an *abysmal and originary liberty*, divine liberty, precisely. The only events or acts that can take place within the divine life are *events and acts of liberty*. Yet liberty, inasmuch as it de-fines, de-limits and de-termines, as an event or act, cannot but be *finite*. Should *finiteness* be then attributed to divine liberty? Rosenzweig effectively maintains this apparently paradoxical thesis by making use of a fundamental clarification. Divine liberty is according to the thinker intrinsically finite because of its own structural configuration as liberty which de-fines, de-limits, de-termines and de-cides. Even so, it is also absolutely infinite, with respect to its *possibilities*. For God, of course, everything is *possible*. Yet what "everything" could we ever speak of in the problem structure we are exploring, that is the context of the divine infinite? What could ever be an infinite horizon within which a suitable application of God's unfathomable liberty could be possible?

In the total absence of other possibilities, the horizon in question could not be represented by anything other than the infinite divine *essence* or *nature*. God's unfathomable liberty, though structurally finite, finds its favored intentional objective, its fundamental finality in the infinite ocean of the divine *nature* or *physis*. Through the use of algebraic-mathematical logic which the thinker had previously used to describe the divine nature, he now wishes to designate *divine liberty* with the symbol A=. Once again, the letter A is chosen to express the absolutely originary and unconditioned character of everything that regards divine life. The = sign indicates the intentional tension of divine liberty toward the other, in this case, toward the infinite nature of God. In this case the *other* is not *other than* God, or outside of him, but rather *another within* the same God.

4.5.3 Divine vitality

The force field that intimately constitutes Rosenzweig's figure of the "elemental" God can at this point unfold in the totality of its internal components. The different and opposite polarities which dwell in him and move his depths have now revealed their intimate layout. The "elemental" God's profile is complete. The elemental God unfolds himself in the rich complexity of his two components – his *nature* and his *liberty*. These two components are working in the irreducible tension that exists between the *positivity* of the divine nature and the *negativity* of divine liberty. God is dynamic, kinetic, perennially moving. The divine liberty hurls itself against the divine nature, shaking its most remote foundations. The divine nature infinitely resists the divine liberty's impetus, breaking it, slowing it down, harnessing it. Divine liberty, in its struggle with the divine nature, transforms itself in *will*; the divine nature's resistance to the divine liberty's impetus is called *destiny, moira*.

The polar dynamics which occur between divine nature and liberty make up, in all of its complexity, what Rosenzweig calls "divine vitality". The "elemental" God appears to be entirely permeated by an infinite flow of life. The living God who appears at this point, in his irreducible tension between nature and liberty, is presented, in the thinker's beloved algebraic-mathematical-logical symbology, with the equation A=A.

In light of what has been said so far, we can now more exactly grasp the meaning of the title which Rosenzweig attributes to *Star I.1*: "God and his being or metaphysics". The elemental God does not present himself as metaphysical because he transcends worldly *physis* – which at this stage in Rosenzweig's discourse has not even appeared on the horizon. The metaphysical character of the "elemental" God of Rosenzweig – his *metà tà phisikà* –surprisingly refers to the divine *physis*. It is as if God were perennially *beyond* his own essence, his own nature, his own *physis*. It is as if God incessantly auto-transcended himself, it is as if he were crossed by a deep inner fracture that divides him into self-transcendent God and self-transcended God. The deep motor of this kind of divine auto transcendence, occurring within God himself in the absence of anything outside of him, is represented by the same unfathomable freedom of God. Freedom is what gives movement and life to the "elemental" God[49].

5. Epilogue

The elemental-theological meditation developed by Rosenzweig in *Star I.1* is much broader and complex than what we have been able to articulate here. Some fundamental elements of Rosenzweig's discourse developed in the Book have been completely omitted. For example one may think, not as an exhaustive list but only as an indicative one, about the philosophical and linguistic falls produced by Rosenzweig's theorization of the "elemental" God, about the rather problematic and questionable philosophical interpretation of the great oriental religious traditions (India and China), which the thinker elaborates, and finally about the budding reflections on philosophy of art which the same thinker draws from his reflection on the "elemental" God.

We would like to conclude our exposition of the subject with some considerations regarding the comparison between the figure of God and the divine that Rosenzweig treats in *Star I.1* and with some developments that the theological reflection of the thinker will come to know in the rest of the work.

Rosenzweig thematizes the "elemental" God in *Star I.1* and presents him expressly as the result of a philosophical re-elaboration of the mythical God, as thought of in the "pagan" religious tradition of Ancient Greece. According to the thinker this figure was able to grasp, in a particularly ingenious way, some fundamental traits which effectively distinguish the face of what Rosenzweig deemed to be the true God. In philosophical key, Rosenzweig's rethinking of the *revealed* image of God, which emerges from Biblical Scriptures, will take up and enhance these fundamental traits, not without transfiguring them radically. The "elemental" mythical God will be able to present himself as a sort of singular prophetic pre-announcement of the living God of the biblical tradition, who maintains with the same mythical God a relationship both of continuity and of rupture.

Some quick remarks will help to give a very general idea of the process of transfiguration that, according to the thinker, the biblical revelation will work on the base of the mythical understanding of God.

For Rosenzweig, the biblical God is the result of the mythical God's exit from the impenetrable mystery of his hiddenness. This exit is proposed by

---

[49] A careful reader of the *Star* will notice the creatively reworked main sources from which the thinker draws his understanding of the "elemental" God. Because of their relevance, Schelling's later thought on the one hand, and Nietzsche's speculative challenge, on the other, stand out among these sources, which are openly mentioned (GS II, 19–21).

Rosenzweig as follows. The supreme and unfathomable divine liberty of the "elemental" God is in tension yet remains in equilibrium with the resistance of the divine nature, but the moment of revelation breaks this equilibrium and in a certain sense, breaks through the wall of the divine nature in question, spilling it outside the mythical God's horizon. This breaking through immediately produces a revolutionary restructuring of the polar aspect that distinguished the mythical God. The divine liberty, passing through the divine nature, undergoes a positive inversion of its negative polarity and thus transforms itself in essence. In other words, the mythical God's sovereign free will is transformed in creative power with respect to the world. Divine liberty is thus harnessed and channeled, explicating itself in well determined directions of development, that is to say, in the coordinates that uphold the world's order. Divine creativity thus transforms itself into one of the *essential attributes* of the revealed God's *nature*[50].

The «elemental» divine nature, on the other hand, itself remains, so to speak, branded by the huge impact produced on it by the sovereign and abysmal divine liberty. This also produces a revolutionary restructuring of the overall polar framework which originally marked the mythical God. As a result of divine liberty's impact against the elemental divine nature, the latter also, symmetrically, inverts its polarity which thus is transformed from positive to negative. This means that the divine nature of the elemental God transforms itself into the *event* or *act* of the revealed God. If we ask ourselves what this concretely means, we meet with one of the most suggestive concepts which the *Star* offers its readers. The mythical God's nature, transforming itself into the *act* or *event* of the revealed God, transforms itself into an *act of love* on the part of God toward the human soul to which he reveals himself. In lovingly revealing himself, it is as if God offered or gave man his own *nature*, his own *essence* – that which is dearest to him. In this way God dangerously exposes himself to man's acceptance or refusal[51], but he can enter into dialogue being almost on the same level as a being from which he is separated by an unfillable ontological abyss. God hands himself over lovingly – he consigns his very essence – to human liberty; thus begins the drama which is salvation history.

It is not, of course, possible here to adequately expand on these brief thoughts. Yet, it is sufficient for us to have evoked the ulterior (the "revealed") developments of the "elemental" theological meditation – which the thinker had begun to outline in *Star I.1*.

Further readings

Del Prete, M., (2012), *Über die Wahrheit des gesunden Menschenverstandes: Zu Rosenzweigs theologia naturalis*, in: Yehoyada Amir et al., Faith, Truth and

---

[50] See GS II, 124–173.
[51] The theme of revelation is especially treated in GS II, 174–228.

Reason. New Perspektives on Rosenzweig's „Star of Redemption", Freiburg 481–492.

Schmied-Kowarzik, W., (2012), *Vom Gottesbeweis zum Erweis Gottes*, in: Yehoyada Amir et al., Faith, Truth and Reason. New Perspektives on Rosenzweig's „Star of Redemption", Freiburg 15–36.

Erster Teil, zweites Buch: Die Welt und ihr Sinn oder Metalogik

Emanuele Pompetti

1. Einführung

In diesem Aufsatz wird das zweite Buch des ersten Teils des *Stern der Erlösung* (GS II, S. 44–66) von Franz Rosenzweig dargestellt. Der rote Faden der Darstellung wird der Begriff der *metalogischen Welt* sein und dies aus mehreren Gründen. Einerseits trägt der Teil, der hier behandelt wird, eben diese Überschrift: «Die *Welt* und ihr Sinn oder *Metalogik*»[52]. Andererseits ist anzumerken, dass der gesamte *Stern* metalogisch aufgebaut ist.

Was dies bedeutet, soll im Folgenden dargestellt werden. Dafür ist allerdings ein Ausgangspunkt nötig und dieser kann nur der sein, der am Anfang des *Sternes* von Rosenzweig selbst vertreten wird: der Tod bzw. die Angst vor dem Tod. Rosenzweig tut dies, weil der Tod eine bestimmte Beziehung zum Nichts, also zum Punkt Null der Erkenntnis, darstellt[53], und Rosenzweig schreibt:

---

[52] GS II, 44.
[53] Rosenzweig schreibt: «Das Nichts ist nicht Nichts, es ist Etwas. Im dunkeln Hintergrund der Welt stehen als ihre unerschöpfliche Voraussetzung *tausend Tode*, statt des einen Nichts, das wirklich Nichts wäre, *tausend Nichtse*, die, eben weil viele, Etwas sind.» (GS II, 5; kursiv von mir). Der Tod hat also

---

How to cite this book chapter:
Pompetti, E. 2021. Erster Teil, zweites Buch: Die Welt und ihr Sinn oder Metalogik. In: Brasser, M., Bojanić, P. and Ciglia, F. P. (eds.) The Star *for Beginners: Introductions to the Magnum Opus of Franz Rosenzweig*. Pp. 41–54. London: Ubiquity Press. DOI: https://doi.org/10.5334/bco.e. License: CC-BY

«Von den Nichtsen des Wissens stösst unsere Entdeckerfahrt vor zum Etwas des Wissens.»[54]

Das Nichts als Ausgangspunkt der Erkenntnis über den Sinn der Welt wird sich in zwei Wege spalten, die aber komplementär sind und die jeweils auf verschiedene Erkenntnisse bringen werden. Diese zwei Wege werden von Rosenzweig «de[r] Weg der Bejahung dessen, was nicht Nichts ist, und de[r] Weg der Verneinung des Nichts»[55] genannt. Hier wird nun der Weg vom Tode über das Nichts bis zur metalogischen Welt im *Stern* rekonstruiert.

Bevor mit dem Eigentlichen begonnen wird, ist eine kleine Anmerkung nötig. In diesem Aufsatz ist der vielleicht etwas einfache Stil der Darstellung zu entschuldigen, der aber, dem Ziel dieses Bandes dienend, Klarheit in der Darstellung schaffen möchte. Aus diesem Grund und aus Gründen des eingeschränkten Umfangs dieses Aufsatzes sind die Verweise, die der erfahrene Philosoph sicherlich vermissen wird, auf andere Philosophen und deren Werke bzw. auf Sekundärliteratur vermieden bzw. massiv eingeschränkt.

2. Vom Tode

«Vom Tode, von der Furcht des Todes, hebt alles Erkennen des All an»[56]. Wir können versuchen, mit Rosenzweig diesen Weg zu gehen: aus der Angst des Todes, Erkenntnis über die Welt zu gewinnen.

Was ist der Tod? Wir wissen wahrscheinlich wenig darüber, ja vielleicht sogar nichts. Aber heisst das, dass der Tod nichts ist? Nein, nur wir wissen nichts darüber. Wir fürchten den Tod wahrscheinlich deswegen, weil wir nichts über ihn wissen und weil er uns auf jeden Fall angeht: nur eins ist sicher, wir werden irgendwann sterben. Diese Wahrheit, die bei Rosenzweig durch so etwas wie eine Urangst, die jeder hat, bewusst oder unbewusst, ans Licht kommt, kann keine Lehre verleugnen. Man mag dem Tod jegliche Bedeutung geben (ein Scheintod, ein Gehen ins Jenseits, ein Auseinandergehen der Moleküle, aus denen wir bestehen, ein gehen ins Nichts, usw.), sicher aber ist nur eins: jeder, alles muss einst sterben. Wenn der Tod dermassen beängstigt, dass er dazu drängt, nach Erkenntnis zu suchen, um sich zu beruhigen, weil niemand in und mit dieser Spannung ein schönes Leben verbringen kann, wenn der Tod die unausweichliche Frage ist, können wir nicht behaupten, dass er nichts sei. Also ist der Tod etwas. Aber Was?

---

eine Beziehung zum Nichts. Allerdings ist das Nichts im *Stern* nicht nur der „Punkt Null" der Erkenntnis. Hier können wir die anderen Aspekte des Nichts im *Stern* nicht vertiefen, deswegen verweisen wir auf: L. Bertolino, Il nulla e la filosofia. Idealismo critico ed esperienza religiosa in Franz Rosenzweig, Torino 2005.

[54] GS II, 22.
[55] GS II, 23.
[56] GS II, 3.

Der Tod, hier von Rosenzweig als Ausgangspunkt unseres Wissens genommen, ist ein Nichts: das Nichts *unseres Wissens* und gerade dieses Nichts-Wissen über den Tod, der uns aber unmittelbar angeht, macht uns Angst und drängt uns zur Suche nach der Erkenntnis, denn das, was uns geschieht und das wir nicht verstehen, beängstigt uns. Ausserdem ist mit dieser Urangst ein gewisses Gefühl des Untergehens verbunden. Denn was bedeutet, sich vor dem Tod zu fürchten? Es bedeutet das Gefühl des Untergehens zu haben, sich auch für einen kurzen Moment panisch die Fragen zu stellen: „Sterbe ich?", „Was passiert im Augenblick des Todes? Und danach?", „Gehe ich ins Nichts?", „Wie kann ich dem Tod entgehen? Ist das überhaupt möglich?", usw. Rosenzweig schreibt dazu: «der Mensch […] muss sich einmal in seiner furchtbaren Armut, Einsamkeit und Losgerissenheit von aller Welt gefühlt haben und eine Nacht lang Aug in Auge mit dem Nichts gestanden sein.»[57] Allerdings, schreibt Rosenzweig, «ihm [dem Menschen] ist ein […] Ausweg aus dem Engpass des Nichts bestimmt»[58]. Welcher denn? Er schreibt weiter: «Der Mensch soll die Angst des Irdischen nicht von sich werfen; er soll in der Furcht des Todes – bleiben. […] Die Angst des Irdischen soll von ihm genommen werden nur mit dem Irdischen selbst»[59].

Wie ist so etwas möglich? Die Philosophie hat Rosenzweigs Meinung nach versucht, die historische Aufgabe zu erfüllen, dem Menschen die Angst vor dem Tod zu nehmen. Wie denn? Wie soll die Philosophie die Angst vor dem Irdischen, vor dem Sterblichen nehmen? Hier finden wir den zentralen, „philosophischen"[60] Ansatz Rosenzweigs: «Die Angst des Irdischen soll von ihm genommen werden *nur mit dem Irdischen selbst*»[61]. Er setzt sich mit der philosophischen Tradition auseinander und nimmt dazu Stellung und seine Lösung, die einzig mögliche für ihn, ist eine *metalogische*. Im Folgenden werden wir also den Gedankengang Rosenzweigs rekonstruieren, der uns von der Angst des Todes zu einer metalogischen Antwort führen soll.

3. Der Weg zur *Meta*-logik

«Die Angst des Irdischen abzuwerfen, dem Tod seinen Giftstachel, dem Hades seinen Pesthauch zu nehmen, des vermisst sich die Philosophie»[62]. Wie geht

---

[57] GS II, 4.
[58] GS II, 4.
[59] GS II, 4.
[60] „Philosophisch" in dem Sinne, dass Rosenzweig hier, im ersten Teil des *Sternes*, seine Gedanken «in philosophos» (GS II, 3), also „für die Philosophen" bzw. „im Namen der Philosophen" formuliert. Denn die Philosophie hat, seiner Meinung nach, nicht das letzte Wort (dies werden wir aber später vertiefen).
[61] GS II, 4; kursiv von mir.
[62] GS II, 3.

das? Kann die Philosophie das wirklich? Für Rosenzweig ist die Antwort der Philosophie vielleicht unzulänglich, aber es ist sehr wichtig, dass der Mensch diesen Weg geht, denn dies wird ihn dazu bringen, den philosophischen Ansatz zu überwinden und durch die Theologie (zweiter Teil des *Sternes* – «in theologos»[63]) und die Politik (dritter Teil des *Sternes* – «in tyrannos»[64]) hindurch der Weg «[v]om Tode»[65] (wie es am Anfang des *Sternes* heisst), «ins Leben»[66] (wie es am Ende des *Sternes* heisst) zu gehen. Dieser Weg ist ein fruchtbarer Weg voller Erkenntnis. Denn der Mensch ist ein erkennendes Wesen und diese Erkenntnis hat eine Geschichte, sie entsteht durch einen bestimmten Prozess, den wir hier schildern werden. Ja, das Leben ist auch Erkenntnis, die Erkenntnis ist ein wichtiger Teil unseres Lebens. Der Mensch, der lebt, strebt ein bewusstes Leben an, ein Leben, in dem er weiss, woher er kommt und wohin er geht. Der Mensch möchte wissen, ob er in der Erkenntnis einen Anhaltspunkt haben kann, um sich im Leben zu orientieren. Deswegen muss der Weg zur Erkenntnis beschrieben und geprüft werden. Dies tut Rosenzweig, indem er sich zum „Punkt Null" des Wissens stellt und daraus versucht, unser Wissen über die drei Elemente, die die Wirklichkeit ausmachen, Gott, Welt und Mensch, zu rekonstruieren.

Hier ist anzumerken, dass innerhalb des bis jetzt aufgebauten Szenarios bereits alle Elemente der «immerwährenden Vorwelt»[67] vorhanden sind: Gott, Welt und Mensch. Denn die Frage nach dem Tod setzt ein Wesen, einen Menschen voraus, der *lebt* (und *die Welt* besteht aus abertausenden *lebendigen Einzelwesen*), der sich um sein Leben kümmert (innerhalb eines bestimmten Milieus, *der Welt* eben, in der der Mensch sich *orientieren* möchte, ja sogar *orientieren muss*) und ängstigt, der sich vielleicht sogar die Frage nach einem möglichen Schöpfer des Lebens (*Gott*) oder Retter stellt (*Gott* oder der Nächste, der andere *Mensch*). Diese sind die drei „Nichtse", über die Rosenzweig im ersten Buch des *Sternes* nachdenkt. Denn, nachdem ich mir die Frage gestellt habe, ob es Gott, Welt und Mensch gibt, was weiss ich darüber? Erstmal nichts, ich muss erst weiter denken, um Aussagen über sie machen zu können, und das ist eben das, was Rosenzweig in diesem ersten Teil des *Sternes* macht. Aber auf diesem ersten Niveau (ausgehend vom „Punkt Null der Erkenntnis") ist *in der Frage*, was Gott, Mensch und Welt seien, noch keine Antwort enthalten. Keine Antwort, aber schon eine gewisse *Orientierung*. Gott, Mensch und Welt bezeichnen drei Baustellen, drei Probleme (Gott das Problem der Schöpfung, der Rettung, ja sogar seiner Existenz und das Problem, was er sei – das Problem der Physis Gottes; die Welt das Problem der Lebenden und die Frage der Orientierung des Menschen in ihr, also ob und wie sie verständlich sei – das Problem der Logik;

---

[63] GS II, 103.
[64] GS II, 295.
[65] GS II, 3.
[66] GS II, 472.
[67] GS II, 2.

der Mensch das Problem der Rettung und dementsprechend – der Ethik). Hier finden wir eine erste Erklärung der Vorsilbe „meta"[68]. Rosenzweig schreibt: «Nicht als Gegenstände rationaler Wissenschaft denken wir sie wiederherzustellen, sondern gerade umgekehrt als ‚irrationale' Gegenstände. Als Mittel zur ersten Absteckung ihrer Orte diente uns die Methode, die in der Vorsilbe ‚meta' bezeichnet ist»[69].

4. Die zwei Wege zum Etwas des Wissens

Bevor wir mit der Rekonstruktion der Erkenntnis über die Welt (Gott und Mensch werden im ersten und dritten Buch des ersten Teils des *Sternes* behandelt, deswegen werden sie hier ausgelassen) starten, muss geklärt werden, wie Rosenzweig zu den aufwändigen und etwas dunklen Formulierungen der „Verneinung des Nichts" und der „Bejahung des Nichtnichts" kommt.

Angst vor dem Tod zu haben heisst, sich die Frage zu stellen: was ist der Tod? Ist der Tod nichts? – „Nein", lautet die Antwort. Ist also der Tod etwas? – „Ja", lautet die Antwort. Was ist aber der Tod? Was weiss ich darüber? – „Nichts."

Auf diese Weise haben wir schon unsere zwei Wege, von denen Rosenzweig spricht (die „Verneinung des Nichts" und die „Bejahung des Nichtnichts") und die uns zur Erkenntnis führen sollten: Ist der Tod nichts? – *„Nein."* Unter dieser Perspektive wird der Tod als *„Verneinung* des Nichts" bezeichnet. Ist der Tod etwas? – *„Ja."* Was denn? – „Ich weiss es nicht, ich weiss nur, dass er nicht Nichts ist." Unter dieser zweiten Perspektive wird der Tod also als *„Bejahung* des Nichtnichts" bezeichnet.

Unter der ersten Perspektive wird der Tod als nichts verneint (der Tod ist etwas, deshalb kann ich davor Angst haben), aber das bedeutet gleichzeitig ein erster Schritt unseres Wissens über den Tod, ein sich Verabschieden vom Nichts des Wissens über den Tod: kann ich etwas über den Tod behaupten? Kann ich eine positive Aussage über den Tod machen? „Der Tod ist nicht Nichts" ist eine negative Aussage, also eine „Verneinung des Nichts" des Todes.

Kann ich dies nun positiv formulieren? Ja: der Tod ist ein „Nichtnichts". Das „Nichtnichts" des Todes kann bejaht werden. Wieso sind diese zwei Wege so wichtig und komplementär für Rosenzweig? Weil sie verschiedene Perspektiven eröffnen. Dass der Tod kein Nichts sei, zeigt nur, dass es ein Etwas gibt. *Was* das denn sei, ist in der Frage nicht enthalten. Eine Verneinung unterbricht das Fragen. Eine Bejahung, eine positive Formulierung, möchte nun mit präzisen

---

[68] Rosenzweig spricht vom „*meta*physischen Gottesbegriff", vom „*meta*logischen Weltbegriff" und vom „*meta*ethischen Menschenbegriff" (siehe GS II, 20).
[69] GS II, 22.

Inhalten gefüllt werden. Ich möchte nun nicht nur wissen, ober der Tod nichts sei (Ja-Nein-Frage), sondern auch, was denn der Tod sei.[70]

4.1 Die „Verneinung des Nichts"

Wir gehen nun zuerst[71] den Weg der „Verneinung des Nichts". Die Welt ist nicht Nichts, sondern etwas. Sie besteht aus einzelnen Wesen, die nicht nichts sind, sondern etwas, so wahr ist es, dass sie auch sterben können. Ist diese eine grosse Erkenntnis? Für Rosenzweig schon, denn somit kritisiert er den Ansatz «der ganzen ehrwürdigen Gesellschaft der Philosophen von Ionien bis Jena»[72], also von den Griechen bis Hegel, die die Welt «als eine Allheit»[73] betrachtet haben. Diese ist die Antwort, für Rosenzweig ja die Lüge, die die Philosophie gepriesen hat, um den Menschen von der Todesfrage zu erleichtern. Rosenzweig schreibt: «die Philosophie leugnet diese Ängste der Erde [...], indem sie den blauen Dunst ihres Allgedankens um das Irdische webt. Denn freilich: ein All würde nicht sterben, und im All stürbe nichts. Sterben kann nur das Einzelne.»[74] Die Philosophie hat meistens behauptet, dass eigentlich ein All existieren würde (z.B. das Sein bei Parmenides, das Eine bei Plotin, Gott bei Spinoza, der Geist bei Hegel, usw.) und nicht das Einzelne. Das Einzelne wäre nur immer als Offenbarung, als Teil usw. des Alls zu verstehen. Das All hätte ein (wahres) Leben, nicht das Einzelne, und weil das Einzelne nur im All zu verstehen ist und nur in ihm und durch es leben kann, «ist der letzte Schluss dieser Weisheit: der Tod sei – Nichts»[75], denn der Tod des Einzelnen kann das Leben des Seins, oder das Leben Gottes oder des Geistes nicht beeinträchtigen. Mit dem Weg der „Verneinung des Nichts" – der Tod ist nicht Nichts – wehrt sich Rosenzweig gegen diese Lüge der philosophischen Tradition. Der Tod ist nicht nichts, und

---

[70] Diese zwei Wege setzen verschiedene Akzente. Rosenzweig schreibt, dass der Weg der Bejahung unendlich ist, der Weg der Verneinung aber endlich. Denn in der Antwort auf die Frage, was der Tod sei, ist das Feld nicht eingeschränkt, sondern potentiell „unendlich" breit, die Möglichkeiten, die geprüft werden wollen, sind erst mal potentiell unendlich. Dies ist bei der Frage „Ist der Tod nichts?" nicht der Fall, denn diese ist eine Ja-Nein-Frage, es stehen also potentiell nur zwei Antworten zur Verfügung. Rosenzweig schreibt: «Bejahung des Nichtnichts setzt – wie jede Bejahung, die durch Verneinung geschieht, – ein Unendliches, Verneinung des Nichts setzt – wie jede Verneinung – ein Begrenztes, Endliches, Bestimmtes.» (GS II, 26)

[71] Rosenzweig stellt im *Stern* zuerst den Weg der „Bejahung des Nichtnichts" dar und dann den Weg der „Verneinung des Nichts". Hier kehren wir aus Klarheitsgründen die Ordnung der Darstellung um.

[72] GS II, 13.

[73] GS II, 13.

[74] GS II, 3–4.

[75] GS II, 4.

die Welt ist kein All, sondern sie besteht aus vielen einzelnen Teilen, die eine gewisse gegenseitige Autonomie haben. Es gibt kein Leben ausserhalb dieser einzelnen Wesen. Ein All, das lebt, gibt es nicht. Diese ist die erste, ja vielleicht die wichtigste Erkenntnis, wodurch Rosenzweig den Begriff „Metalogik" charakterisiert: ein Ganzes, das lebt, gibt es nicht, es gibt nur einzelne Teile bzw. Einzelwesen, die leben und die als Nebeneffekt durch die Beziehungen, die sie zueinander pflegen, evtl. ein Ganzes ausmachen[76]. Alles, was existiert, ist metalogisch[77]. Die einzelnen Teile leben und existieren, das Ganze nicht. Rosenzweig fügt hinzu: «dass die Philosophie das Einzelne aus der Welt schaffen muss, diese Ab-schaffung des Etwas ist auch der Grund, weshalb sie idealistisch sein muss»[78].

Aber wieso wird dies, dass nur die Einzelnen leben und nicht das Ganze, als „metalogisch" bezeichnet? Denn in jedem „idealistischen" (im Sinne Rosenzweigs – d.h., dass die Ideen ein Leben haben bzw. lebendig sind) System hat das All eine bestimmte „logische" Dynamik. Die einzelnen Wesen können im Rahmen dieses Alls „abgeleitet" werden, die einzelnen Wesen verhalten sich „logisch", weil das System „logisch" gestaltet ist und diese Wesen im System fest verankert sind (Rosenzweig spricht von «Emanation»[79]). Wieso verhält sich dieses All „logisch"? Rosenzweig schreibt: «Worauf beruhte denn jene Allheit? Weshalb wurde denn die Welt nicht etwa als Vielheit gedeutet? Hier steckt offenbar eine Voraussetzung [...]: die der Denkbarkeit der Welt. Es ist die Einheit des Denkens [...]. Die Einheit des Logos begründet die Einheit der Welt als eine Allheit. Und hinwiederum bewährt jene Einheit ihren Wahrheitswert in dem Begründen dieser Allheit.»[80] Die Welt muss als Allheit gedacht werden, damit sie überhaupt denkbar sein kann, denn denken heisst, die Beziehungen zwischen den Elementen, die das Ganze ausmachen, zu verstehen. Wenn das Ganze verständlich ist, muss dieses Ganze sich nach „logischen Mustern" verhalten und entwickeln (und dementsprechend die Einzelteile dieses Ganzen ebenso), meinen die Idealisten, da ich diese Beziehungen nachvollziehen kann. Die Philosophie setzt deswegen die Identität von Sein und Denken voraus, um die Übereinstimmung zwischen Sein und Denken zu begründen.

---

[76] Rosenzweig schreibt: «hier [beim Metalogischen] gilt das All nicht mehr als das eine und allgemeine, sondern als „ein" All» (GS II, 50–51).

[77] Der gesamte Stern ist metalogisch aufgebaut, es gibt nur Teile, die drei «Elemente» (GS II, 2) Gott (GS II, 25), Welt (GS II, 44) und Mensch (GS II, 67) die später (im zweiten Teil des *Sternes*) in Beziehung treten. Diese Beziehungen werden «Schöpfung» (GS II, 124), «Offenbarung» (GS II, 174) und «Erlösung» (GS II, 229) genannt.

[78] GS II, 4.

[79] GS II, 55 (dieser Ausdruck ist aus der philosophischen Tradition übernommen, wie z.B. bei Plotin).

[80] GS II, 12–13.

Aber für Rosenzweig gilt die «Nichtidentität von Sein und Denken»[81] [...]. Er fügt hinzu: «Da der Grund der Einheit von Sein und Denken im Denken gesucht wird [bzw. gesucht wurde, von den Idealisten], so müsste zunächst im Denken der Grund der Nichtidentität aufgedeckt werden»[82] und das ist es, was Rosenzweig mit dem Weg der „Verneinung des Nichts" macht, denn damit hat er den Allheitsgedanke kritisiert. *Wie ist aber die Welt denkbar, wenn es keine Identität zwischen Denken und Sein gibt?* Diese Frage wird anhand des Weges der „Bejahung des Nichtnichts" beantwortet.

Die Welt ist ein All. Diese ist eben die grösste Scheinweisheit, die Rosenzweig verleugnen möchte: es gibt kein All, es gibt kein System! Die Welt ist nicht „logisch", wie die Idealisten sie sich vorgestellt haben. Allerdings heisst das nicht, dass sie unlogisch sei, denn wir haben ja gesagt, dass wir eine Erkenntnis haben und diese Erkenntnis auch irgendwie „logisch" ist (wir werden im Folgenden sehen, in welchem Sinne Rosenzweig hier von „Logik" spricht). Die Welt ist nicht „unlogisch", aber auf keinen Fall „logisch" im Sinne des Idealismus: sie ist *meta*logisch, das heisst jenseits der Logik, weil das erste, der Ausgangspunkt, die Notwendige und unabdingbare Voraussetzung für die Existenz einer Welt, die Existenz des Einzelnen ist und nicht die des Alls. Das All des Idealismus mag logisch sein, es existiert für Rosenzweig nicht. Was existiert, sind die einzelnen Wesen und was wir über sie bis zu diesem Zeitpunkt der Argumentation behaupten können, wurde bereits dargestellt: sie sterben, sie sind sterblich.

Der Weg der „Verneinung des Nichts" ist also sehr fruchtbar und unabdingbar für Rosenzweig. Allerdings konnten wir somit das Lebendige nicht positiv definieren. Dafür müssen wir den zweiten Weg beschreiten: den Weg der „Bejahung des Nichtnichts". Wir stellen uns nun die Frage, *was* denn der Tod sei.

4.2 Die „Bejahung des Nichtnichts"

Was ist der Tod? Ich weiss es nicht, ich weiss nur, dass man stirbt. Was stirbt also? Wenn ich die allgemeinste Antwort versuchen würde, die fast wie eine Tautologie klingen könnte, würde ich antworten: das Lebendige. Das Lebendige stirbt. Was ist aber das Lebendige? Kann ich das sagen? Ich kann behaupten, dass ich lebe. Ich lebe, ich existiere, ich bin. Um zu sterben, muss ich ja sein. Und weil der Tod mir Angst macht, weil ich sterben werde, heisst es, dass ich keine „quantité négligeable"[83] bin und dass ich bzw. meine existenzielle Situation des Leidens, der Angst und des Sterbens der Ausgangspunkt jedes meines Erkennens sein darf. Wenn ich lebe, stellt sich die Frage: Wer bin ich? Was bin ich? Was ist das Lebendige überhaupt? Wenn es eine Welt gibt, die aus verschiedenen lebendigen Wesen besteht, was sind diese Wesen? Wenn diese Wesen

---

[81] GS II, 13.
[82] GS II, 13; Anmerkung in Klammern von mir.
[83] "Ich bin nicht unwichtig".

sterben, wie kann die Welt weiter bestehen, wenn es diese Wesen sind, die die Welt ausmachen? Die Welt kann offenbar bestehen, weil andere Wesen geboren werden. Rosenzweig schreibt: «Ohne Aufhören gebiert Neues der Schoss der unermüdlichen Erde, und ein jedes ist dem Tode verfallen.»[84] In diesem Satz ist bereits am Anfang des *Sternes* die Dynamik der Welt geschildert. Wir haben nun herausgefunden, was die Welt ist.

Kann ich mich aber somit zufriedengeben? Habe ich nun positiv bestimmt, was das Lebendige ist? Gibt es ein Wort, das diese Dynamik beschreibt, das für alle existierenden Wesen zutrifft, und das mir Erkenntnis, d.h. Ordnung in dieses Chaos der Welt bringen würde? Für Rosenzweig ist dies der Fall: der Begriff heisst «Gattung»[85]. Denn nur der Einzelne stirbt, die Gattung aber nicht, sie erneuert sich durch den Tod des einzelnen Wesens.

Dieser Schritt zur „Gattung" ist deswegen sehr wichtig, weil er der entscheidende Schritt zum metalogischen Aspekt *der Erkenntnis, zum Sinn* der Welt ist. Mit diesem Begriff können wir die Dynamik der Welt feststellen: Die Gattung ist das Allgemeine, das über den Einzelnen steht. Wenn ich mich frage, was die Welt sei, muss ich feststellen, dass denken (in diesem Falle der Versuch, diese Frage nach der Welt zu beantworten), immer denken an etwas ist. Ich kann mir also dieses „etwas" bzw. die vielen „etwas", die einzelnen Wesen vorstellen, aber das sagt mir noch nichts darüber, was die Welt ist. Diese *begrifflose* Welt, die wir anhand der „Verneinung des Nichts" gefunden haben, ist chaotisch für mich, erscheint mir ungeordnet, ich habe in diesem Sinne kaum Erkenntnis von ihr, mir fehlt die Orientierung. Um diese Welt *begreifen* zu können, brauche ich allgemeine Begriffe wie „Mensch, Tier, Staat, Bürger, usw.", die die innersten Beziehungen zwischen den einzelnen Wesen aufweisen. Die Beziehungen, von denen im ersten Teil des *Sternes* die Rede ist, sind keine Beziehungen, die jeder Einzelne in seinem Leben bewusst pflegt oder vermeiden kann. Es sind die Beziehungen „des Seins" der einzelnen Wesen.

Der Weg der „Bejahung des Nichtnichts" ist bei Rosenzweig fruchtbar für *den Sinn* der Welt, für die Erkenntnis. Ich kann nur durch Begriffe, die eine Ordnung in die vor mir liegende und erscheinende Welt bringen, die Welt verstehen. Denn ohne die *allgemeinen* Begriffe der Vernunft, kann ich nichts über diese Anhäufung an *besonderen* Wesen sagen. Rosenzweig schreibt: «hier [...] beschreiben wir gewissermassen die ganze Kurve des Vorgangs. Der eine [...] Punkt ist der, wo nach einem Stück reinen, *richtungs- und bewusstseinslos* blinden Stürzens das Besondere sich seiner gezogenen Bewegung nach dem Allgemeinen hin gewissermassen *bewusst wird* und ihm dadurch die Augen *über seine eigene Natur* aufgehen. In diesem Augenblick wird das vorher blinde Besondere überhaupt zum seiner Besonderheit *bewussten* [...] Besonderen. Ein Besonderes, das vom Allgemeinen „weiss", [...] [d]as ist das „Individuum", das Einzelne, das die Merkmale des Allgemeinen, seiner Art, seiner Gattung, am

---

[84] GS II, 3.
[85] GS II, 52.

Leibe trägt und trotzdem noch wesentlich Besonderes, aber nun eben „individuelles" Besonderes ist»[86].

Rosenzweig fügt hinzu: «Es gibt einen Vorgang, worin sich diese beiden Elemente des Weltwesens [...] spiegeln. Das Individuum entspringt in der Geburt, der Genus [...] in der Begattung. Der Akt der Begattung geht der Geburt voraus und geschieht als einzelner Akt ohne die bestimmte Beziehung auf sie als Einzelne, dennoch in seinem allgemeinen Wesen streng auf sie bezogen und gerichtet. Die Geburt aber bricht nun in ihrem individuellen Ergebnis hervor [...]. Begattung gab es immer und dennoch ist jede Geburt etwas absolut Neues. Die Eigenheit des Geborenen [...] sammelt sich ganz im Augenblick der Geburt [...] insofern er Individualität, also ein besonderer Teil der Welt gleich jedem andren aussermenschliche Wesen oder Ding, ist»[87].

Jedes einzelne Wesen ist also ein Individuum, es hat eine bestimmte Beziehung zum Allgemeinen, es trägt diese Beziehung ja sogar „am Leibe", aber das, was lebt, sind die „Individuen" und nicht die allgemeinen Begriffe selbst, wie z.B. Hegel behauptet. Der Beweis dafür ist, dass ein allgemeiner Begriff nicht sterben kann. Die Gattungen, die Begriffe, sind keine Subjekte, die leben. Was sind sie dann? Sie sind eben reine Begriffe, die man „wunderbarerweise" auf die Welt anwenden kann. Rosenzweig schreibt: «Das Denken ist als ein vielverzweigtes System einzelner Bestimmungen in die Welt ergossen [...] Es verdankt seine Bedeutung für die Welt, seine „Anwendbarkeit", jener Verzweigung, jener Vielfältigkeit, zu der es sich entschlossen hat»[88]. Die Begriffe der Vernunft sind „anwendbar", „existieren" aber nicht, nur das einzelne Wesen existiert. Deswegen gibt es lediglich Übereinstimmung zwischen Denken und Sein, und nicht Identität, wie der Idealismus behaupten würde, und das Sein, wenn man unbedingt davon sprechen möchte, wird vom *Da*sein, also von den einzelnen Wesen, abgeleitet, und nicht umgekehrt.

Nun können wir uns die Frage stellen, die wir vorher unbeantwortet gelassen haben: wie kann die Welt denkbar sein, wenn es keine Identität zwischen Sein und Denken gibt? Wie entsteht diese Übereinstimmung zwischen Denken und Sein, wenn nicht durch eine Identität zwischen Sein und Denken? Rosenzweig schreibt: «indem [...] [das Allgemeine] Anwendung verlangt, geht eine anziehende Kraft von ihm aus. So bildet sich um das Allgemeine ein Kraftfeld der Anziehung, in das das Besondere unter dem Zwange seiner eigenen Schwere hineinstürzt.»[89] Rosenzweig liefert uns also keine Begründung, *wie* das Denken auf die Welt angewendet werden kann[90], keine Begründung dafür, wieso

---

[86] GS II, 51–52; kursiv von mir.
[87] GS II, 53.
[88] GS II, 46
[89] GS II, 51.
[90] Rosenzweig scheint hier eine Metapher aus dem Bereich der Chemie zu verwenden. Er stellt diese „anziehende Kraft" fest, ohne zu zeigen, wie sie entsteht.

Welt und Logos übereinstimmen. In der Tat ist das für Rosenzweig nicht zu begründen[91], denn: «[d]as bloss vorausgesetzte Denken mag gedacht werden müssen, denkt aber nicht; bloss das wirkliche, das weltgültige, weltangewandte, weltheimische Denken denkt. So bleibt die Einheit des Denkens ausserhalb; das Denken muss sich dafür trösten mit der Einheit der Anwendung in den geschlossenen Mauern der Welt.»[92] Was sind Begriffe? Was sind Namen? Sie bestehen in der reinen Möglichkeit ihrer Anwendung auf die Welt und das ist das, was Rosenzweig mit «Logos»[93] meint. Er schreibt: «Der Logos ist *das Wesen* der Welt»[94]. Die Welt ist also metalogisch: sie existiert jenseits und unabhängig von der Logik; die Begriffe, der Logos, „existieren" nicht (sie haben kein eigenes Leben). Die Logik besteht nur darin, auf die Welt angewendet werden zu können und deswegen ist diese Welt nicht unlogisch, sondern metalogisch. Denken bedeutet, *anhand der Sprache* denken. Rosenzweig spricht von «Sprachvernunft»[95]. Ohne Sprache keine Vernunft. Ohne Vernunft kein Denken. Ohne Denken kein *Sinn* der Welt.

4.3 Mathematische Zeichen

Der Logos, das Denken in Begriffen, ist für uns das Wesen der Welt. Die Welt ist begreifbar. Danach suchen wir, wenn wir uns die Frage stellen, was die Welt sei, denn wir versuchen sie zu begreifen. Was die Welt ist, diese „was-ist-Frage", kann nur unsere Erkenntnis beantworten: „Die Welt ist..." und das, was folgt, sind notwendigerweise Begriffe. Allerdings ist das Wesen der Welt „dynamisch" und nicht statisch. Wir haben bereits gesehen, dass «[j]edes Besondere [...] bei seiner Geburt [...] nichts als seiend [ist]. Seine Kraft ist nur das blinde Schwergewicht seines Seins»[96] und dass «die logischen Formen [...] das Unbewegte, das „ewig Gestrige", das „Allgemeine" [sind]»[97]. Allerdings «*in der Bewegung*, die das Individuum in die geöffneten Arme der Gattung hineinführt, vollendet sich die Gestalt der Welt.»[98]

Um diese Bewegung innerhalb des Seins der Welt zu beschreiben, bedient sich Rosenzweig der Symbole der Mathematik, denen er aber eine völlig

---

[91] Eine weitere Passage des *Sternes*, die dies zu betonen scheint, ist die folgende: «Diese seine [jedes Weltteils] Individualität wird nun mit *dunkler* Gewalt angezogen von der Macht ihrer Gattung» (GS II, 53–54; kursiv von mir), „dunkel", weil nicht zu erklären.
[92] GS II, 46–47.
[93] GS II, 46.
[94] GS II, 46; kursiv von mir.
[95] GS II, 36.
[96] GS II, 49.
[97] GS II, 50.
[98] GS II, 52; kursiv von mir.

eigenartige Bedeutung verleiht, die mit der üblichen Mathematik, die wir aus der Schule kennen, wenig zu tun hat.

Rosenzweig beschreibt den Logos als „B=A"[99], also „Besonders=Allgemein"[100]. Was „A" betrifft, schreibt er: «[w]ollen wir für diesen schlechthin allgemeinen und doch überall der Welt verhafteten, in sie eingebundenen Logos eine formelhafte Bezeichnung, so müssten wir ihn als Ergebnis einer Bejahung auf der rechten Gleichungsseite auftreten lassen; um seiner Allgemeinheit willen, die keinen Raum neben sich freilässt, dürften wir ihn nur mit A bezeichnen»[101]. Das Zeichen „=" beschreibt das Merkmal der Anwendbarkeit der Allgemeinheit der Begriffe auf die Welt, ja die Anziehungskraft, die diese den Einzelwesen gegenüber haben: «der Charakter der Anwendbarkeit, den wir ihm als wesentlich erkannten, bedeutet einen Hinweis auf die Notwendigkeit, dass die Anwendung an ihm auch wirklich geschehe; diese passiv anziehende Kraft, die von ihm ausgeht, wurde im Symbol ausgedrückt durch den Vorantritt des Gleichheitszeichens. So erhalten wir "=A".»[102] Was „B" betrifft, schreibt er: «Jedes Besondere [...] bei seiner Geburt ist es blind, es ist nichts als seiend. Seine Kraft ist nur das blinde Schwergewicht seines Seins. Das Symbol nach unsrer Terminologie ist B, schlechtweg B, das nackte Zeichen der Einzelheit, ohne ein hinweisendes Zeichen der Gleichheit.»[103] Die Welt hat diese dynamische Bewegung in sich, «ihr Schoss ist nimmersatt zu empfangen, unerschöpflich zu gebären. Oder besser – denn Männliches und Weibliches ist beides in ihr – sie ist als „Natur" ebenso die endlose Gebärerin der Gestalten wie die nie ermattende Zeugungskraft des in ihr heimischen „Geistes".»[104] «So entsteht die Gestalt der Welt, [...] aus dem Eingehen des Individuums in die Gattung.»[105]

Rosenzweig verwendet nicht nur mathematische Zeichen, sondern auch ein bestimmtes Fachvokabular, um diese Dynamik der Welt zu beschreiben. Diese Dynamik, genannt die «Wirklichkeit der Welt»[106], entsteht aus der Synergie zwischen dem allgemeinen und besonderen Charakter der Welt, also zwischen jeweils der «weltliche[n] Ordnung»[107] und der «weltliche[n] Fülle»[108].

Eine letzte Frage bleibt noch ungeklärt: was ist der Tod (denn diese war unsere Ausgangsfrage)? Der Tod kann für Rosenzweig auf diesem Stadium des *Sternes* nur innerhalb dieser Dynamik der Welt verstanden werden.

---

[99] GS II, 54.
[100] Siehe GS II, 51: «Das Besondere – erinnern wir uns des Symbols „B" [...] und das Allgemeine – „=A"».
[101] GS II, 47.
[102] GS II, 47–48.
[103] GS II, 49.
[104] GS II, 48.
[105] GS II, 53.
[106] GS II, 50.
[107] GS II, 45.
[108] GS II, 48.

Andere Aspekte dieses Teils des *Sternes*, wie z.B. die griechische Welt, die orientalische Welt und die Kunst können hier nicht behandelt werden. Es sei nur Folgendes gesagt: Rosenzweig zeigt, dass die griechische Welt bereits metalogisch gedacht hat und die indische bzw. chinesische Welt jeweils einen Aspekt des Metalogischen (die indische das Besondere und die chinesische das Allgemeine) in ihrer Denkweise unterschätzt haben. Ob dies philologisch bzw. philosophisch korrekt sei, kann hier auf keinen Fall besprochen werden.

In Bezug auf das Thema der Kunst: die Ausführungen Rosenzweigs über die Kunst sind überall im *Stern* „systematisch verstreut" und sind im Einzelnen nur schwer zu verstehen. Diese können nur im Gesamtbild des *Sternes* nach einer sorgfältigen Rekonstruktion verstanden werden.[109]

5. Jenseits der Philosophie

Sie können sich nun fragen, ob das Leben, ob die Welt wirklich nur eine reine Anhäufung an Einzelwesen ist, die Gott sei Dank verstanden werden können. Laut Rosenzweig lautet die Antwort: nein. Die Unzulänglichkeit dieser bisher geführten Argumentation ist der philosophischen Haltung zu schulden. Der Philosoph fragt „Was ist?", und diese „Was-ist-Frage" ist bereits der Fehler für Rosenzweig, denn diese Frage will eine ewige Antwort haben; die Philosophie will ewige Antworten, und dies ist eben verwerflich, denn all das, was existiert, ist nicht ewig, sondern steht unter der Knute der Zeit.

Diese ist die ganze Spannung, die es zwischen gesundem Menschenverstand und der Philosophie gibt, laut Rosenzweig. Rosenzweig schreibt: «Der gesunde Menschenverstand steht im Veruf bei den Philosophen. Er soll wohl dazu genügen, ein Viertelpfund Käse einzukaufen, einen Heiratsantrag zu machen, [...] – aber die Antwort auf die Frage, was der Käse, die Frau [...] *eigentlich* sei, diese Antwort dürfe man von ihm nicht erwarten, hier habe der Philosoph einzutreten»[110].

Was ist *eigentlich* der Tod? Was ist *eigentlich* die Welt? *Eigentlich* bedeutet: hier wird keine einfache, schlichte Antwort verlangt, die vielleicht in zwei Monaten nicht mehr wahr ist, sondern eine, die ewig ist. Dieses Wort „eigentlich" setzt voraus, dass die Welt doch etwas Anderes ist als das, was sie erscheint[111]. «So

---

[109] Diese Arbeit wurde sehr akkurat und sorgfältig im folgenden Aufsatz geleistet: F.P. Ciglia, Kunst als Propädeutik der Erlösung. Ästhetik und Theologie im Denken Franz Rosenzweigs, in: M. Brasser (Hg.), Rosenzweig Jahrbuch 1/ Rosenzweig Yearbook 1, Rosenzweig heute / Rosenzweig today, Freiburg/München 2006, 134–154.

[110] BGK, 28; kursiv von mir.

[111] Die ganze Erkenntnistheorie der abendländischen Philosophie, ausgehend spätestens von Platon, fusst darauf: denn sie können nicht behaupten, ein Mensch sei ein Wesen mit zwei Beinen. Sind Menschen die ohne ein Bein geboren werden also keine Menschen? Doch. Also ist dies nicht relevant

bleibt ihm [dem Philosophen] nun nichts anderes übrig als [...] sich einzubohren in das Problem, in den aus dem Fluss des Lebens herausgenommenen [...] „Gegenstand" des Denkens. [...] Er fragt: was ist. [...] Der künstlichen Zeitlosigkeit der „Was-ist"-Frage antwortet die [...] Antwort: „Das Wesen." [...] Im Leben gilt diese Frage so wenig, wie dort die Frage vorkommt. Auch der Philosoph wird sie im Ernstfall nicht stellen. Er wird nicht fragen, was das Viertelpfund Käse „eigentlich" kostet. Er wird seine Erkorene nicht fragen, ob sie „eigentlich" seine Frau werden möchte. [...] Nicht „eigentlich", sondern „wirklich" ist das Wort des Lebens [...]. Hier [...] trennen sich seine Wege von den Wegen des gesunden Menschenverstands. Der gesunde Menschenverstand vertraut dem Wirklichen und seinem Wirken.»[112] Aber «[...] ins eine All der Wirklichkeit trägt uns nur der eine Strom der Welt*zeit*»[113].

Die Unzulänglichkeit der philosophischen Perspektive, die sogar jeglichen gesunden Menschenverstand brüskiert, sollte uns dazu bringen, diese Perspektive zu verlassen und den zweiten und dritten Teil des *Sternes* zu lesen, in der diese philosophische Perspektive eben überwunden wird.

Achtung: dies heisst nicht, dass die bis jetzt erbrachte Mühe umsonst war. Der *Stern*, die Wirklichkeit, sind metalogisch aufgebaut und die Angst vor dem Tod erfährt jeder. Ein Erkenntnisbewusstsein zu erlangen, ist nötige Voraussetzung des wahren Lebens. Der gesamte *Stern* kann wie ein Weg betrachtet werden, der gegangen werden muss, um diesen dann zu verlassen, wenn man am Ziel angekommen ist. Wie die wittgensteinische Leiter, die gebraucht wird, um aufzusteigen und dann aber eben zur Seite gelegt zu werden, können wir auf den *Stern* erst dann verzichten, wenn wir mit Rosenzweig den Weg «[v]om Tode»[114] «ins Leben»[115] gegangen sind.

Weiterführende Lektüre

Bertolino, L., (2000). La Filosofia del Nulla in Franz Rosenzweig, in: Annuario Filosofico 16 (2000) 257–287; [https://philpapers.org/archive/BERLFD-10.pdf]

Losch, A., (2011), Der Stern, im Licht der Offenbarung betrachtet – zur geometrischen Konstruktion des Sterns der Erlösung, in: Naharaim 5 (2011) 36–54. [https://www.degruyter.com/document/doi/10.1515/naha.2011.005/html]

---

für die Definition des Begriffes „Menschen". Daher die Suche nach dem „Wesen" des Menschen (im zweiten Buch des ersten Teils des *Sternes* stellt sich Rosenzweig die Frage nach dem Wesen der Welt), d.h. einer Antwort, die ewig ist.

[112] BGK, 30–32.
[113] GS II, 95; kursiv von mir.
[114] GS II, 3.
[115] GS II, 472.

Erster Teil, drittes Buch: Der Mensch und sein Selbst oder Metaethik *und* Übergang

Martin Brasser

In diesem dritten Buch des ersten Teils[116] behandelt Rosenzweig die Frage: was ist der Mensch? Seine Antwort lautet: der Mensch ist in seinem Wesen metaethisch. Ausgangspunkt ist die Feststellung, dass der Mensch ein in sich geteiltes Wesen hat. Er besteht aus zwei Elementen oder Bereichen oder Diskursen.

---

[116] Die Entstehungsgeschichte dieses Teils lässt sich aus Rosenzweigs Briefen recht präzise datieren: am Abend des 13. September 1918 verlässt Rosenzweig die Stellung auf dem Dub in Richtung des nahe gelegenen Skopje (türkisch Üsküb). Auf dem Weg dorthin wird am 14. September 1918 SE I 2 fertig (GB 152). Über Nisch gelangt Rosenzweig nach Belgrad und verbringt die Tage im Lazarett (GB 153). Dort schreibt er bis zum 31. September den SE I 3 fertig und beginnt am 1. Oktober mit dem «Übergang». Parallel dazu entsteht die Abschrift von I 2 und I 3 (GB 155). Am 10. Oktober 1918 ist auch die Abschrift des «Übergangs» erstellt zusammen mit der Abschrift der Hälfte von SE I 3 (GB 167). Mit Brief vom 11. Oktober kann Rosenzweig also seiner Mutter also insgesamt fünf Abschriften ankündigen: «du … kannst diese fünf in einen gemeinsamen Umschlag legen und auf den Umschlag schreiben: Die Elemente oder das Immerwährende» (GS 612). Am 19. Oktober ist nur die Abschrift von SE I 3 noch nicht per Post an die Mutter verschickt (GS 613).

How to cite this book chapter:
Brasser, M. 2021. Erster Teil, drittes Buch: Der Mensch und sein Selbst oder Metaethik *und* Übergang. In: Brasser, M., Bojanić, P. and Ciglia, F. P. (eds.) *The Star for Beginners: Introductions to the Magnum Opus of Franz Rosenzweig*. Pp. 55–68. London: Ubiquity Press. DOI: https://doi.org/10.5334/bco.f. License: CC-BY

Auf der einen Seite gibt es den Bereich, in dem alles vorkommt, auf das man sich abstützen und verlassen kann – ein Bereich des Stabilen. Auf der anderen Seite gibt es einen Bereich, von dem aus auf das Stabile im Menschen geblickt wird. Das ist der Bereich, den Rosenzweig die Freiheit nennt. Beide Bereiche bestehen zusammen. Der eine kann den anderen nicht ersetzen. Damit nimmt Rosenzweig den Gedanken auf, den wir in den vorausgehenden Kapiteln schon gelesen haben: den Gedanken von der inneren Zerbrechung, der inneren Differenz. Er wird im dritten Buch des ersten Kapitels wieder aufgegriffen und anthropologisch vertieft.

Um den Kern und die Pointe dieser These zu erfassen, braucht es ein Verständnis für das methodische Vorgehen von Rosenzeig und für seine inhaltliche Argumentationsfolge.

Das methodische Vorgehen

Methodisch greift Rosenzweig wie bei der Analyse der Elemente Gott und Welt auf eine mathematische Symbolsprache zurück. Sie soll – wie bei Gott und Welt auch – das beschreiben, was der Untersuchungsgegenstand eigentlich ist: «das wahre Sein des Menschen» (55). Die formale Struktur des verwendeten Symbols ist am Aussprechen des Wortes «Ja» formalisiert, das für Rosenzweig im Aussprechen von jedem anderen Wort mit ausgesprochen ist und so dessen Grundlage darstellt. «Ja sagen» heisst mindestens: die Relation zwischen dem, was man sagt, und dem Umstand, dass es gesagt ist, als bestehend bestätigen – und damit eine Relation herstellen, die formal mithilfe der Buchstaben A oder B und einem Gleichheitszeichen ausschreibt. Gott wird in der Gleichung «A=A», Welt in der Gleichung «B=A» und der Mensch in der Gleichung «B=B» dargestellt. Diese Formalisierung ist lediglich eine Hilfskonstruktion, die in dem Moment wieder verworfen wird, in dem sie ihren Dienst geleistet hat. Sie kommt im zweiten Teil des SE nicht mehr vor. Sie dient nur dazu, das «Sein» oder «Wesen» des Menschen zu erfassen und tut dabei so, als liesse es sich in eine allgemeingültige Formel fassen. Dem ist nicht so. Aber in dem Stadium, in dem sich die Gesamtargumentation des SE jetzt gegen Ende des ersten Teils befindet, ist diese Formel noch hilfreich.[117] Sie ist abstrakt formal genug, um klarzumachen, dass das «Sein» oder «Wesen» des Menschen nicht angemessen erfasst wird, wenn man sie in allgemeingültige Sachbegriffe zu bringen versucht. Der Anspruch daran ist eigentlich nicht deshalb verfehlt, weil man Sachbegriffe statt formaler Termini zu nutzen versucht, sondern weil man für die Begriffe den Anspruch von Allgemeingültigkeit erhebt, den sie als philosophische Begriffe traditionell haben aber gleichwohl nicht mehr erfüllen können. Im Verlauf des Kapitels wird Rosenzweig deshalb seine Argumentation schrittweise so aufbauen, dass der eigentliche Begriff für das

---

[117] Die Symbolsprache «B=B» für den Menschen wird ausführlich rekonstruiert bei Samuelson, User's Guide 66ff.

«Sein» oder «Wesen» des Menschen maximale Anschlussfähigkeit an die nicht-philosophische biblische Sprache hat: der Mensch ist in seinem wahren Kern nicht Selbst, sondern Seele.

Bevor dieser Denkschritt nachvollziehbar ist, braucht es noch das Verständnis für einen methodisch noch davorliegenden Schritt: Rosenzweig bestimmt das «Sein» oder «Wesen» des Menschen wie sein expliziter Gewährsmann Kant und wie sein impliziter Gesprächspartner Hegel transzententalphilosophisch. «Transzendental» heisst hier zunächst das, was als Bedingung dafür angenommen werden muss, dass Menschen Menschen, also sie selbst sein können. Und es heisst zugleich und damit einhergehend, dass dieses «Sein» oder «Wesen» so verfasst ist, dass der Mensch in de Lage ist, über sich selbst hinauszugehen. Dabei denkt Rosenzweit vom Ende seiner Systematik her, d.h. von seinem radikal theo-zentrischen Verständnis des «Seins» und «Wesens» des Menschen, dem dieses «Sein» oder «Wesen» solange nicht zugänglich ist, als es nicht von Gott selbst eröffnet worden ist. Auch diese Verschlossenheit ist Teil des Wesens des Menschen – und eine Methodik, die das Element des Gottesbezugs aus der Erfassung des «Seins» oder «Wesens» des Menschen ausblendet, kommt bis zu genau diesem Punkt der Erkenntnis: der Mensch ist in seinem «Sein» und «Wesen» nur er selbst. Damit ist der im Kern dreistufige Argumentationsschritt Rosenzweig in diesem Kapitel schon genannt: das «Sein» oder «Wesen» des Menschen ist sein Menschsein («Adam»), das aus philosophischer Sicht ein «Selbst» ist, wobei der Kern dieses Selbst «die Seele» ist. Es gehört zu den Grundüberzeugungen Rosenzweigs, dass die Philosophie diese eigene Begrenztheit ihres Blicks auf «Sein» und «Wesen» des Menschen selbst nicht in den Blick bekommt und folglich der Kernbestand des Selbstkonzepts, also die «Seele» des Selbst, selber gar nicht auf den Begriff gebracht hat. Dafür muss man auf die Literatur ausweichen, die zwar nahe bei der Philosophie ist, aber näher noch bei dem Kern der Philosophie, für den die Philosophie selbst blind ist.

Wenn Literatur der Ort ist, an dem vor-theozentrisch «Sein» und «Wesen» des Menschen verständlich und gewissermassen vor-begrifflich richtig verstanden werden, dann ist auch klar, dass dieses «Sein» und «Wesen» nichts Abstraktes ist, sondern Gegenstand von erlebbarer Erfahrung. Literatur begreift sie, wenn sie Menschliches wie Geburt, Tod, Liebe auf der Bühne oder zwischen Buchdeckeln evoziert. So wie Geburt, Tod oder Liebe Erfahrungen der empirischen Welt sind, so sind sie die Erfahrungen des realen «Seins» und «Wesens» dessen, was uns als Menschen ausmacht. Der Schnitt läuft für Rosenzweig nicht zwischen Erfahrung und Transzendentalität – was wäre das für eine Transzendentalität, die nicht zur Erfahrung werden könnte –, sondern zwischen zwei Formen von Erfahrung: diejenige, in der wir uns als Menschen mit anderen verbunden und in Austausch befindlich erfahren, und derjenigen, die uns auf uns selbst und unsere individuelle Eigenart und Unbezüglichkeit zurückwirft. Welche davon die anthropologisch-transzendental argumentativ relevante ist, dürfte aus dem Bisherigen klar geworden sein. Rosenzweig baut seine Argumentation so auf, dass er dabei zeigt: solange das «Sein» und «Wesen» des Menschen als «Selbst» konzipiert wird (und das tut alle Philosophie), hat man erst den Anteil an diesem «Sein» und «Wesen» erfasst, der im Vorfeld der «wahren» Philosophie angesiedelt ist, die ihrerseits nur als Theologie möglich ist. Denn nur sie erfasst das «Sein» und das «Wesen» des Menschen als solchen, d.h. als in Beziehung stehenden.

Der Argumentationsverlauf

Argumentativer Ausgangspunkt des dritten Buchs im ersten Teil des SE ist die These, dass der Mensch eine innere Differenz ist. Dieser Gedanke erinnert an Descartes und dessen Unterscheidung zwischen «res cogitans» und «res extensa» und an Kants Unterscheidung zwischen der Welt der Erscheinung und der Welt der Freiheit. Die Frage, die sich deshalb sogleich stellt, lautet: Wie ist die Einheit beider Teile beschaffen. Hier sieht Rosenzweig anders als Descartes oder Kant eine Steigerung in der Art, wie diese Einheit beschaffen sein kann. Diese Steigerung zeigt Rosenzweig in diesem Kapitel dadurch an, dass er zunächst vom Menschen als solchem spricht, dann vom Menschen als einem Selbst und im dritten Schritt vom Menschen als Seele. Der Übergang vom Begriff Mensch zum Selbst ist eine Konsequenz aus der Begriffsanalyse, die Rosenzweig im vorliegenden dritten Buch des ersten Teils vornimmt. Der Übergang vom Selbst auf die Seele kann, so Rosenzweig, nicht mehr durch eine Analyse des Begriffs «Seele» erfolgen. Sondern dieser Übergang braucht das, was Rosenzweig am Ende des Kapitels «die Umkehr» nennt. Hier beginnt das Ende des philosophischen Räsonnierens und der Einstieg in das, was Rosenzweig denkerisch an Neuem bringen in die Philosophie einführen möchte.[118]

Es geht um das, was Kant so ausgedrückt hat: dem Glauben Platz machen. Kant ist dann auch der erste Bezugspunkt, mit dessen Hilfe Rosenzweig in seine Argumentation einsteigt. Kant ist der Gewährsmann, auf den sich Rosenzweig für seine eigene Analyse vom Wesen des Menschen beruft, und zwar sowohl in Bezug auf dessen Erkenntnistheorie, auf die sich Rosenzweig in diesem Kapitel explizit bezieht, als auch auf dem Feld der Moralphilosophie. Mit Kant teilt Rosenzweig die Vorstellung darüber, wohin die Begriffsanalyse weisen soll: in den Glauben hinein. Dort angekommen, wird – so ist das Versprechen von 52 – wir das nicht-glaubende Wissen in eine ganz einfache und klare Erkenntnis münden. Worin diese Erkenntnis besteht, das wir dann in den späteren Kapitel dargelegt.

Am Anfang dieses Wegs steht eine Verwirrung (54): Wo soll man anfangen, wenn man sich fragt «was ist der Mensch»? Man weiss nicht, wo genau

---

[118] Im Brief vom 1. Oktober 1918 schreibt Rosenzweig an Gritli seine Zusammenfassung des dritten Buches. Er hat «eben I 3 zu Ende geschrieben und es gefällt mir ganz gut» (GB 155). In seiner Zusammenfassung stellt Rosenzweig insbesondere den Bezug zum «Rudibrief», der sog. Urzelle des Sterns heraus.

man anfangen soll. Man hat, so Rosenzweig, zunächst nichts in der Hand, von woaus man anfangen könnte. Und genau dieses «Nichts» macht Rosenzweig zum Ausgangspunkt seiner Überlegungen, wie das zum ersten Mal schon bei «Gott», dann zum zweiten Mal bei der «Welt» der Fall gewesen war.

Diese Überlegungen sind also methodisch geführt, und zwar in einem Dreischritt: ausgehend von einem bestehenden Faktum, das schon allein dadurch, dass es besteht, eine komplexe Welt eröffnet, wenn man das, was da besteht, analysiert («schaffendes Ja»). Man muss nur gedanklich analytisch genug vorgehen, um nachvollziehen zu können, was gedanklich-analytisch alles in diesem Ausgangspunkt implizit bereits mitgegeben ist. Dann entsteht gewissermassen begriffslogisch-automatisch der nächste Schritt: man sieht das, was verneint worden ist. Auch hier öffnet sich erneut eine komplexe Welt («das zeugende Nein»). Und schliesslich braucht es den Schritt, der die Verbindung zwischen den Ergebnissen des ersten und denen des zweiten Schritts herstellt («das gestaltende Und»).

Diese Gedankenbewegung nimmt ihren Reiz und ihre Überzeugungskraft daraus, dass man mitvollzieht, wie konsequent der eine Schritt aus dem anderen folgt. Daran hängt die Plausibilität der Argumentation, die sich einer Hegel'schen Dialektik bedient, ausgehend von einem negativen Befund, dem «Nichts des Menschen».

Als Ausgangspunkt nimmt Rosenzweig zunächst das, was der gesunde Menschenverstand antwortet, wenn er fragt: was unterscheidet den Menschen von Gott und was unterscheidet ihn von der Welt? Die Antwort auf diese Fragen ergibt eine Antwort auf die Frage nach dem Wesen des Menschen, wenn die jeweiligen Antworten miteinander kombiniert werden. Gott ist – gemäss Rosenzweig – immer «dieser Gott», also individuell. Und die Welt ist ein Wechsel von Entstehen und Vergehen. Die Kombination aus beiden Aspekten ergibt das Wesen des Menschen: der Mensch lebt den Wechsel von Entstehen und Vergehen als Individuum. Das heisst: genau einmal. «Vergänglichkeit ist sein Wesen». Zu dieser Vergänglichkeit kommt nach Rosenzweig ein unbestreitbares Fakt: die Fähigkeit des Menschen, sich auf diese individuelle Vergänglichkeit zu beziehen.

Von der Art, wie Rosenzweig genau diesen Bezug beschreibt, hängt der ganze weitere Weg der Analyse ab. Dieser Bezug ist rein nur auf das je eigene Individuelle gerichtet. Man sieht die ganze Welt jeweils nur aus der individuell-eigenen Optik, geradezu – sit venia verbo – «autistisch». Rosenzweig bezeichnet den Menschen auf dieser Stufe als «einzelnes und doch alles». Dieser Bezug ist ausserdem darauf aus, sich selbst auf Dauer zu stellen. Am besten wäre hier die ungekürzte Dauer, also die Unendlichkeit. Kürzere Dauer haben die Eigenschaften, die den individuellen Menschen Zeit seines Lebens prägen. Diese Eigenschaften machen das am Menschen aus, was Rosenzweig «den Charakter» nennt. Damit ist bereits in einem ersten und einfachen Denkschritt eingelöst, was eingangs festgestellt worden war: der Mensch ist ein geteiltes Wesen. Wir wissen jetzt besser, worin dieser Teil seines Wesens besteht. Die Teile selbst sind geklärt: es gibt das, was man ein «Nichts» bezeichnen kann, und das «Feste» im Menschen, das Rosenzweig dessen «Charakter» nennt.

Rosenzweig liebt es, in der geometrischen Figur des Sterns zu denken.[119] Mit dem bisherigen Gedankengang ist ein Teil der noch zu erarbeitenden Formel für das Wesen des Menschen bereits gefunden. Die Eigenheit des Charakters des Menschen kann mit einem einfachen «B» bezeichnet werden. Der Sinn dieser Operation erschliesst sich eigentlich erst, wenn man am Schluss steht und die ganze Formel vor sich hat. An dieser Stelle wird zunächst einfach eingeführt: der Charakter des Menschen ist ein einfaches «B».

Methodisch folgt jetzt der zweite Schritt, der des «zeugenden Nein». Man muss dafür das erreichte Ergebnis seinerseits verneinen bzw. genauer: das verneinte erreichte Ergebnis als Teil des Ganzen ansetzen, das eben der Mensch ist. Und was ist das im Menschen, das den Charakter verneint? Das ist, so Rosenzweig, der freie Wille. Das Faktum der freien Stellungnahme gehört genauso zum Wesen des Menschen wie die Tatsache, dass er oder sie einen ganz spezifischen Charakter hat. Dieser Wille selber ist endlich, weil er nicht so allmächtig ist wie bei Gott. Als Symbol für den freien Willen benutzt Rosenzweig wieder ein «B». Und weil der Wille etwas ist, was sich auf etwas bezieht («ich will etwas»), kommt noch ein Beziehungszeichen hinzu: den Teil des Menschen, der seinen Willen ausdrücken soll und seinem Willen entspricht, schreibt Rosenzweig als «B=».

Damit hat Rosenzweig die beiden zentralen Teile oder Elemente am Menschen bestimmt: seinen Charakter und seine Freiheit.

Man kann das als eine freie Verdichtung der Gedanken ansehen, die schon Kant zur Frage nach dem Menschen vorgetragen hat. Rosenzweig führt deshalb hier mit guten Grund Kants Name ein – einmal mehr. Bei der nächsten Frage aber kann Kant nicht mehr weiterhelfen. Sie lautet: wie hängen beide Teile des Menschen zusammen? Hier geht Rosenzweig über Kant hinaus. Sofern der Mensch als die Einheit aus Charakter und Wille verstanden wird, nennt Rosenzweig ihn «das Selbst». Das Selbst ist sozusagen das «Und» aus dem ersten «Ja» und dem anschliessenden «Nein». Dass es eine solche Einheit gibt, ist wenig strittig. Aber wie sieht diese aus? Die Antwort auf diese Frage entfaltet Rosenzweig im Folgenden. Er geht dabei von einer Beobachtung aus, die beim Willen ansetzt. Rosenzweig beobachtet einen Widerspruch im Willen selbst. Dieser Widerspruch wird deutlich, wenn man sich vor Augen hält, dass Freiheit etwas ist, das ausdrücken soll, dass man an nichts gebunden ist. Freiheit heisst, «causa sui et non altrius» zu sein. Als Menschen sind wir aber, wie soeben dargelegt, an den Charakter gebunden. Das ist nun aber nicht nur ein

---

[119] Am 4. Oktober 1918, also 14 Tage nach dem Beginn der Niederschrift des SE am 21. August 1918 schreibt Rosenzweig an Gritli darüber, dass er im Motiv des Sterns den ganzen Inhalt des zu schreibenden Buches vor Augen hat: «Also ich sah den Stern und merkwürdigerweise drehte er sich um sich selbst und darin war alles was ich noch zu schreiben habe, zu sehn.» (GB 159).

Problem, entstanden aus dem Gegensatz von Charakter und Wille, wobei der Wille tendentiell das Unendliche will, es aber nicht (erreichen) kann aufgrund der Tatsache, an einen Charakter gebunden zu sein. Sondern – und darin liegt Rosenzweigs spezifische Beobachtung – das ist ein Problem im Willen als solchem. Der Wille ist Ausdruck dessen, dass wir frei sind – und zugleich will jeder Wille als Wille sich binden. Er will etwas. Dieser Widerspruch trägt jeder Mensch als solcher in sich aus und zwar nicht erst dann, wenn er seinen Charakter bejaht oder verneint. Sondern überhaupt bereits dann, wenn er überhaupt einen Willen hat. Sofern und weil der Wille diese doppelgleisige Tendenz hat und somit nie wirklich befriedigt werden kann, nennt Rosenzweig ihn den «Trotz». Der Trotz ist «des freien Willen Gestalt».

Die gesuchte Einheit, das Selbst, ist also näher betrachtet «ein Und aus Trotz und Charakter».

Noch einmal betont Rosenzweig – und an der regelmässigen Wiederholung dieses Gedankens erkennt man, wie wichtig dieser Gedanke für die Argumentation Rosenzweigs ist: dieses Selbst hat «keine Beziehung zu den Menschenkindern, immer nur zu einem einzigen Menschen, eben dem Selbst». Dieses Selbst ist «Adam, der Mensch selbst».

Um diese Unbezogenheit des Selbst klarer zu machen, grenzt Rosenzweig diese Unbezogenheit, die sich gewissermassen nach oben richtet, gegen die Unbezogenheit ab, bei der das, was man selbst ist, aus dem Bezug zu Anderen gewonnen wird. Rosenzweig nennt dies «die Persönlichkeit». Und zusätzlich grenzt Rosenzweig das Selbst sozusagen nach unten ab, gegen die Individualität, d.h. gegen das blosse Vorhandensein des numerisch Einzelnen. Als solches Selbst ist der Mensch eine Bezogenheit, wenn man es formelhaft ausdrücken will «ein =», aber als solche eben unbezogen, d.h. «reine Insichgeschlossenheit, bei der sich der Mensch nur auf sich selber bezieht». Die Formel des Selbst lautet folglich «B = B». Das ist ganz und gar nichts Negatives. Es ist vielmehr der Ausdruck für die besondere Nähe des Menschen zu Gott. Rosenzweig verstärkt hier noch einmal die Gleichsetzung von Selbst mit Adam und bezeichnet das dergestalt autonome Ich als «Ebenbild Gottes». Also nicht die Bezogenheit, sondern die Unbezüglichkeit und damit die Gabe, bei sich selbst zu sein und zu bleiben, ist das, was den Menschen so sein lässt wie Gott. Rosenzweig adelt die Unbezüglichkeit zu einem exklusiven Prädikat menschlicher Würde. Er schliesst sich damit der Auffassung der Aufklärer an, die der Meinung sind, dass es die Autonomie ist, die dem Menschen die Würde gibt.

Eine erste Zwischenüberlegung

Im Grunde ist die oben gestellte Frage jetzt beantwortet. Das begriffliche Gerüst ist aufgebaut. Was jetzt noch folgt, sind Konsequenzen und Plausibilisierungen dessen, was auf rein begriffslogischer Ebene bisher bereits über das Wesen des Menschen gesagt worden ist. Rosenzweig zieht im Folgenden zwei

Konsequenzen in 62 – 64. Dann blickt er auf die Kulturgeschichte Indiens (65–66), Chinas (67–68), des Vorderen Orients (69) und des Alten Griechenlands (70–71). In letzterem erkennt Rosenzweig die Figur des Selbst als tragendes kulturelles Identifikationsmuster. Schliesslich versucht er durch eine kunsttheoretische Überlegung seine Idee des Selbst weiter plausibel zu machen. Damit könnte die Argumentation an ihr Ende gelangt sein – und sie wäre es auch, wenn da nicht ein Thema oder Problem noch offen geblieben wäre: Der Mensch als Selbst kommt ohne Beziehung nach aussen aus. Der reale, konkrete Mensch aber tut das nicht. Folglich ist das Selbst noch nicht die Beschreibung des tatsächlichen Menschen. Mehr noch: wenn man nur nach dem Ebenbild Gottes leben würde, könnte man immer noch «alles Fremde allein dort im Eigenen und als Eigenes erblicken». Das wiederum wäre der Autismus, den kein Mensch jemals wollen kann. Und zwar gerade auch als Ebenbild Gottes nicht. Wie entsteht bei Wahrung der Autonomie Bezogenheit? Das zu zeigen muss der nächste Denkschritt sein, wenn man die Frage nach dem Menschen so beantworten will, dass man nicht nur einer kohärenten Begriffsphantasie folgt, sondern die passende Beschreibung dessen vor Augen geführt bekommt, was Menschen wirklich sind. Genau und erst dann ist Philosophie im Rosenzweig'schen Sinn empirisch. Und dabei gilt, wenn die bisherige Beschreibung passend war und das Beste des Menschen tatsächlich darin besteht, ein Selbst zu sein: aus dem Menschen selbst kann diese Bezogenheit nicht kommen. Der Schritt in die eingangs bereits angesprochene Dimension des Glaubens wird an dieser Stelle unausweichlich. Auf diese Spitze und «Kehre» läuft Rosenzweigs Argumentation letztlich zu. Bevor diese Wende vollzogen wird, benennt Rosenzweig zwei Konsequenzen aus seiner Argumentation.

Die erste Konsequenz betrifft die Frage, wann das, was bisher über das Selbst rein argumentativ-begrifflich gesagt wurde, auch tatsächlich erlebt und erfahren wird. Rosenzweigs Antwort lautet. Zum einen kann dies ab dem Moment eintreten, in dem ein Mensch erstmals seine eigene individuelle Sexualität erlebt. Und zum anderen ganz besonders in dem Moment, in dem ein Mensch sein Selbst gerade endgültig verloren hat – «auf dem erstarrten Antlitz eines Toten».

Die zweite Konsequenz betrifft die Frage, welche Rolle dann noch allgemeine sittliche Verpflichtungen spielen, wenn das Selbst so sehr auf Autonomie und Selbstbezogenheit abgestellt ist. Hier kann man nach allem Bisherigen nicht anders antworten als so: das Selbst steht über der objektiven sittlichen Welt. Es ist metaethisch.

Für die kulturgeschichtliche Plausibilisierung der These vom Selbst «in seiner gebirgshaft edel stummen Einsamkeit» greift Rosenzweig im Wesentlichen auf seine auch in anderen Stellen des Sterns vorgenommene Dreigliederung der Varianten von Möglichkeiten zurück: Indien – China – Griechenland. Die jeweils best gelungene Variante findet sich immer im Alten Griechenland. Indien und China sind jeweils noch defizitärere Varianten, die je eine der beiden Bestandteile – hier des Selbst – übergewichten und zueinander komplementär sind, während das alte Griechenland die Synthese aus den beiden komplementären Polen bereits herstellt, aber noch nicht in der gelungenen Form. Vollgestalt des Selbst ist der Held in den Tragödien der attischen Dichtung. Dort ist das Selbst sozusagen literarische Gestalt geworden. In Indien war dies nicht möglich. In der dortigen Kultur liegt der Akzent darauf, nur die Seite des Charakters zu betonen. So jedenfalls deutet Rosenzweig die Tatsache, dass die indische Kultur stark vom Kastenwesen geprägt ist. Sogar die buddhistische Religionsvariante in Indien konnte, so Rosenzweig, daran nichts Wesentliches ändern, sofern auch der Buddhismus dort von der Idee geprägt ist, einen bestimmten Charakter, nämlich den der Erlöstheit, zu erreichen. China dient hier als Kontrastfolie: Konfuzius, Litaipe, Laotse – sie alle wollen letztlich die Reduzierung des Charakters bis zu dessen vollständiger Auflösung, die letztlich nur der vollkommene Mensch erreicht. Was hier idealtypisch übrig bleibt, ist ein Nicht-Ich, das im Rosenzweig'schen Konzept von Anthropologie der reine Wille ist. Die Einheit beider Seiten gibt es erst in der Figur des tragischen Helden der antiken attischen Tragödien.

Diese Figur ist schon in der Bibel in den Gestalten von Simson oder Saul und im Vorderen Orient in der Gestalt des Gilgamesch vorentworfen.[120] Die Attischen Dichter, allen voran Aischylos, bringen sie dann in die europäische Kulturgeschichte ein. Wieso aber ist gerade dieser Held der Inbegriff des Selbst und woran erkennt man das? Rosenzeig bringt hier mehrere Beobachtungen bei. Er führt zugleich und en passant einen zentralen Gedanken ein. Die Selbstabgeschlossenheit der Helden der antiken Tragödien ersieht man daran, dass die Helden der attischen Tragödien nie selber Dialoge führen. Das tut gemäss der Dramaturgie jeweils der Chor. Ein Ausstieg aus der Selbstabgeschlossenheit ist zudem in keiner der attischen Tragödien jemals vorgesehen: es gibt keine Liebesszenen. Im Showdown der Tragödie wird die Selbstabgeschlossenheit vom Helden selbst jeweils ausdrücklich so gewollt. Der Grundsatz lautet hier: Ausdruck der Bezugslosigkeit ist die Sprachlosigkeit. Dabei will der antike Held doch nur das, was jedes andere Selbst auch will: bleiben, Bestand haben und letztlich unsterblich sein.

Unsterblichkeit meint aber in der Sache durchaus mehr als nur dies, dass man für unbegrenzte Zeit fortbesteht. Was genau sie bedeutet, wird von Rosenzweig an dieser Stelle seiner Argumentation noch nicht gesagt, sondern nur angedeutet, wenn er von «Unsterblichkeit im neuen Sinn» spricht. Man ahnt es freilich schon: es geht um eine Unsterblichkeit, die nicht nur unendliches Weiterleben meint, sondern die zugleich frei ist von der entscheidenden Begrenztheit, die das Selbst noch in sich trägt – von der Sprachlosigkeit.

Tatsächlich aber hat die antike Philosophie keinen derartigen qualitativen Begriff von Unsterblichkeit entwickelt. Sie ist, so Rosenzweig, der Idee verhaftet geblieben, dass es etwas geben könnte, das das Ich dauerhaft trägt so wie das Wasser die Schiffe oder die Wurzel den Baum trägt. In der antiken Philosophie heisst dieser Träger «Seele». Aber in diesem Denken ist die «Seele» dann

---

[120] Zu den Vorgestalten ausführlicher vgl. Samuelson, User's Guide 70–76.

doch wieder reduziert auf einen Teil des Menschen und beschreibt nicht sein ganzes «Selbst».

Eine zweite Zwischenüberlegung

Damit liegen alle argumentativen Fäden bereit, um die Idee des Selbst in die der Seele zu überführen. Man ahnt es als Leser: die Seele ist das Selbst, das durch Sprache in die Welt der Beziehung eingeführt wird. Als solches ist das Selbst «Seele» in einem nicht mehr antik-griechischen, sondern in einem der Bibel entnommenen Sinn.

Bevor aber nun der Schritt aus der Welt der Philosophie in die Welt der Theologie, aus der Welt des Heidentums in die Welt der Bibel gemacht wird, gibt es einen weiteren Versuch, das begriffslogische Gerüst des Selbst anschaulich zu machen. Dem kulturgeschichtlichen folgt der kunsttheoretische Zugang. Dadurch wird auch präzisiert, welche Sprache Rosenzweig im Sinn hat, wenn er Sprache als Mittel der Befreiung aus der Autonomie verstanden wissen will. Es ist die Sprache des gesprochenen, des akustisch laut gewordenen Wortes. Die Kunst ist die Sprache, der es gelingt, das Selbst anzusprechen, ohne dafür Worte verwenden zu müssen. Kunst ist so stumm wie der antike Held und spricht genauso wie er: durch ihre Wirkung, die ohne Worte wirkt. Kunst wirkt wie das stumme Selbst und sie bewirkt in den Menschen, auf die sie wirkt, dass sie selber stumm bleiben. Kunst «geschieht von Selbst zu Selbst, von einem Schweigen zum anderen Schweigen.» Aber so ist die Welt noch nicht die Welt, wie sie ist, wenn sie erfüllt und bewohnt wird nicht nur vom Selbst, sondern vom konkreten Menschen. Wie das Selbst aufwacht zur Bezogenheit, wie die Sprache so wirkt, dass sie sprechend macht, wie Worte die Selbstbezogenheit in Bezogenheit auf den Anderen macht, davon handelt der zweite Teil des Sterns der Erlösung. Um das zu verstehen, verlassen wir zugleich die Welt Chinas, Indiens, Griechenlands und allen Heidentums und gehen über die Welt des jüdisch-christlichen Glaubens.

Übergang

Es folgt das letzte Kapitel des ersten Teils des SE mit dem Titel „Übergang". Damit ist dessen Funktion bereits angezeigt: dieses Kapitel verbindet die bisherigen Argumentationen über Gott, Welt und Mensch mit denen des zweiten Teils des SE. Dies tut Rosenzweig dadurch, dass er Bewegung in die Zuordnung der drei Elemente zueinander bringt. Sie stehen nicht isoliert jedes für sich, sondern jeweils für eine Epoche in der Weltgeschichte: für die Vergangenheit steht die entwickelte Gottesvorstellung, für die Gegenwart das Konzept des Menschenbildes und für die Zukunft das, was als Element „Welt" erarbeitet worden ist. Diese Dynamisierung und Historisierung der Ergebnisse macht diese noch anschlussfähiger an das, was in den folgenden Teilen des SE weiter entwickelt werden wird. Dort entwirft Rosenzweig ein weltgeschichtliches Szenario mit

Gott an dessen Anfang, dem Menschen in dessen Mitte und der (erlösten) Welt als einer in der Zukunft liegenden Zielgestalt. Wenn die bisherigen Elemente nicht nur einzeln nebeneinander liegende Abstrakta, sondern in einem zeitlich spezifizierten Verhältnis zueinander stehen, dann sind sie noch mehr das, was sie immer schon sein sollten bzw. eigentlich auch immer schon sind: die heidnische Vorwelt dessen, was im Kern und in Wahrheit die Welt der Theozentik ist. Wäre diese Vorwelt ganz und gar über sich selbst aufgeklärt, dann wüsste diese Welt auch das. Aber sie weiss ja nicht einmal, dass die drei Elemente in einem geordneten Verhältnis zueinander stehen. Das zu zeigen, ist Aufgabe des Abschnittes „Übergang".

Dies nicht zu wissen, ist nicht Schuld oder moralische Verfehlung, sondern liegt gewissermassen in der Natur der Elemente. Im Ergebnis der bisherigen Argumentation stehen sie einfach nebeneinander. Sie sind aber auch Erklärungskonkurrenten: jedes Element kann als Ursprung jedes anderen Elementes verstanden werden, sobald es als universal gültig genommen wird. Dann aber werden zwei Elemente auf ein drittes reduziert, ohne dass eine der drei dabei möglichen Varianten eine höhere Plausibilität für sich beanspruchen könnte.

Gleichwohl ist es besser, diese drei Elemente in eine Ordnung zu bringen, als sie nebeneinander stehen zu lassen. So legt sich der „Wirbelwind der Widersprüche" (Se 93). Denkerische Ruhe stellt sich für Rosenzweig ohnehin erst dann ein, wenn Erkennen in die Form eines Systems gebracht worden ist. Dessen Umrisse zeichnet Rosenzweig im Folgenden: a) dieses System erhält seine Ordnung dann, wenn seine Elemente untereinander in eine Beziehung gebracht sind und b) wenn dafür die einzelnen Bestandteile selbst nicht statisch, sondern dynamisch als Prozesse verstanden worden sind, die c) einen Platz in der Geschichte einnehmen.

Ordnung entsteht durch Beziehung

Ordnung entsteht durch Relation. Ordnung ist dabei das Ergebnis einer interpretatorischen Eindeutigkeit, die nicht aus dem Fakt, sondern aus der Relation, in der das Fakt eingebunden ist, entsteht. Rosenzweig bringt zwei Hinweise: ob die Zahl „3" eine Vielheit („drei einzelne Dinge") oder eine Einheit („die Drei") bedeutet, ersieht man aus der Gleichung, in der die Zahl 3 Verwendung findet: „3 = 3 x 1" oder „3 = 1 x 3"[121]. Das ist der erste Hinweis.

---

[121] Samuelson, User's Guide 79 weist zurecht auf die Analogie der Fragestellung hin: ist «3» als Einheit oder als Vielheit zu verstehen – sind auch die Elemente als Einheit oder als Vielheit zu verstehen? Die Antike konnte diese Frage nicht beantworten. Wenn «Antike» für das Äusserste steht, was nicht-theozentrische Weltsicht aus sich selbst heraus denkerisch leisten kann, dann wird die Radikalität dieser Beobachtung deutlich – verschärft durch die Beobachtung Rosenzweigs am Kapitelanfang, dass jedes Element «sich monistisch als das Ganze» (SE 92) zu setzen in der Lage wäre.

Der zweite lautet: Fakt und Ordnung verhalten sich wie Integral zu Differential. Mittels Integralrechnung werden die Grössen von Flächen errechnet und als Fakt ausgegeben. Die Differentialrechnung berechnet die Veränderung von Funktionen, indem es Eingabewerte und Ausgabewerte aufeinander bezieht. Das gilt auch übertragen auf die drei Elemente: erst wenn sie „miteinander in eindeutige, ... wirkliche Beziehung treten" (SE 94), verlieren sie den Schwindel erregenden „Wirbel der Möglichkeiten" (SE 94). Mehr noch und trotz allem, was bisher denkerisch geleistet worden ist: dann können diese drei Elemente überhaupt „erst erkannt werden" (SE 94). Dabei sind die drei Elemente in sich selbst durchaus beziehungsfähig, weil selber eigentlich nicht statisch, sondern dynamisch, d.h. sie tragen „in sich selbst ... die Kraft ..., aus welcher Bewegung entspringt" (SE 96).

Die Elemente sind dynamisch

Die Herleitung dieses Aspekts der Elemente bezieht sich eigentlich nicht so sehr auf die Elemente selbst, sondern auf den Vorgang ihrer Thematisierung in den vorausgehenden Büchern. Als reinen Erkenntnisprozess will Rosenzweig dies jedoch nicht verstanden wissen. Dieser Erkenntnisprozess ist Teil der Elemente selbst und deren Hervortreten als das, was sie in ihrem Sein und Wesen sind. Wenn man einmal eingesehen hat, dass die Elemente tatsächlich so sind, wie sie analysiert worden sind, dann sind sie in ihrer Tatsächlichkeit in Erscheinung getreten. Reflektiert man diesen „ontologischen Erkenntnisprozess", dann kann man – so Rosenzweig – eine Art Verdrehung oder Umkehr der Verhältnisse feststellen. Die Herleitung der drei Elemente startete jeweils beim Nichts des Wissens und war so angelegt, dass dieses Nichts als produktive Grösse letztlich der Ursprung dessen war, was dann als Element in seiner Tatsächlichkeit erkannt und als faktisch (so) existierend postuliert werden konnte. Der Vorgang dieser Postulierung aber dreht diese Sachlogik der Entstehung um (obwohl die Verlaufslogik von vorher-nachher natürlich bestehen bleibt): jetzt wird nicht mehr das Nichts das Bewirkende, sondern das Bewirkte – also jedes Element – als die Ursache von Wirklichem angesehen und auch faktisch so in Kraft gesetzt[122]. Das ist bei Gott und beim Menschen gut nachvollziehbar (weniger gut beim Element Welt). Dabei ist wichtig zu sehen: das Fakt der Reihenfolge von Nichts und Element hat sich nicht verändert, nur die Ordnung, in die Anfang und Ende der Bewegung eingebettet ist: das Verhältnis von Ursprung und Wirklichkeit dreht sich um – der Moment der Umkehr ist

---

[122] Vgl. Samuelson, User's Guide 81 mit dem Akzent auf dem In-Sich-Sein der Elemente als Ausgangspunkt der Transformation: «... the objects of knowledge become transformed from being something in themselves to being origins for the movement of reality (Wirklichkeit)."

der Moment, in dem ein Element seinen Status der Tatsächlichkeit erlangt hat. Durch diesen Status kommt sozusagen Bewegung in die Zuordnung – und damit wird das Verhältnis der Elemente zueinander dynamisch. „Aus fertigen Ringen werden Glieder einer Kette." (SE 97). An welchem Ort in dieser Kette sich welches Element näherhin befindet, wird im dritten und letzten Argument, der Historisierung der Elemente, noch kurz skizziert.

Die Historisierung der Elemente

Für Rosenzweig sind die drei Elemente – Gott als lebendiger Gott des Mythos, die Welt als plastische Welt der Kunst und der Mensch als der Held der Tragödie – Ausdruck von „reife(m) Heidentum" (SE 97). Das ist in einem doppelten Sinn zu verstehen: geschichtlich-historisch und systematisch. Rosenzweig sieht beide Aspekte zusammen: die griechische Antike ist im Grundcharakter der Wissenschaften von Gott, Welt und Mensch auch heute noch gegenwärtig. Und nun historisiert Rosenzweig noch einen Schritt weiter: sofern schon für die Antike die drei Elemente historisch geordnet waren, sind sie es als systematische Grundlage der Wissenschaften auch heute noch. Die historische Ordnung der drei Elemente sieht so aus: schon für die klassischen Griechen war ein Gott als lebendiger Gott des Mythos geschichtliche Vergangenheit und deren Gegenwart vom Selbstverständnis des tragischen Helden geprägt (so dass für die dritte Zeitdimension Zukunft dann das Element Welt übrig bleibt). Diese historische Ordnung ist auch die systematische: „Gott war von uran, der Mensch ward, die Welt wird." (SE 99). Was bisher aus Gründen, also philosophisch entwickelt worden und entstanden („geboren") ist, ist im Licht dessen, was jenseits der Philosophie gewusst wird, eine „Schöpfung" – und damit lüftet Rosenzweig am Ende des Übergangs schon ein ganz klein wenig den Schleier und gibt den Blick in den Bereich jenseits der Philosophie frei, indem er die Begriffe einführt, die ab jetzt leitend sein werden: Schöpfung und Offenbarung. Der „Übergang des Geheimnisses in das Wunder" (99) ist denkerisch-argumentativ vollzogen. Denn „Schöpfung" in einem vor-theozentrischen Sinn ist bisher bereits demonstriert worden: es ist gezeigt worden, wie die Elemente aus ihren Nichts heraus entstehen – und genau darin lag auch (die Beschreibung des Prozesses) ihr(es) Offenbarwerden(s). Die Elemente sind nun als solche für das Erkennen offenbar. Das dritte Stichwort, das in der nun folgenden theo-zentrischen Argumentation der Teile 2 und 3 des SE eine gleich zentrale Rolle spielt, ist die Erlösung. Sie kann hier noch nicht erwähnt werden, weil sie nicht aus den Elementen heraus, auch nicht aus der Perspektive der umgekehrten Elemente heraus, zugänglich gemacht werden kann. Dafür wird Rosenzweig eine ganz eigene Methodologie entwickeln, deren Grundlagen in der gesprochenen Sprache Rosenzweig erst im zweiten Teil des SE legen wird.

Weiterführende Lektüre

Freund, E.-R., (1959), Die Existenzphilosophie Franz Rosenzweigs. Ein Beitrag zur Analyse seines Werkes „Der Stern der Erlösung", 2. durchgesehene Auflage, Hamburg, Meiner.

Santner, E., (2010), Zur Psychotheologie des Alltagslebens. Betrachtungen zu Freud und Rosenzweig, Zürich, Diaphanes.

Zweiter Teil. Die Bahn Oder Die Allzeiterneuerte Welt /
Part Two. The Course, Or The Always-Renewed World

Part Two, Introduction: The Renewal of the Miracle

Yehoyada Amir

The Decline of Miracle-Faith

Surprise, a slice sense of perplexity, sometimes even frustration. These are quite common reactions on listening to some modern symphonies, and they arise, in particular, when reaching the first tones and sentences of the second chapter. Have we not already been introduced to the assumed "point of departure" of the entire work? Has the composer not presented the melody, rhythm, and musical and spiritual mood that will prevail throughout the entire musical work? Have we not adjusted our ears and souls to this fresh new music – a totally unfamiliar path – while nevertheless knowing that these very new tones, themes, and musical discourse will eventually become an integral part of the "All" of that symphony? We are hence called upon to digest it gradually. First, to encounter that which the new chapter is bringing; and only then to ask how these seemingly alien paths meet and integrate in the All that these two chapters, as well as the ones to come, create.

The same experience awaits the reader of the *Star*. Part I created a demanding, coherent, and thoughtful environment. If carefully followed and confronted, it made its own sense. Firstly, it offered a harsh and principled critique of

How to cite this book chapter:
Amir, Y. 2021. Part Two, Introduction: The Renewal of the Miracle. In: Brasser, M., Bojanić, P. and Ciglia, F. P. (eds.) The Star *for Beginners: Introductions to the Magnum Opus of Franz Rosenzweig*. Pp. 71–82. London: Ubiquity Press. DOI: https://doi.org/10.5334/bco.g. License: CC-BY

Idealistic philosophy "from Ionia to Jena" (p. 18)[123] – from the beginning of pre-Socratic philosophy to that of Hegel and beyond. Idealism is ill-conceived and misleading since it presumes that being and thinking are identical, and hence argues that the only legitimate point of departure for systematic, philosophic thinking is the empty nothing [Nichts]. Secondly, Part I offered a "healthy" and valid alternative philosophy: one that would actually provide a systematic account that which the primary life-experience intuitively knows and believes. At the heart of that philosophy lay two foundations. The first is that philosophy in no way begins with empty nothing, but rather with that which is given by "the experience of factuality prior to all of actual experience's matters of fact;"[124] its task is not to create the being but to reconstruct it – to offer a convincing, full, and systematic account of that which we know and experience. The second foundation is that philosophy's point of departure must be plural rather than singular: its "problems" should be rather than one "nothing" three "nothings" [Nichts] – those of God, man,[125] and the world. Rosenzweig emphasized that confronting each of these three and unfolding each of these facts should be done in a parallel and isolated way. Part I offered a careful and challenging work with these three separate points of departure, to the extent that the reader holds "something" of God, of man and of the world. These theoretical "somethings" correlate more or less to the major aspects of ancient world pagan culture. The closing discussion of Part I offered a sincere critique of the clear limitations of that which this part achieved. Yes, it offered "pictures" of God, Man, and the world, but these pictures are totally isolated from each other, closed in their own spheres. By developing them, philosophy indeed responded systematically to our intuitive belief in God, in Man, and in the world. Nevertheless, the account it succeeded in offering in no way matches our belief. We know these three as interrelating and revealed; Part I portrayed them as hidden and isolated, and

---

[123] Citations from the Star are given from Barbara Galli's translation, unless otherwise indicated; the page number is cited within the text.

[124] Franz Rosenzweig, "The New Thinking", Philosophical and Theological Writings, Tr. By Paul W. Franks & Michael L. Morgan, Indianapolis & Cambridge: Hackeltt, 2000, p. 135. "The New Thinking" (1925) is a late retrospective on that which the Star is developing. Scholars disagree concerning the extent to which the philosophic stand expressed in this article is indeed identical to that of the systemic book, but I find this expression fruitful for its comprehension.

[125] The German word Mensch Rosenzweig uses is gender-inclusive and refers equally to man (Mann) and woman (Frau). This is also the case, though not systematically, with the Hebrew word אדם, which Rosenzweig, when referring to the Biblical Creation narrative, translates by Mensch. English does not offer such a term, and all the translations of Rosenzweigian texts use the gender-exclusive word man. This chapter follows this convention, but I wish to emphasize that it does not do full justice to Rosenzweig's discourse.

accordingly what it achieved is insufficient. Something new should be brought into the system in order to overcome this deadlock.

The first paragraphs of the introduction to Part II indeed bring something new and unexpected. Nevertheless, the reader should ask herself how this new discussion relates to the discourse of Part I and to its philosophic argumentation and insights. The best strategy for dealing with this perplexing question is suspension. Let us first understand what is going on in the new discussion, what is the inner logic of the new "music" to which we are exposed. Only once we have digested the new path we are invited to pursue may we ask how this part relates to the "music" of the previous one; how the new problems, argumentations, and insights help solve the enigmas left to us by the previous part.

The specific question Rosenzweig raises from the very first sentences of his introduction, concerns a substantial shift in the status and role religious thought – theology, religious literature, religious consciousness – attributes to miracles. He identifies a major change that occurred in this regard in the last generation, seemingly across the board of Western religions and theologies, affecting the heart of religious faith. For classic religious argumentations, miracles were anchor and rock. They proved the authenticity and validity of "our" faith and grounded the divinity of "our" Revelation. Miracles were major "summa contra gentiles" pleading, and to a no lesser extent a profound "summa theological" pillar.

> When Augustine or another Church Father had to defend the divinity and the truth of revealed religion against the attacks and doubts of the pagans, they seldom missed the opportunity to refer to miracles … [T]hey were its most powerful argument. For, it could well be that the pagan magicians also turned their rods into snakes; the rod of Moses swallowed the rods of idol worshippers. His own miracles were even more miraculous than the miracles of the adversary (p. 104).

No more. Modern religious consciousness appears to have lost this anchor. For modern believers, miracles were no longer stable, self-evident facts assuring the strength and undeniable nature of religious tradition. The miracle-stories tradition tells became questionable elements to be defended or abandoned. At best, tradition-loyalists hold to the belief in the miracles their tradition transmits for the sake of their loyalty. At worst, they are embraced by the load of these narratives, undermine them, award them a naturalizing interpretation, or simply depart from them. For Rosenzweig, this process is a powerful given, a substantial characteristic of our time's spirit. His question is: why? What stands behind this dramatic shift? How did intellectual and religious consciousness change to leave no more room for miracle? What does this tell us about contemporary religion? Should it simply be accepted?

In order to respond to this question, Rosenzweig must first offer his understanding of the nature of miracle altogether, and firstly, as seen by classic "theology," namely by the central Jewish and Christian scriptures. He claims that the heart of the notion of miracle is not so much its supernatural character, its deviation from normal rules of nature. What makes the miracle is that an extraordinary occurrence was foreseen and prophesized. A miracle is therefore a fulfilled promise.

> [T]he miraculous character of miracle rested on ... the fact that it was predicted. Miracle is a "sign" ... [Singular miracle not] stand out more due to its unusual character – this is only "make up" and not core, although this unusual trait may often be most useful for the effect it produces, but no, miracle stands out because it is predicted. That a man could lift the vail that commonly extends over the future, this is miracle ... Miracle and prophecy go together. (p. 104–105)

The Hebrew Bible portrays the Exodus from Egyptian slavery and the Sinai event as a fulfillment of the promise, to the Patriarchs in the first place and later to the suffering Israelites. The entire Exodus event is predicted and prophesized by God, and only as such it can serve as the basis for the covenant with His people. A Christian reading of the Bible similarly depicts the Christus-event as foreseen and promised – by the Hebrew prophets as well as by the Sibyls. It is a true and formative revelation because it was prophesized. It is a fulfilled promise, anchored in the beginnings of the Creation narrative. Magical acts, too, are "unusual" and break the regular laws of nature. Magicians seek to force natural reality and to overcome its limitations. Magic acts may seem like miracles, but there is an essential difference: they brake the Divine law of nature, while foreseen miracles manifest Divine providence. Miracle and prophecy are the two historical stages constituting that on which pre-modern theology relied, that which classic Christian and Jewish religiosity believed to be a cornerstone of their reliability. We believe, in part, because miracles proved the authenticity, divine nature and undeniability of our faith.

Miracles, in their dual stages – promise fulfillment, are historical in nature across two interrelating layers. A miracle itself is a testimony that gives witness to faith and to the faith-community and its guides. And the reliability attributed to the story of the miraculous event depends on the personal reliability of the direct and indirect conveyers of the word, as well as on the historical context of the event and its testimony.

> [Miracle] needed witnesses ... All forms of juridical proofs are found here: the weakest is proof by circumstantial evidence, the strongest comprise testimony by oath and interrogation by torture ... For the proof of the miracle, it is ... fundamental to go back to eyewitnesses. In their hearing under oath, it is personal credibility, the judgement of their capacity for observation, and even their numbers that are

decisive¹²⁶ ... [T]he testimony adhered to during the tortures of the interrogation is an absolute guarantee; the witness who spills his blood is the true witness. Thus, reference to the martyrs is the greatest proof of the miracle, and above all the martyrs whose torture was to confirm the quality of eyewitness, but later, the appeal to the subsequent martyrs as well: by spilling their blood, they demonstrated the solidness of their faith in the credibility of those who transmitted the miracle to them¹²⁷ ... finally became a single proof in Augustine's famous appeal from all reasons based on the present, historical phenomenon, the *auctoritas ecclesiae*... (pp. 106–107)

The decline of miracle's role for modern theology, the fact that not secularists alone but rather also persons of faith and of faith-ful thought lost their appetite to base faith on the miracle-stories, means that the perception of the past has gone through major shift, that history does not play anymore the same role its used to. This is a decisive change in human consciousness, and to a certain extent also a dangerous one. It is therefore essential to analyze the reasons and forces behind it.

It is common to attribute that shift to enlightenment, secularization, and modern science. Rosenzweig distinguishes between three stages and characteristics of enlightenment. Ancient enlightenment was philosophical in nature. It gave rise to mediaeval discussions that strive to bridge miracle narratives with their notions of Divinity and its "general providence." Secondly, in the context of the Renaissance, enlightenment dramatically changed the perception of nature and its laws. It challenged specific miracle narratives, striving to imbue them with a natural explanation. Most powerful in that sense is the nineteenth-century "enlightenment of history" that challenges altogether the historicity of traditions, scripture, and myths. Though all three did play a certain role in shaking the miracle-faith, none of them could bring about the essential and

---

[126] Rosenzweig refers to a popular argument brought in mediaeval Jewish philosophy, attempting to prove the superiority of the Jewish narrative of Revelation. Contrary to the "empty tomb" visited by two individuals, brought as cornerstone evidence for Christ's resurrection, the Hebrew Sinai narrative reports the presence of hundreds of thousands of participating witnesses (see, for example: Yehudah ha-Levi, *The Kuzari*, 1:9; Norbert Max Samuelson, "Halevi and Rosenzweig on Miracles," in: David Blumenthal (ed.), *Approaches to Judaism in Medieval Times*, Atlanta: Scholars Press, 1984, Vol. I, pp. 157–173).

[127] The martyr is portrayed here as the supreme witness, for spilling blood and giving life for the sake of his/her testimony. In the last 'book' of the 'Star' (III:3) Rosenzweig will update this distinction and will portray as supreme witness, that which an individual or community verifies in their entire life.

across-the-board undermining of the notion of miracle. At the heart of the nullification of miracle-faith lies a substantial inner transition within faith. Rather than anchoring its authority, authenticity, and truth in a sacred formative past, it turned to an attempt to ground them in personal religious experience (Erlebnis),[128] in the present. Luther changed only the *kind* of authoritative past to which Christians adhere. For him, it was *sola scriptura* that conveyed to the present-day Christian community the word of God and His revealed will, rather than the history of the Church and its sacred writings and Dogmas. It was still the past that constituted religious life. Centering faith in the presence, in religious experience, and in its power to lead to moral progress and redemptive future, this new form of faith found its first powerful representative at the end of eighteenth century in the teachings of Friedrich Schleiermacher:

> With Schleiermacher, this whole system found its classical representative dedicated as it was to denying the permanent value of the past and to anchoring the always present experience of the feeling of belief in the eternal future of the moral world. (p. 110)

This new faith, intertwined with the philosophical and theological notions of progress, of a mandatory, constant move forward, made the past a problem. It was no longer relevant as a formative anchor for values, commandments, and convictions. It was no longer sacred and superior. The past needed to be interpreted in a manner that would give the present and future their full space. From this point on, the miracle was useless. It gave witness to an irrelevant past and strived to anchor that which no-one needed any more. The shift now concerned not merely miracles, specific narratives told by traditions, but rather the very notion of miracle. It indeed seemed as though there was no more possibility to experience the miracle.

Contrary to the prevailing Idealistic philosophy so firmly attacked and negated by Rosenzweig, his perception of *Erlebnistheologie* is delicate and careful. He shares some of its basic intuitions and insights. He adheres to the demand "to maintain ... the primacy of hope" and to "a faith, that is personal and ex-perienced in the moment [*momenthaft er-fahrenen*], oriented on the pole of certitude that 'the kingdom of the ideal will finally come'" (p. 112).

---

[128] The German word *Erlebnis*, as distinct from regular experience [*Erfahrung*], hints etiologically to the strong connection between life [*Leben*] and experience. Barbara Galli, the translator of the Star into English, invented the term "life experience" in order to transmit this richness of expression, one normal English could not provide. In this article, I use alternately her term and the standard one, experience, or the original *Erlebnis*. The same connection was emphasized by the creation of the Hebrew new term הֲוָיָה, invented at the beginning of the twentieth century by the philosopher A.D. Gordon, a close ally and teacher of Martin Buber. His usage of the word life-perception maintains the same interrelated poles of life [חיים] and experience.

The primacy of the present, anchoring both past and future in the primordial experience of Revelation, lies at the heart of the Star. In this sense, Rosenzweig is very close to the position Martin Buber would express a few years later when speaking about "religion as presence;"[129] when placing at the heart of human life a dynamic, occurring "relation" [*Beziehung*] between the I and the You.[130] Rosenzweig shares the intuition that "facts" and "objects" belong to the past, constituting a sphere of non-relational truth.

If he will strive to renew the formative role of a "past," and hence of the miracle, this will in no way imply the simple restoration of pre-modern naïve notions, of a non-critical reading of the scriptures – Christian and Jewish alike. He refers neither to the miracles nor to historical past, but rather to the miracle,[131] the notion of miracle, and to the ultimate past, namely the notion of Creation. *Erlebnistheologie* presents revelation, cannot give up past-based factuality; religiosity based on personal experiencing should in no way abandon truth; miracle-faith substantiated Jewish and Christian religious conviction in the old days. A new way to the miracle must be found.

Integrity and Objectivity

It is time now to turn back and set the argumentations developed in this introduction in their wider context within the Star; to zoom in and consider the meaning of this discussion in light of Part I. As stated above, we left Part I understanding that philosophy – the "healthy"[132] and valid one Rosenzweig

---

[129] Martin Buber first expressed his emerging dialogical philosophy in the series of lectures he gave in 1922 at Rosenzweig's Lehrhaus, entitled: "Religion als Gegenwart" [Religion as Presence]. A year later, this discussion received its complete formulation in his famous book I and Thou, which he saw as the point of departure for his entire philosophical work (see; Rivka Horwitz, *Buber's Way to 'I and Thou*, Philadelphia, New York and Jerusalem: Jewish Publication Society, 1988.

[130] Contrary to the You [Thou], the It belongs to the past and has no part in the present-event.

[131] Both English translations of the Star (Galli and Hallo) mistranslate the title of the introduction to Part II by referring to miracles in the plural, whereas Rosenzweig actually speaks about "the miracle" [das Wunder].

[132] The notion that Idealism is "sick" while the philosophy Rosenzweig constructs is "healthy" manifests itself in the fullest sense in Rosenzweig's later *Das Büchlein vom gesunden und kranken Menschenverstand* (1912). Rosenzweig never published the book, which he considered too popular. It was published for the first time in 1955 in Nahum Glatzer's translation, under the title "Understanding the Sick and the Healthy" (see: Yehoyada Amir, "Rosenzweig's Büchlein vom gesunden und kranken Menschenverstand as a prolegomena", in: Yehoyada Amir, Yossi Turner, & Martin Brasser (eds.)

himself develops –is still "insufficient." It suffers from two essential shortcomings: First, it is a philosophy of Viewpoint [*Standpunkt*], a reaction of an individual philosopher to her/his life-experience rather than a scientific system. As such, it offers a "worldview" (or even a "life-view") rather than objective philosophy. Second, it is capable only of constituting "pictures" of God, man, and the world as isolated and hidden; it does not succeed in giving an account of them as we actually know them and believe in them: revealed and interrelating.

> These are the elements of our world, but we do not know the world this way; this is the world we believe in, but we do not believe in it as it is presented to us here. We know a living movement, an electric circuit in which these elements swim; now they are pulled out of this current … we no longer recognize them (p. 93).

As we have seen, these substantial shortcomings are grounded in the very nature of the philosophy Rosenzweig believes to be healthy and valid, and therefore cannot be overcome by philosophy itself.

A similar situation concerns the introduction to Part II regarding *Erlebnistheologie*, the prevailing kind of modern religiosity, one that Rosenzweig both shares and criticizes. He holds firm "the primacy of hope, or, more precisely, a faith that is personal and ex-perienced in the moment, oriented on the pole of certitude that 'the kingdom of the ideal will finally come'" (p. 112). Nevertheless, he would in no way give up grounding this very present-experience on truth, on factuality; he refuses to abandon the ethos of witnessing; he insists on returning to centrality of the miracle. Experiencing God's revealed love is in no way merely psychological;[133] it is a real encounter between the God we know and believe in and the man we are aware of; it occurs in and carries a redeeming message for the real world in which we live.

> [T]ruth cannot be denied, not even in the name of the ideal, let alone in the name of lived experience. Truth is and remains the solid ground on which alone authentic experience can grow, where alone the ideal can be verified. The miracle of the personal experience of Revelation may be strengthened, for the will, in the certitude of its future confirmation through Redemption; but cognition wants to see another foundation on which that experience rests, including when it throws that anchor of hope (p. 117).

Faith, *Truth, and Reason: New Perspectives on Franz Rosenzweig's 'Star of Redemption,'* Freiburg & München, 2012, pp. 37–60).

[133] In his later article Die Schrift und Luther, Rosenzweig compares the assumption that religious experience is merely psychological to the attempt to find the stars within the telescope, simply because we see them through this instrument (*Zweistromland* [GS 3], p. 760).

Theology must find a stable basis that can ground the life experience of revelation. It is only philosophy, viewed now as "Creation,"[134] that can provide such a grounding in factuality and award experience with truth:

> Theology ... calls in philosophy ... in order, theologically speaking, to throw a bridge from Creation to Revelation ... From the theological point of view, what philosophy must accomplish for it is ... its anticipation, or more accurately, its foundation, the exhibiting of the pre-conditions on which this content rests. And since theology itself does not its content as content, but as event – that is to say not as life, but as lived experience – the pre-conditions are not conceptual elements, but existing reality; in the place of philosophical concept of truth, therefore, the notion of Creation arises for it. Philosophy contains the entire content of Revelation in this way, but it does possess this content as Revelation, so not as revealed, but as created content. In Creation, Revelation is – "foreseen" in its entire content, exactly in accordance with today's notion of faith, hence including Redemption. Philosophy, as the theologian practices it, becomes the prediction for Revelation ... [B]efore our astonished eyes, Revelation ... gains its character of authentic miracle – authentic, for it becomes wholly the fulfillment of the promise that took place in Creation. (p. 117–118)

Philosophy needs theology to a no lesser extent. As a viewpoint, philosophy is dependent on the point of view of the philosopher and can never overcome subjectivity and its non-scientific and aphoristic quality unless that viewpoint acquires the quality of objectivity. This can be achieved only once the one philosophizing is a receiver of an ultimate and objective message:

> The man as receiver of Revelation, carrying its faith-content in her/his life experience .... is the only possible philosopher of the new philosophy. Philosophy today requires ... for its scientific character, that "theologians" do philosophy. (p. 116; slightly different translation than Galli's)

---

[134] Rosenzweig refers to the terms Creation, revelation and Redemption in two interrelating meanings. On the one, expanded sense Creation is identified with philosophy, dealt with in part I; Revelation – the entire content of part II; and Redemption – the supreme encountering with eternity and truth, to be dealt with in part III. The more restricted sense of these terms, as dealt with in details in the books of part II, is Creation as the specific relationship between God and the world; Revelation – the encounter between man and God; Redemption – the work of Man and the world on each other. The usage of the terms in the introduction to part II, and hence in this article, is in accordance with the expanded, former meaning.

Philosophy requires theologians for whom Revelation, the dialogue between the ultimate-objectivity of the Divine and the pure subjectivity of the human *is* the presence experience.

This mutual need of theology and philosophy forms the basis for the miracle. Viewing philosophy as Creation, namely as grounding and foreseeing Revelation, as well as viewing Revelation as a fulfilled promise grounded by the factuality philosophy has established, are in no way necessary logical outcomes of either of these. They are a free decision, indeed *the* essential decision that constitutes the entire system of the Star and revives "the possibility to experience the miracle."[135]

The decision to intertwine philosophy and theology, Creation and Revelation, is *the* act of faith-ful cognition [gläubigen Wissen] the Star conveys.[136] Once we make this decision, once we adopt this epistemological stance, the miracle actually happens. Creation, the ultimate past beyond all layers of historical past, is the promise, foreseeing Revelation. Revelation is indeed a fulfillment of the promise inherent in Creation. Philosophy, as an anticipating theology, gains its objectivity; theology, grounded in the truth and factuality of philosophy, is imbued with integrity. Miracle is therefore neither proved nor proving any claim. It is merely experienced.

Miracle, in its renewed epistemological sense, is the pivotal point of the Star. It portrays the framework for the complex relationships between Parts I and II, offering the two alternating points of departure for the entire system: approving life in the shade of death-fear; and being anchored in the experience of Revelation. Miracle also serves as the methodological key to the detailed discussions of the three "events" discussed in Part II's books, opening and revealing God, man, and the world. In all the points of this discussion, Rosenzweig makes creative use of the idea that the relationship between the closed, isolated images of God, man, and the world in Part I, and their interrelating, revealed appearance in Part II, is that of a fulfilled promise. Promise and fulfillment are identical in content yet of opposing directions: a complete, fully-ended element transmutes into a beginning, a point of departure for something new. The specific contents of the "pictures" of God, man, and the world developed and portrayed in Part I, reappear in Part II's books in a reversed manner. Thus the rebellious and proud pole of the notion of man reappears in Part II, in the context of Revelation, as humility; its origin as independent defiance as well as its transmission to humility establish the figure of the beloved sole, the receiver of Revelation.

---

[135] The title of the introductions to the various parts speak in a profound Kantian manner about "possibilities." Here: Über die Möglichkeit das Wunder zu erleben [On the Possibility to Experience the Miracle]. At first Rosenzweig planned to award the introduction with the title "On the Possibility to experience God" (*Gritli Briefe*, letters from 31 Aug. 1918; 4 Oct. 1918).

[136] *Zweistromland*, (Gs 3), p. 835.

The same is true of every pole of the "pictures" of the three isolated elements of Part I as they encounter each other in Part II.

Miracle is therefore an epistemological decision. It realizes itself in the Star's system of faith-ful cognition. Nevertheless, it is not merely theoretical, but manifested in the multifaceted appearance of language.

> [L]anguage, as it is entirely there, entirely created, yet only awakens to its real life in Revelation. And so there is nothing new in the miracle of Revelation … it is entirely sin, entirely a making visible and a becoming audible of the Providence originally hidden in the mute night of Creation, entirely – Revelation. Revelation is therefore always new only because it is immemorially old. It renews the immemorial Creation into the ever newly created present because that immemorial Creation itself is already nothing other than the sealed prediction that God renews from day to day the work of the beginning The word of man is symbol: at every moment it is newly created in the mouth of the one speaks, yet only because it is from the very beginning and already bears within its womb each speaker who one day brings about the miracle of renewal in it. (p. 121)[137]

Further Reading (Annotated List)

Leora F. Batnizky, Idolatry and Representation: the Philosophy of Franz Rosenzweig reconsidered, Princeton: Princeton University Press, 2000, pp. 32–62 [especially 40–47].
  * Batnizky gives full account of Rosenzweig's notion of the import of miracle-faith and witnessing in Jewish existence. She does not refer to miracle-faith's role for the building of Rosenzweig's system neither to the place of miracle and its renewal in Christian environment and hence in overall Western culture.

Paul Mendes Flohr, "Rosenzweig's concept of miracle," in: Jens Mattern, Gabriel Motzkin & Shimon Sandbank (eds.), Jüdisches Denken in einer Welt ohne Gott: Festschrift für Stéphane Mosès, Berlin: Vorwerk, 2000, pp. 53–66.
  * Mendes Flohr follows my reading of the introduction (though failing to mention his sources) and sets it in the wider context of modern Jewish philosophic discourse.

---

[137] Compare Benjamin's note that "'God created' is a potential miracle, not an actual one. The actual miracle is God's speech, which transforms and thus fulfills what is already given" (Mara H. Benjamin, *Rosenzweig's Bible: Reinventing Scripture for Jewish Modernity*, Cambridge: Cambridge University Press, 2009, p. 49).

Renate Schindler, "Das Wunder: Paradigma geschichtlicher Ewigkeit", in: *Zeit Geschichte Ewigkeit in Franz Rosenzweigs 'Stern der Erlösung,'* Berlin: Parerga, 2007, pp. 199-229.
* Schindler gives a systematic account about the role of miracle in in constructing the relationship between philosophy and theology, close to the interpretation given here. She includes extensive references to previous scholars' perceptions.

Francesco Paolo Ciglia, *Auf der Spur Augustins.* Confessiones *und* De civitate Dei *als Quellen des* Stern der Erlösung, in: *Rosenzweig als Leser. Konzeptuelle Kommentare zum «Stern der Erlösung»*, Max Niemeyer Verlag, Tübingen 2004, S. 233-244.

Part Two, Book One: Creation, or the Everlasting Ground of Things

Jules Simon

Rosenzweig begins Book One of Part Two in a familiar yet strange way.[138] It is familiar in how he immediately takes up an already established narrative from the Bible through simply repeating the statement that "God spoke". It is strange, however, because the first thing he draws our attention to in the phrase "God spoke" is how it expresses a temporal condition. It occurs in the form of the grammatical past tense whose content refers us to a previously silent and invisible—because interior—act of the will. That act is one of the strangest and most mysterious of all acts, namely, the act of creation. To create something new—for example, *something* literally out of *nothing*—entails putting into motion a powerful expression of spontaneous willfulness. As Rosenzweig notes, this spontaneous expression is what constitutes something totally new, that is, that something could be created out of nothing is understandable as the apparently miraculous prophecy of a *process* that has become a visible actuality. And that process is the process of our experiencing anything at all. Moreover, the very fact of communicating an understanding of our experiencing anything at all and having that be understood by another is a novelty of human community

---

[138] The content of the following chapter is largely derived from Chapter Two, "Renewing Narrations or Chaos in Creation", of my book Art and Responsibility: A Phenomenology of the Diverging Paths of Rosenzweig and Heidegger, New York 2011, 57–84.

How to cite this book chapter:
Simon, J. 2021. Part Two, Book One: Creation, or the Everlasting Ground of Things. In: Brasser, M., Bojanić, P. and Ciglia, F. P. (eds.) *The Star for Beginners: Introductions to the Magnum Opus of Franz Rosenzweig.* Pp. 83–97. London: Ubiquity Press. DOI: https://doi.org/10.5334/bco.h. License: CC-BY

only able to be enacted through speech because how we talk to each other refers us to our experience of things in the world. To better understand this point, Rosenzweig distinguishes between a creator, in this case, the creator from the biblical story called god, and whatever it is that a creator creates. In order to do that, however, Rosenzweig says that we have to better understand what speaking itself is all about.

As a visible actualization, the process of speaking itself becomes a miraculous beginning. Initially, it is miraculous in the sense that Rosenzweig has already delineated, namely, it is something about which we can wonder and marvel. It is an actually existing *something* that is not *me* or simply an element of my psychological makeup. To make his point, and to get to his next point about separating the act of a creator and the creation itself as something other than the creator, Rosenzweig returns us to his earlier metaphysical discussion from Book One, Part One about negation and affirmation in their immediate relation to their origin in the nothing. Here, at the beginning of Part Two of his book, Rosenzweig more strongly emphasizes the non-dialectical character of the relation of these two moments, that is, the moment of speaking as a moment of communication between two humans correlated with the moment of creation as the relationship of creator to creature or created thing. The process is not dialectical but is one of confrontation – of a *Begegnung* –and thus happens as a meeting of two opposites that creates a transformation. This most significant of all transformations originates as an inner struggle of negation with its achievement of a defining sense of self-freedom, to an outwardly directed expression of positive freedom.

Rosenzweig uses packing and unpacking a trunk in order to emphasize the existential awareness of the empirical changes in our condition in which we are involved when we undertake an intellectual journey.

The metaphor of "packing and unpacking" prepares us for his claims about the nature of undergoing any experience whatsoever, namely, that the actual, empirical experience of packing this or that thing in a suitcase changes the order of how we understand, and thereby interpret, things when we unpack them. This means that our understanding is conditioned by the fact that at one time in my life I experienced something one way, like putting clothes into a suitcase, and then at another later time in my life I experience those contents otherwise as I remove them—after having undergone an experience—in a reordered fashion from the suitcase. In other words, I do not *experience* things as the self-same things over time because temporal and spatial "intuitions"—to borrow some Kantian terms—are filters for our dynamic experiences that do not allow us to reduce those experiences to a timeless account that could be repeated in an endless loop of identical iterations.

The correlation of analyzing the process of speaking with the process of creating enables Rosenzweig to talk about a human phenomenon that occurs when we speak of god's self-expression—visible now through how he conceptualizes 'god's' speech-act, that is, that god created. Such a speech-act is the beginning of god "shining forth" in self-expression. This shining forth is the self-expression of god's structure, god's configuration, and is god's essential attribute. But what, more precisely, does it mean to express oneself as 'shining forth?" Shining forth has to do with the power of self-expression that becomes how more than one of us understands the experience of moving from spontaneous and willful caprice to the peacefulness of enduring essence that Rosenzweig traces in his description of how one, as subject, objectively expresses one's essential nature as creator.

Through talking about the relationship of a creator and speech, Rosenzweig explicates how self-expression is a visible process, not as deed, but as essence. It is visible as essence in the way that phenomenal existence *of self-expression* can be 'seen' *and* 'heard' through the very act of speaking that becomes the tangible marker of a prior willful act. To put it simply, the very act of speaking embodies in its expressive 'shining forth' the 'wisdom' that is the experience of having done something, of having created some thing. More concretely, Rosenzweig explicates the expressive act of the shining forth of an experience through a complex analysis of necessary versus freely spontaneous acts. He notes that god 'must' create, "like the artist" in order to satisfy a divine need within himself, namely, in order to set the burden of loneliness within himself free. And while to be free it is necessary to create, Rosenzweig notes that there can not be even one drop of passion in this creative act, neither a yearning to love nor a Maimonidean sort of overflowing love,[139] because if creation happened out of such a need, then the created thing would lose its own independence. The world, for example, would lose its elemental characteristic of independent createdness, its having been created at one time and its character of being left on its own to develop as it will.

---

[139] Which is not a Maimonidean rational construction, even if depicted via negative theology.

For this reason, Rosenzweig returns to the notion of caprice, noting that it is not merely a cornerstone but the foundation stone for any theory of creation. But now caprice has to be reinterpreted to fit Rosenzweig's narrative structure, not as a fixed attribute but as dynamic occurrence that "burned with ceaselessly renewed flame in God's bosom before creation"[140] —a "flaming caprice" with which the creator vitalizes himself within himself, and which occurs as miraculous, creative power. This creative power manifests itself in serene vitality but at the base of that power is *unconditionally free* caprice. That is, that which is within is not necessity, but radically free caprice, not passionate need understood as a completing or clinging kind of love, but simply an expression of inner freedom.

Rosenzweig begins Book One of Part Two by asking us to think about a very specific kind of speech-act, that is, he begins by providing us with a speech-act that is a form of speech-thinking that syntactically occurs in the past tense but that semantically refers us to a historical and philosophical narrative about how to think about god as a Creator God, the grammatical subject of the phrase, "God created". This leads us to consider how we understand what it means to create something at all, namely, how to understand and then to speak about what it means to bring something into existence and for that something to exist. The project is a meta-linguistic exercise that leads us to the thought of how that something could be the world (or universe) as an existing entity consisting of a plethora of particulars that must ever be renewed to maintain their enduring, transitory existence.

To be distinctive,[141] is to be counted as a chaotic particular, willfully involved in a process of creative self-transformation that negates all others. This is what Rosenzweig means when referring to the particulars birthed out of the world itself, represented by the essential nature of this or that 'universal' species. But the particular also retains traces of its origination out of the universal essence and thus retains the character of that essence itself. Thus endowed, it is not merely logically deduced from its source; rather, it is endowed with existence and can be counted as an existing particular individual.

This picture of a plastic, dynamic world, in Rosenzweig's account, is "universal" but is not "always and everywhere" because it is constituted as particularity and so must continually become new in order to continually 'contain' this concrete particularity called *existence*. But in order to continue to contain its concrete existence, its character of absolute empiricism, the world must continually undergo a necessary process of transformation—birthing absolutely free and arbitrarily willful, ever-new particulars, or existents, that crystallize

---

[140] SE 128; The German words in this context are: caprice—*Willkür*; cornerstone—*Eckstein*; foundation-stone—*Grundstein*; attribute—*Eigenschaft*; occurrence—*Vorgang* or *Ereignis*.

[141] The German expression is: *eine Besondere* which has the connotation of something that is singular and separated out of a larger whole.

as they grow older to form a completion in death as a denial of life, fixed with the character of thingliness. Upon completion of this specific form — the form of an ephemeral denial of enduring life — new particulars emerge, constantly denying the stability of the world and yet ever-becoming that stability again, and so on. This is also a way to understand the dynamism of the entire structure of Rosenzweig's book with its symbolic configuration as a Star of David.

Rosenzweig adopts an old term, providence, and coins a new one, "creature consciousness", in order to suggest the logical and aesthetic differences between his account of the world process and Idealist accounts.[142] On providence, he says that the "divine grasp of existence does not occur in creation, which took place once and for all. Rather, it is a momentary grasp, a providence that, though universal, renews itself with every smallest distinctive moment for the whole of existence in such a way that God 'day by day' renews the work of the beginning"[143]. And it is this very consciousness of their creatureliness that radically differentiates humans from other life forms because that consciousness gives us a capacity for aesthetic presentation. Humans speak in different ways with each other that includes creating works of art that "speak" from the particularity of one human to their commonality with other humans. That distinction is accentuated in differentiating between the "dead" language-form of mathematics and the "living" grammatical distinctions of spoken language referred to in the transition from Part One to Part Two.

Obviously, we have kinds of laws that take the form of rules of logic, namely, premises, deductions, inferences, and conclusions that can be modeled mathematically. But there are also kinds of laws of grammar that result from investigating the emergence of hearable root-words from what Rosenzweig introduced earlier as the silent source-words. The source-words are "Yes, No, And" and they function as variables in a differential calculus that corresponds to his model of the hypothetical structures of the pre-world. Those hypothetical structures enable us to think about any one of the three primary elements of reality according to their respective 'logics': god world human. What makes Rosenzweig's philosophy distinctive and still compelling is how he correlates the 'logic' or laws of grammar with a midrash on the story of creation, claiming that, through the familiarity of a re-narrated and newly interpreted traditional narrative, we can better understand how words work and how and why they occupy the space that they do in the sentences composed of them. That is, we can better understand why we choose and use the words that we do in creating or not creating understandings in our inter-subjective relations. Said otherwise, the grammar of words and sentences can be related to the emergence of particulars in creation as a way of accounting for the renewal of the unconquerable and anarchic dimension of the chaotic, spontaneous freedom at the root of

---

[142] Both Hegelian and all others: Kantian, Fichtean, Schellingian, but also Platonic/Aristotelian and Maimonidean.

[143] GS II, 135.

human distinctiveness. Words are related to creation because what we say about creation—about the world—also has to do with things and the space that they occupy. The sensual nature of words, both written and spoken, makes them the special case of being both thing-like—having to do with world-space—and temporal and ephemeral, that is, speech includes an essentially chaotic dimension that is open to change over time. And in order to catch the sense that chaos plays in our speech-acts, we must begin with sentences, not words.

To make his case, Rosenzweig employs a speech-thinking (*Sprachdenken*) analysis of the syntax and semantics of the adjective[144] as the grammatical analogy for the particular nothings of creation. He moves our attention from the relationship of an adjective, with its initial indefinite case, to the noun as the *carrier* of adjectives, to the pronoun "this". The underlying logic is deductive, namely, to understand anything in particular we must first be given and then understand something in general. Such is the sentence. Such is also the world. The indefinite and inherently comparative nature of the adjective "this" points us towards the *fact that* a "something" should be sought as a concrete, definite referent. Moreover, along with the "this" is implied a spatial indicator, the "here", which entails that *space* is posited as the universal condition under which the definite thing, so far only an undefined "something", is to be sought. Given the initial evaluative affirmation of the adjectival attribute we are led by logical inference to consider the noun and then the pronoun, which consequently points us to space as the dimension of objectivity and the general nominative 'space' called "thinghood" where we *find* actual things in the world.[145] Guided by grammatical structures in the use of our everyday language, we are determined to seek out things in the general context of their thinghood as that which constitutes the space of the world in which we live, psycho-physiologically.

For example, in getting us from using an indefinite adjective to a more definite sense of substantiality—of the general, predicate 'space' thinghood—is important because of the apparent problem that in any speech-act an individual adjective is merely one of many that could be used, indicating that there is an unacknowledged plurality always at work in our speech-acts. This is what Rosenzweig earlier referred to as the complex ordering problem of the "perhaps". In the context of the set of language practices as a whole, however, we have more than just sentences composed of variables. Indeed, adjectives can also become definite by being affixed to a definite article. Rosenzweig notes: "fixed by the definite article, the adjective is a definite, affirmed thing in the endless space of cognition or creation."[146] What makes Rosenzweig's account special is that he correlates this syntactical arrangement as a semantic analogue to his creation thinking, such that when we realize how the adjective "comes to rest" as a grammatical object in the sentence and stands "free and affirmed"

---

[144] Attribute word, or adjective: "*Eigenschaftswort*".
[145] Cf. GS II, 142; SR, 127.
[146] Ibid., 143; 129.

we can, by analogy, think about how the created stuff of creation stands in an objective relationship "free and affirmed" to the creator.[147]

But to truly understand how the world is a created thing, Rosenzweig tells us that we have to understand how it is "totally, in its primal origin, the fullness of the this", which is expressed by means of adjectival words. For Rosenzweig, another way of describing this fullness is to call it chaos, what he calls the "firstling" of creation. In fact, the world is not created until this existence, this chaos, is itself first called into existence. And existence, in its universality and all-embracing formfulness, remains the immediate, created ground, the "beginning", out of which the ever-new births of the fullness shoots forth.[148] No chaos, no creation, no world. The fullness, as chaos, is its transitory appearance as particular existents, which is also the first utterance we can make about the world's existence.

There is an ethical significance for Rosenzweig's grammatical analogy in how the very existence of the world corresponds to the rootword of creation, the "primal yes" or the "Yes!" that he interprets as an affirmative and evaluative "Good!" uttered in judgment upon completion of an act of creation. It is an estimating judgment that logically occurs *before* the fullness, before the chaos of adjective-words. And thus, according to Rosenzweig's linguistic account for creation, "chaos is in creation not before it; the beginning is—in the beginning", which is the act of creation.[149]

Rosenzweig is critical of Idealist kinds of aesthetics because of how those philosophies contend that we should only think about the world in which we live in terms of a deductive logic that presupposes both a rationally defined source and a rationally defined goal. That kind of thinking is problematically based on a principle of generation whereby a succession of particulars identical to the original generator is produced and that has a built-in teleological goal of an ordered cosmos.[150] Rosenzweig's concept of creation, by contrast, reveals an ordered cosmos, but does not entail either a rational *connection* between

---

[147] Ibid. The German word Rosenzweig uses to characterize this condition is "*Gegenstand*", which literally means that-which-stands-over-against an implied or specified other. Rosenzweig constructs a mental bridge from the actuality of the grammatical distinctions to those of relations which hold in thinking about creation: It (the object) now "stands" *there* on its own feet over-"against" a supposed creator, a definite, affirmed thing in the infinite space of cognition or of creation. This is his metaphysics of the elemental thought-constructs involved in any process of creation or creative act.

[148] Ibid., 148; 134.

[149] Ibid.

[150] In Schelling's case, the generating principle is the ongoing production of the identifying of non-identical principles, for example, the Real and the Ideal, in what he calls a doubling (*Doublirung*) of the initial unity, whose ultimate goal is the exclusion of non-being as evil. However, the final redemption

the world and its creator or the *presupposition* of an ultimately ordered cosmos except for the *fact* of the act of creation itself. Rosenzweig tells us that creation includes, by definition, an anarchic dimension since, as an event that is freely produced, it is not set in a previously ordered horizon determined by this or that principle.[151] For Idealist philosophers, "Generation should accomplish the same as creation; it should give to the plastic, objective world, the world as Antiquity saw it, the point from which its multiplicity closes together and orders itself in unity"[152]. By positing the concept of a creator whose only relation to the world is that of having created it, we are able to think of a created world as being separate and thus having pictureability and plastic self-containedness, aesthetic traits already also elaborated in Antiquity.[153] Given a concept of a god that is not so inextricably bound up in managing the laws of the world allows us to represent to ourselves a picture of a world that is not chained to a causal determinism that would undermine the basic insights of standard empirical philosophy or the possibility of radical, ethical freedom.[154] In Rosenzweig's model, we are given the conditions that enable us to imagine a sense of ourselves in a world in which we are able freely to act and to create new things and new relationships.

In order to differentiate the phenomenon of speech-thinking from the generative logic of Idealist thinking, Rosenzweig uses garden imagery to suggest

---

that Schelling has in mind is ultimately very Christian: God becoming man and then everything, i.e. nature, becoming God the Father.

[151] Whereas in the Idealist tradition, precisely in order to circumvent the concept of creation and to provide an ordering connection, all Idealist philosophers resort in one way or another to a concept of generation that leaves no gaps in its logical development.

[152] GS II, 149; SR, 135.

[153] Rosenzweig literally means "pictureability" when he uses "*Bildhaftigkeit*".

[154] See Rosenzweig's thoughts on empiricism in *Das neue Denken* in GS III. See also Robert Gibbs, Correlations in Rosenzweig and Levinas, Princeton 1992, 128, for his argument that Rosenzweig's theological sociology presents a theory of redemption as social action that "is an empiricism of the future — that we can make society conform to these concepts, and so redeem the world". See also Norbert Samuleson, A User's Guide to Franz Rosenzweig's *Star of Redemption*, Surrey 1999, 60, for his judgment that Rosenzweig would restrict all variants of philosophy, including empiricism as a modern form of Atomism, to his general critique of traditional philosophy at its philosophical best, i.e. as idealist philosophy. However, in his logic of creation, Rosenzweig maintains a firm link to the empiricist tradition by citing Bacon in order to express the empiricist principle that the future is absolutely unlike the present and cannot give us knowledge of what is actual or of actuality: "Gar die Zukunft gilt als absolut ungeeignet 'unfruchtbar' für die Erkenntnis des Wirklichen." (GS2, 146; SR, 132).

how language is rooted in the primal word, which is a counter-argument on his part for an alternative sort of logic, yet is only able to grow and flourish through practical actualization in human relations.[155] It grows and renews itself because language is a kind of living and growing "art" form in the way that language and life mutually nourish each other. In order for language to happen at all, there must be a lived world where humans share their experiences with each other. It is precisely this point that distinguishes Rosenzweig's philosophy of language from an Idealist or analytic philosophy of language. Where an Idealist or analytic philosophy of language contends that all forms of human speech can be reduced to symbolic designators and algebraic formulas, Rosenzweig contends that doing so robs language of its rootedness in human sensuality and its ability to transform humans—through its trans-sensuality—from tragically isolated selves to existing, colorful, soundful souls able to touch and move each other. That happens as the process of revelation, the theme for the next chapter.

Proleptically, however, the work of creation-thinking shows that, because Idealist thinking lost contact with the living vitality of unpredictable existence and was "sunk-down in the under- and pre-world shadow realm of logic, it …[had to seek and]… to hold open an access to the over-world"[156]. It sought this access because it had lost trust in language since it was not the work of its own hands.[157] Acting from the spur of a guilty conscience, Idealists needed another supposition to mediate and thereby confirm the dynamics of reality, a substitution that had to be a human garden in which humans themselves plant the structures of mediation but which retains the character of unconsciously arising as if without human involvement. That was art.[158] Art became the vehicle for Idealist philosophers to visibly and empirically justify their need

---

[155] Although language is rooted in the primal-words in the subterranean grounds of being, it already shoots upward into the light of terrestrial life in the root-words, and in this light blooms forth in colored multiplicity. It is, therefore, a growth in the midst of all growing life, from which it is nourished as that life nourishes from it! Language is differentiated from all this life because it does not move itself freely and arbitrarily above the surface, but rather stretches down roots in the dark grounds below life.

[156] GS II, 162; SR, 146.

[157] Cf. for this the Introduction to Part Three where Rosenzweig refers to Goethe's drama *Faust* for how the ideal human condition is to exercise total independence in the course of one's life. Rosenzweig goes on to reconstruct for us a plausible scenario for what happened next in the historical record of the development of Idealism.

[158] See Immanuel Kant, Critique of Judgment, J. H. Bernard (trans.), New York 1951, 78. For Rosenzweig, the Idealists apotheosized art by making art into a god-like phenomenon and removing, thereby, its particularity as its embededness in human distinctiveness. Moreover, art became a garden with the kinds of signs that the art-work is directed to a purpose and yet at

for methodological completeness in their panlogistic ordering of reality.[159] The artwork provides the "visible" proof of an "absolute" verification of certainty that one's roots are drinking from "the" reality of the All and therefore quells the doubts that dwell at the root of all philosophical undertakings.

Hence, instead of believing in the "speech of the soul, which is a self-revelation of human innerness that encompasses, supports, and completes all other self-expression", an Idealist trusts merely in art in itself, in one torn-off limb of humanity.[160] But for Rosenzweig, what it means to become fully human is precisely to become "ensouled", which means accepting that a human life is not, in essence, a work of art, even though without that limb humans would be crippled. Without art a human would still remain human but without the spoken word of language, which testifies to a human's soul, a human ceases being fully human.

the same time comes about without purpose, quite like the Kantian idea of a purposeless purpose set out in his *Critique of Judgment*.
[159] Rosenzweig says: "When doubt overcomes him about the admissability of its method of the 'panlogistic' pure generator, he only needs to look at the art-work, produced by spirit and yet also part of natural reality, in order to again obtain a good *conscience*."
[160] GS II, 163; SR, 147.

Just as creation can be said to be only the beginning in the framework of world-time, so the *creation* of an artwork is *only* the beginning of the work of humans in the world and the beginning of the effects of the work itself through time. Involved in understanding the formative process of a work is also the effect of the work on the viewer. Returning again to speech, Rosenzweig tells us that the present effect is also the revelatory effect and that has to do with language.[161] Indeed, Rosenzweig distinguishes between "spoken language" as such and "the living, streaming actuality of actual speech"[162] in order to highlight the difference between grasping the intention and expression of a speech act (or act of creation) and the actual effects of its becoming or its completion in the other, in the viewer. We only "see" the beginning—in creation—but not the ongoing or completed life of the work. That entails revelation. Only in the revelatory "saying" of actual, living, streaming language is "human content" able to be expressed by way of the beautiful "artwork". What is "exposed" or freely brought out in the "life-day of the work of art", in building up a work of art, are individuals. These individuals take the form of a kingdom of details—the adjectives—that emerge from a pre-aesthetic totality in an historical procession from the "ground-concepts" to an aesthetically rich actuality. Rosenzweig identified for us three foundational examples of such productions in Part One: god-as-mythic, world-as-plastic, and human-as-tragic.[163]

Towards the end of this chapter, the sections on genius, poet and artist in *The Star* connect Rosenzweig's theoretical discourse in Part One with his practical demonstrations in Part Two, especially with how he interprets biblical texts as exemplifying how creative acts are tied up with language and established narratives. Rosenzweig first tells us that the creation of the artwork happens in the author, using the word "*Urheber*" for author.[164] Rosenzweig wants us to think of the activity of the genius-as-author in terms of one who draws something up or out of an already existing reservoir, out of the primal depths and wealth of one's own pre-existing reservoir, that is, from out of one's own autonomously developed substance.[165] Hence, creation of the artwork happens not so much as an act of remembrance that breaks out of the author, as with Plato and other Idealists, but is an activity of becoming that presupposes the status of the author already having become someone who is capable of bringing forth a new and original work. Rosenzweig names this state: being-already-created.

---

[161] Ibid. This is his fusion of aeshetics and theology.
[162] Ibid.: "*gesprochene Sprache*" and „*der lebendig strömenden Wirklichkeit der wirklichen Sprache*".
[163] GS II, 165; SR, 148.
[164] Ibid.
[165] Since one of the etymological roots of *Urheber* means to raise out of the primal depths. The work of art is raised out of the primal, pre-reflective and pre-linguistic depths of a particular author revealing the created work as a process of bringing something forth that is already there.

He points out that the happening of the work of art in its relation to the viewer depends on the viewer for its completion, a completion that is measured by its degree of actual liveliness. This provides an important part in Rosenzweig's theory for the role of art as cultural and political phenomenon. As one of the criteria for measuring the actual effectiveness of a work of art, the liveliness is that aspect of the work that is capable of arousing a feeling of common humanity in others, that is, liveliness presupposes that there is another human other than myself who, through that work, awakens me as I awaken her by way of experiencing a lively feeling of our common sense of humanity. That awoken feeling then initiates a process within the other which leads to the formation of self-identities through instigating a process of self-reflexivity initially based on the formation of a perceived sense of commonality. That commonality is that the other is like me but shares a human commonality that is, however, in the next instance negated in order to allow for one's own self-affirmation.

In order to better elucidate his ideas about this matter of self-identity, Rosenzweig turns to an ideal case, namely, the case of the genius and the "eruptive" act by which someone becomes marked as a genius by an evaluating public. The issue of the "genius" is not new with Rosenzweig, but instead indicates his roots in the German Idealist preoccupation with using such a term to categorize extraordinary works of human production.[166] Rosenzweig rejects the assumption that only an elite, pre-determined few in a process of natural selection have been predetermined, that is, pre-selected, to become geniuses. He argues that if geniuses were *born* to inevitably become geniuses then the category of personality would provide the criteria to determine who is or is not a genius, whereas personality is simply that determination of a human being that results from cultural and environmental factors and not genetic heritage. Instead, the category of genius is tied to the category of self and to become a self is open to almost everyone, as Rosenzweig notes: "Miracle-children have just as much, or just as little, chance to become a genius *as any other human*."[167] Just as a self "suddenly surprises someone one day", so genius "surprises someone one day". What is common between the genius and every other self is that both presuppose a pre-existing totality of human being whereas what differentiates the genius from every other self is that the genius, drawing on his/her "complex of in-genius characteristics", which constitute its ownmost self, is able to draw from within him-/her-self and set free a work.[168] It now becomes apparent how important the earlier presentation and analyses of freedom, caprice, and necessity is for Rosenzweig's position.[169] Being able to *draw from within* oneself and

---

[166] See Immanuel Kant, Critique of Judgment, J. H. Bernard (trans.), New York 1951, 150–64.

[167] GS II, 165; SR, 148. (My italics.)

[168] Ibid.,166; 149.

[169] See Chapter Two in this text, where Rosenzweig establishes the metaphysics for his Cohenian-inspired, mathematically based epistemology.

to *set free* a work is what constitutes the difference between genius and non-genius and not personality as such.[170]

Rosenzweig expands that definition of genius/author to include every human being capable of becoming a self but restricts members of that set to those who are capable of "increasing and completing oneself within oneself"[171]. What this means is that the genius is able to "begin a new beginning" because the emergence of genius, with respect to personality and self, is the beginning of a new phase of one's life. But the true genius has to become a poet, as opposed to being just an artist—since every genius is an artist but not every artist is a genius.[172] This means that the genius has to have access to an "inner manifoldness, a world of creations, of imaginative insights and thoughts which ... harmoniously strive towards each other in simply being with one another"[173]. Rosenzweig calls this harmonious inner striving of co-existing thoughts "family resemblances", a concept that connects his ideas about art with the ethical relationship of dialogue, developed later in Part Two and instrumental in his social theory of responsibility that he develops in Part Three. He also notes that unless one is capable of inexhaustibly producing new creations out of this "covenant" of family relations, then one is a "crippled" genius. It seems that the life of the genius, although open to everyone, is actually very demanding and complex.

Finally, Rosenzweig ends the chapter with his midrashic interpretation of the opening passages of Bereshit (Genesis). In exercising his midrash, it becomes clear that he does not negate or reject art or mathematics, which would then be submitting to the inexorable appropriation of a dialectical logic; rather, he

---

[170] The distinct divergence from attributing genius to personality may also indicate Rosenzweig contesting, again, Hegel's phenomenology of social ethics articulated in *The* Philosophy of Right. In sections on "Abstract Right" Hegel claims that self-determination in any society has its origins in the stipulation of personality as "'the' defining human characteristic, which then leads to his theory of property rights, etc. See G.W.F. Hegel, Grundlinien der Philosophie des Rechts, Stuttgart 1970, 115–23.

[171] GS II, 166; SR, 149.

[172] Which sets him against Hegel as well. Rosenzweig provides us with a pair of examples to differentiate between poet and artist: Flaubert as mere artist versus Balzac as poet, and Huch as artist versus Lagerlöf as poet. The difference is that in the case of Flaubert and Huch, their artistry consists in their attempts to retell history *realistically* in some kind of mirroring effect. Balzac and Lagerlöf, on the other hand, create new adventures and comedies to depict society as such but also possible social relations. Additionally, Rosenzweig provides gendered pairs, Balzac and Flaubert are both male, Lagerlöf (who was the first woman to ever be awarded the Nobel Prize for Literature in 1909) and Huch are both female.

[173] GSII, 166; SR 149.

proceeds phenomenologically by taking art and mathematics as presuppositions and proceeds by building their transformation from static placeholders in a metaphysical sort of logical atomism—whose power is the analysis of the individual point—into the building stones for a story which descriptively reveals that which is believed to be a dynamic, self-renewing course of actual emerging creations and relations. The hypothetical and isolated elements are withdrawn from within the author and assembled to form a philosophical/theological/sociological narrative that makes ethical and thus corresponding sense of the different elements in the narrative. It is also ethical because ethical relations depend on establishing relations of believing trust in the language that comes naturally to us. In Rosenzweig's words: "We describe the course in which we believe, with the words in which we trust."[174] But which words should we trust? Which do we believe in and where do such words come from? What do we mean when we talk about trust?

We trust because we are accustomed to using something based on our faith in its reliability. Rosenzweig tells us that it is necessary to trust language, which is easy because of its utter familiarity.[175] We trust in that language that *resounds* for us with a sense for familiar, joyful, and fruitful relations and that bridges our inner radically subjective experience with our objective experiences of others in, with, and of the world.[176] Simply put, what we hear from the other is what we *intuitively* say from our own hearts. That means that even though the inner-structural processes for constructing the elements "god world human" can be and should continue to be differentiated, Rosenzweig asserts that the "word of god and the word of the human are the same" in how they resound with actuality for us.[177] At this end-point, as at the beginning of Book One, what Rosenzweig means by god is simply a speech-act referring to that one who at one time created something out of nothing, an act about which we continue to speak.

Further readings

Bauer, A.E, (1992). *Rosenzweigs Sprachdenken im „Stern der Erlösung" und in seiner Korrespondenz mit Martin Buber zur Verdeutschung der Schrift*, Frankfurt a.M., Lang

---

[174] GS II, 167; SR, 150.
[175] Language is in us and around us, and there is nothing else which comes to us from "without" (*aussen*) in the way that it resounds (*widertönt*) out of our "inner" (*Innen*) to the "outer" (*Aussen*). The word is the same as it becomes heard and as it is spoken GS II, 167; SR, 150.
[176] Interiority and exteriority, as such.
[177] Accordingly, drawing on what is closest to his own heart, Rosenzweig claims that what human beings hear in their heart and take to be their own human language is "the word which comes out of the mouth of god". But what exactly Rosenzweig means by god is not at all clear.

Del Prete, M., (2009). *Erlösung als Werk. Zur offenbarten Ontologie Franz Rosenzweigs*, Freiburg, Alber.
Kalatzis, A., (2021), *Episodic Genius. Autonomous Artistic Agency in the Star of Redemption*, in: "Into Life", Franz Rosenzweig on Knowledge, Aesthetics, and Politics. Supplements to the Journal of Jewish Thought and Philosophy 31 (2021) 111–138; [https://doi.org./10.1163/9789004468559_007]
Schwartz, M., (2003). *Metapher und Offenbarung. Zur Sprache in Franz Rosenzweigs «Stern der Erlösung»*, Berlin, Philo.

Zweiter Teil, zweites Buch: Offenbarung oder die allzeiterneuerte Geburt der Seele

Gesine Palmer

1. Abgrenzung

1.1 Offenbarung philosophisch – Offenbarungsbegriffe in den realen Religionsgemeinschaften

Rosenzweig hielt den zweiten Teil des *Stern* – und in ihm das zweite Buch – für das Beste, was er geschrieben hat. Schon im Weiterschreiben am dritten Teil glaubte er, die Höhe des zweiten Buchs nicht wieder erreichen zu können. Tatsächlich laufen in diesem zentralen Stück verschiedene Fäden seiner Konstruktion zusammen. Es enthält – wenn man es durch die Brille heutigen Fachmenschentums lesen wollte – eine philosophische Theorie der primären Bindung und ihrer Bedeutung für das Wirklichkeitsgefühl des Menschen. Damit ist es aber zugleich auch etwas wie ein „dialogischer oder relationaler Gottesbeweis" jenseits oder vor aller Ausdifferenzierung der verschiedenen Religionen. Zwar erläutert Rosenzweig seinen Begriff des wahren Glaubens und der Offenbarung auch in diesem Buch am Gegenbild des Islam und des Heidentums. Aber hier, sozusagen im Auge des Sternenorkans, geht es so konzentriert um die wechselseitige Hervorbringung von Gott und Mensch, dass die Grunddifferenz zwischen Judentum und Christentum fast völlig in den

---

How to cite this book chapter:
Palmer, G. 2021. Zweiter Teil, zweites Buch: Offenbarung oder die allzeiterneuerte Geburt der Seele. In: Brasser, M., Bojanić, P. and Ciglia, F. P. (eds.) *The Star for Beginners: Introductions to the Magnum Opus of Franz Rosenzweig*. Pp. 99–111. London: Ubiquity Press. DOI: https://doi.org/10.5334/bco.i. License: CC-BY

Hintergrund tritt, während geradezu platt deutlich wird, wie sehr der Islam als eine Folie dient, um einen falschen Offenbarungsbegriff zu illustrieren. In der Realität der historischen Religionsgemeinschaften ist dieser in Rosenzweigs Augen falsche Offenbarungsbegriff selbstverständlich unter Christen und Juden genauso verbreitet wie im Islam – während umgekehrt auch im Islam dem kundigen Forscher Denker bekannt sind, die einen ähnlich elaborierten Offenbarungsbegriff haben wie Rosenzweig ihn für „den wahren Glauben" beansprucht.[178] Tatsächlich muss geradezu umgekehrt erst einmal festgestellt werden: Was Rosenzweig „Offenbarung" nennt, würde vielen einfacher gläubigen Gemütern als das ganze Gegenteil von Offenbarungsglauben erscheinen. In einem resümierenden Satz sagt er es selbst so: *„Die Offenbarung ist gegenwärtig, ja ist das Gegenwärtigsein selber"* (SE 207; Hervorhebung GP).

1.2 Theoretisierung und Metaphorisierung eines Liebesproblems

Das Buch beginnt mit dem Satz „Stark wie der Tod ist die Liebe" und springt mitten hinein in eine Situation zwischen Liebendem und Geliebter. Als zeitgenössische Leserin verschluckt man ein Entsetzen – oder vielleicht besser nicht. Es wäre letztlich ganz unrosenzweigisch, es zu verschlucken, und insofern auch für ihn keine angemessene Antwort. Das Buch versammelt schon auf der ersten Seite äusserst anstössige Sätze, von denen der folgende vielleicht am meisten empört: „Der Geliebten zunächst gilt es, dass die Liebe stark ist wie der Tod. Wie nur dem Weibe, nicht dem Manne die Natur es gesetzt hat, an der Liebe sterben zu dürfen" (SE 174). Rosenzweig war in jenen Jahren von der Idee, dass eine junge Frau an der Liebe sterben und einen Opfertod auf sich nehmen könnte wie Alkestis, tief fasziniert. Das hatte einerseits sicher mit seiner eigenen Lage als Soldat zu tun, in der er gerade als Mann einem möglichen frühen Opfertod täglich gegenüberstand. Andererseits damit, dass er eine bedrängende und komplizierte biographische Situation durch eine weitere Komplikation „gelöst" hatte: Er hatte sich in die Frau seines Freundes Eugen Rosenstock verliebt, der ihn immer wieder bedrängte, zum Christentum zu konvertieren wie er. Seit der ersten intimen Begegnung des Paares schrieb Rosenzweig Gritli eine grosse Zahl von Briefen. Die Liebe der beiden wurde offen ausgelebt, und viel besprochen, wobei auch immer wieder von der Liebe zwischen Eugen und Franz die Rede ist. Auf diese Geschichte ist das „Herzbuch" vielleicht nicht zurückzuführen – aber sie sollte auch deswegen nicht unerwähnt bleiben, weil Rosenzweig selbst gerade dieses Buch in besondere Beziehung zu Gritli stellt.[179]

---

[178] Vgl. Einleitung (GP) und Nachwort (Yossef Schwartz), in Franz Rosenzweig: „Innerlich bleibt die Welt eine". Ausgewählte Schriften zum Islam, Berlin/Wien 2003.

[179] GB 177, Brief vom 2. Nov. 1918: „Dies Buch II 2, an dem ich jetzt schreibe gehört dir noch viel eigener als das Gritlianum, grade weil es nicht von

In einem seiner etwas über 1000 erhaltenen Briefe an Gritli schreibt er von einer gemeinsamen Freundin Doris, diese sei an Gritlis Stelle „heruntergestiegen".[180] Die Vorstellung, dass eigentlich Gritli an der Liebe zwischen den beiden hätte sterben müssen, war ihm also nicht fremd.

Mit derselben Entschlossenheit, mit der ich diese Geschichte hier zu bedenken gebe, möchte ich freilich vor Kurzschlüssen warnen. Rosenzweig hielt sich selbst an seine ebenfalls in II.2 mitgegebene Kunsttheorie, in der die Einfälle, die aus dem Leben des Künstlers und über ihn kommen, sorgsam im Zuge der handwerklichen Arbeit von dem Leben und der Person abgelöst und zu einem Werk verarbeitet werden. Ich werde die Zusammenhänge noch näher beleuchten. Zu Beginn ist erst einmal wichtig, Probleme zu klären, die leicht verhindern könnten, dass man sich auf den tieferen Sinn des Textes einlässt.

Die Anmutung einer furchtbaren Pathetisierung der als natürlich ausgegebenen traditionellen Geschlechterordnung ist von diesen Hindernissen sicher eines der schwersten. Zugleich hängt gerade an diesem „Gleichnis" die ganze Konstruktion, weit über die möglicherweise veranlassende reale Liebeserfahrung hinaus. Die Liebesbeziehung zwischen einem Liebenden und einer geliebten Seele in ihrer fundamentalen Asymmetrie erweist sich im Verlauf der in diesem Buch folgenden Ausarbeitung als eine hochdifferenzierte Darstellung dessen, was die „allzeiterneuerte Geburt der Seele" ausmacht. Möge für die vorausgeschickten Abgrenzungen die Feststellung genügen, dass am Ende des Buches die geliebte Seele gerade nicht stirbt.[181] Sie hat vielmehr erst Gott als den

---

vornherein für dich bestimmt war und es ja auch jetzt nicht ist. Es ist nicht ‚Dir' aber – dein. Dein – wie ich. Manchmal ist mir, als wäre ich ein Kind, das nicht schreiben kann und es doch gern möchte und du führtest mir die Feder. Tu's weiter, Geliebte." Die Grundidee zu diesem Buch nannte er „Gritlianum". An verschiedenen Stellen im umfassenden Briefwerk sagt er, dass er sie ursprünglich „der Schrei" nennen wollte – ein Thema, das sich im hier verhandelten Buch auch wieder findet.

[180] GB 179, Brief vom 8. Nov. 1918: „Wir hatten freilich bei der Nachricht von Doris beide das gleiche Gefühl, deinen Brief bekam ich erst viel später. Aber ich meine, es war das Gefühl, als ob sie wie ein Opfer an deiner Stelle heruntergestiegen wäre. Ein furchtbares Gefühl, aber so kam es mir." Dazu zu lesen sind Erwägungen aus einem Brief vom 31. 10. 1918, in dem Rosenzweig über den Tod von Doris von Beckerath berichtet und wieder sehr allgemeine Überlegungen über das Verhältnis von Mann und Frau anstellt.

[181] Es ist gelegentlich zu hören, dass in Wahrheit Rosenzweig an der letztlich unerfüllt gebliebenen Liebe zu Gritli gestorben sei. Dafür lassen sich jedenfalls dann Indizien finden, wenn man die Berichte über seine Verfassung nach seinem Entschluss zur Verheiratung mit Edith Hahn pathologisierend als den Beginn einer schweren Depression und den Ausbruch der ALS psychosomatisch liest. Ich warne aber auch hier vor Kurzschlüssen (für eine differenzierte Betrachtung vgl. mein *Die Qual der Kreatur bewährt vermutlich nichts. Überlegungen zum Zusammenhang von Krankheit und*

Liebenden zu dem gemacht, was er ist, und „überschreitet" den „Zauberkreis der Geliebtheit", um nun ihrerseits den Mund zu öffnen, „nicht zur Antwort mehr, sondern zum eigenen Wort" (SE 228). Insofern zeigt dieses Herzbuch im kleinen und für die weiblich imaginierte geliebte Seele dieselbe Struktur, die das ganze Werk für den Menschen überhaupt kennzeichnet: es beginnt mit der Todesfurcht und endet mit dem Entschluss oder der Bestimmung, ins Leben zu gehen.

1.3 Gleichnis und Nichtgleichnis – das Hohelied als „Kernbuch der Offenbarung"

Die Idee des Buches ist extrem – das heisst: in voller Konsequenz und präziser sprachlicher Durchführung – prozesshaft. An keiner Stelle dürfte das deutlicher sein als da, wo Rosenzweig über den Gleichnischarakter desjenigen biblischen Buches spricht, das er als „Kernbuch der Offenbarung" (SE 225) ansieht. Der Prozess, um den es hier geht, ist der einer gleichsam dynamischen mystischen Vereinigung, aus der die Realität des einen im Glauben an die Realität des anderen hervorgeht. Unio mystica – mystische Vereinigung – wird also nicht als Endstadium eines kontinuierlichen Loslassens irdischer Bindungen verstanden, in dem dann die endgültige Gelassenheit der reinen Seele erreicht wäre. Vielmehr bedeutet sie gerade umgekehrt die Entstehung der Vielfalt der weltlichen Bindungen aus der wechselseitigen Veränderung der Verschiedenen in der Liebesbeziehung. In der Geschichte der Bibelforschung hat man sich immer wieder mit der Frage beschäftigt, warum ausgerechnet das Hohelied, das doch alle Charaktere eines „weltlichen" Liebesliedes trägt und nirgends von Gott spricht, in den Kanon der heiligen Schriften aufgenommen wurde. Rosenzweig beantwortet die Frage damit, dass er sagt: nur dieser Text behandelt die Liebe *nicht* mehr als ein Gleichnis, wie dies die Prophetenbücher tun, in denen immer wieder die eheliche oder ausserehliche „sündige" Liebe als Gleichnis für die Beziehung zwischen Gott und seinem Volk verwendet wird. Dabei verlässt Rosenzweig die mystischen Deutungen, in denen man die Vereinigung eines präexistent gedachten Gottwesens und eines nachgeordnet präexistenten Menschenwesens sehen könnte, und lässt das Selbstsprechen als die Weise hervortreten, in der das Seelewerden sich allein ausdrücken und offenbaren kann. „Es gibt kein Buch in der Bibel, in dem verhältnismässig das Wort Ich so häufig vorkäme wie hier" (SE 225) – gerade dadurch qualifiziert das Hohelied sich für Rosenzweig zum Kernbuch der Offenbarung. Mit der Überwindung der Sterblichkeit durch die Liebe im Eröffnungssatz „Stark wie der Tod ist die Liebe" ist also nicht gemeint, dass irgendwelche entstofflichten Entitäten unsterblich wären, während der Leib stirbt, und es geht Rosenzweig auch nicht um die

---

Denken Franz Rosenzweigs, in: M. Brasser (Hg.), Rosenzweig Jahrbuch 1 / Rosenzweig Yearbook 1. Rosenzweig heute / Rosenzweig today, Freiburg/München 2006, 232–254.

Vorstellung einer leiblichen Auferstehung. Sein Anliegen in aller Rede von der Liebe, die mehr wäre als ein Gleichnis, geht auf den Augenblick aus, in dem die selbstoffenbarende Ichrede aussetzt. Das wird im folgenden noch ausgeführt werden. Hier ist erst einmal festzuhalten, dass die Voraussetzung dieses Augenblicks ebenso wie die Voraussetzung seiner Dauer immer die *Befreiung* der lebendigen Sprache aus aller die Menschenseele (oder: Gott, Welt und Mensch) verobjektivierenden Rede der Philosophie und der „falschen Offenbarung" ist. Es geht um das „Sagen" der Beziehung in allen ihren „Reifestadien" (wie man sie nur in wissenschaftlich verdinglichter Form darstellen könnte) – nicht um eine objektivierende Darstellung verschiedener möglicher Zustände von Menschen- und Gottesbeziehungen. Die sprachliche Höhe dieses Sagens sieht Rosenzweig im Hohelied erreicht. Dieses spricht die Gegenwart einer Beziehung reiner aus als alle Verkündigungen mit ihren Gleichnissen es vermöchten. Der Augenblick, in dem die Ichrede aussetzt, gilt Rosenzweig als derjenige Augenblick, in dem die Offenbarung sich mit der Schöpfung verbindet (SE 225).[182]

2. Momenthafte Selbstverwandlung, *nicht* Eigenschaft

2.1 Die Liebe des Liebenden und die Liebe der Geliebten

In den ersten Absätzen von II.2 knüpft Rosenzweig an II.1 an, um zu erläutern, inwiefern innerhalb seines Systems[183] die Schöpfung notwendig mit einer Offenbarung verknüpft sein muss. Dabei geht es nicht nur um die Frage nach der Wirklichkeit Gottes – oder die Frage, wie rational es sein kann, einen wirklichen Gott denken zu wollen. Es geht vielmehr um die Frage nach Wirklichkeit

---

[182] „Das Wort ‚Ich' also ist der Grundton, der bald in der einen, bald, durch das Du übergehend, in der anderen Stimme unter dem ganzen melodisch-harmonischen Gewebe der Mittel- und Oberstimmen orgelpunktartig hinzieht. Es gibt in dem ganzen Buch nur eine einzige Stelle, wo er schweigt; sie fällt gerade durch dieses augenblickliche Aussetzen des Grundbasses, den man sonst in infolge seiner Unaufhörlichkeit schon beinahe überhört, ungeheuer auf; so wie man sich des Tickens der Wanduhr erst bewusst wird, wenn sie plötzlich stillsteht. Es sind die Worte von der Liebe, die stark ist wie der Tod.[...] In ihnen ragt die Schöpfung sichtbar in die Offenbarung hinein und wird sichtbar von ihr überhöht. Der Tod ist das Letzte und Voll-endende der Schöpfung – und die Liebe ist stark wie er."

[183] *Dass* es sich schliesslich um nichts Geringeres als ein „System der Philosophie" handle, hat er bereits während des Schreibens in seinen Briefen und später dann auch in den auf den *Stern* bezogenen Essays deutlich ausgesprochen, und viele Forscher haben mit graphischen Darstellungen des Sternsymbols den Systemcharakter erläutert – dies alles hier zu wiederholen wäre also überflüssig.

überhaupt – und wie diese sich verändert, wenn wir in unserem Denken von Aktivität und Passivität mit der Ereignishaftigkeit von Sprache und menschlicher Begegnung ernstmachen. Übersetzt in die Sprache des gegenwärtig vorherrschenden (und darum als allgemeinverständlich geltenden) Psychologismus würde man sagen müssen: Es geht um die Frage nach der („gefühlten") Wirklichkeit emotionaler Verbindungen überhaupt.[184]

Der Tod – dies ist in den vorigen Kapiteln des Werkes überdeutlich geworden – gehört zur Schöpfung. Er ist, wie Rosenzweig in diesem Kapitel sagt, „das Letzte und Volle-endende der Schöpfung". Nun wird also gesagt, „die Liebe ist stark wie er", und Rosenzweig fährt fort: „Dies ist das einzige, was über die Liebe gesagt, aus-gesagt, erzählt werden kann; alles andere kann nicht ‚über' sie gesagt ‚werden', sondern nur von ihr selber gesprochen" (SE 225).

Wie man sich aber das Sprechen der Liebe gegenüber dem Tod als ein Sprechen in menschlicher Sprache vorstellen könne, davon handeln die Schematismen, mit denen Rosenzweig die Liebe zwischen der Liebe des Liebenden und der Liebe der Geliebten aufteilt. Wenn wir seiner Metaphorik zunächst *nicht* in das Gleichnis der Liebe zwischen Mann und Frau folgen, sondern – in Parallele zur späteren Entwicklung in der Psychoanalyse – erst einmal auf die Beziehung zwischen dem abhängigen, seine Bedürftigkeit herausschreienden Menschensäugling und seiner ersten (zumeist mütterlichen) „Bezugsperson" zurückgehen, können wir vieles sehr viel deutlicher verstehen. So wie die spätere Psychoanalyse die Bedürftigkeit auch der Mutter anerkennt, so formuliert

---

[184] Es ist vermutlich kein Zufall, dass die Arbeiten Freuds und die Arbeiten Rosenzweigs etwa zeitgleich entstanden. Das Problem der Offenheit menschlichen Fühlens und der dieses „einhegenden" kulturellen Definitionen war in der Zeit um den Ersten Weltkrieg durch die industrielle Entwicklung und die damit verbundene Erosion der alten Ordnungen bis zu ihrem völligen Scheitern in diesem Krieg so eklatant ins Bewusstsein der gebildeten Zeitgenossen gedrungen, dass alles für sicher gehaltene Sprechen über die „natürlichen menschlichen Beziehungen" nicht mehr als gültig empfunden werden konnte. Aus der Sicht „aufgeklärter Zeitgenossen" nahm Rosenzweig den „Rückweg" in die Religion, wenn auch in eine sehr aufgeklärte Variante davon, während Freud vorwärts ging in die Wissenschaft. Von heute aus stellt sich das insofern etwas anders dar, als die verdinglichende Rede vom Menschen umso deutlicher an ihre Grenzen stösst, je weiter auch die physiologische Erforschung der Vorgänge im menschlichen Gehirn voranschreitet. Werke wie *Der Stern der Erlösung* reden da nicht dem Rückfall in mythisch-religiöse Erklärungen das Wort, sondern erlauben ein modernster Entwicklungs- und Sprachtheorie angemessenes Systematisieren derjenigen Sprachen, in denen wir auf das Paradox, gleichzeitig Forscher und Gegenstände unserer Forschungen zu sein, antworten und aus der isolierenden Stillstellung, die eine pseudoobjektive, vermeintlich rein wissenschaftliche Rede uns antun würde, ausbrechen.

dieses theologische oder philosophische System etwas wie ein Bedürfnis Gottes nach dem Menschen. Um dies gegen die Tradition zu rechtfertigen, verweist Rosenzweig wieder auf die Prozesshaftigkeit des dialogischen Offenbarungsgeschehens. Auf Rosenzweigs Dynamisierung der traditionellen Begriffe komme ich gleich zurück.

Zunächst einmal will ich begründen, warum ich glaube, dass die Beziehung zwischen Mutter und kleinem Kind besser geeignet wäre als die erotische Beziehung zwischen Erwachsenen, um die Figur der den anderen hervorbringenden und das Selbst offenbarenden Liebe zu symbolisieren. Die Kampfansage der Liebe an den Tod, das Schmachten der Liebe nach Gegenwart, sind selbstverständlich in allen Liebesformen anzutreffen. Aber dieses spezielle Wandelnlernen aus der Gewissheit des Geliebtseins, von dem Rosenzweig schreibt, dieses Beimnamengerufensein, dieses erst Festwerden unter der Antwort auf das Liebmich des Liebenden, erinnert doch mehr an das Ichwerden des kleinen Kindes, das von der Mutter beim Namen gerufen wird und sich in dem Masse, in dem es selbst antworten lernt, dann auch von der Mutter entfernen und selbstsprechend in die Welt gehen kann, ohne den Kontakt zur Mutter zu verlieren. Dass es dabei wegen seiner unendlich grösseren Abhängigkeit und Angewiesenheit auf die liebevolle Zuwendung der Mutter auch das Wesen ist, das aus Liebe sterben könnte, liesse sich auf sehr traurige Weise an den vielen Fällen illustrieren, in denen Kinder eher ihr Leben als die Beziehung zu peinigenden Eltern aufgeben. Während umgekehrt das Gelingen einer jeden Liebesbeziehung zwischen Eltern und Kindern nach dem Wunder der Entstehung des Kindes in Zeugung und Geburt die eigentliche, allzeiterneuerte Offenbarung der Menschlichkeit ist. Dazu gehört auch der Charakter der Bedürftigkeit und des Überwältigtseins auf Seiten des Liebenden.[185]

---

[185] Diese Frage wird immer noch besonders differenziert diskutiert in dem Kapitel „Das verlorene Ideal der Mütterlichkeit" in Jessica Benjamins Die Fesseln der Liebe. Psychoanalyse, Feminismus und das Problem der Macht, Frankfurt a.M. 1993, woraus hier nur ein kleiner Absatz zitiert sei: „Das Kind kann die Mutter nur dann als Subjekt mit eigenem Recht wahrnehmen, wenn die Mutter auch ein solches ist. Und hier sollten wir uns klarmachen, dass zur Subjektivität der Mutter (kontrastiert zum Ideal der Mütterlichkeit) auch Unvollkommenheit gehören muss, damit sie für sich selbst und für ihr Kind real sei" (207), es lohnt sich aber, den ganzen Text einmal neben Rosenzweigs zu halten. Obwohl Benjamin philosophisch eher auf einen Diskurs der gegenseitigen Anerkennung rekurriert, liefert sie doch genau das Mass an psychoanalytischem Basiswissen über die Elemente der asymmetrischen Beziehung zwischen Erwachsener und Säugling bzw. Kleinkind, die gewusst werden müssen, wenn man die Entwicklung vom unbedürftigen allerbarmenden Gott zum bedürftigen liebenden Gott auf einer passenden irdisch-zwischenmenschlichen Grundlage verstehen will.

2.2 Das Nichts und die innere Umkehr

Wenn die Prozesshaftigkeit der Liebesoffenbarung – an welchem lebensnahen Beispiel einer asymmetrischen *Beziehung* auch immer – anschaulicher geworden ist, kann nun noch einmal die abstraktere Gestalt des „dynamischen Gottesbeweises" in den Blick genommen werden. Die Konstruktion des Stern hängt einerseits an der graphischen Figur das Davidsterns und damit auch an der Idee, die Beziehung von Gott, Mensch und Welt, von Schöpfung, Offenbarung und Erlösung *more geometrico* darzustellen, wie dies für philosophische Systematiker nicht erst seit Spinoza und nicht nur bis Hegel verlockend war. Andererseits soll der Stern, wie Rosenzweig in einem seiner Briefe über seine „Vision" von der Sache berichtet, rollen. Und drittens – soll das Ganze auf lebendigere Weise als frühere Entwürfe „offen" sein oder ins Offene, ins Lebendige hinausführen, und zwar, so Rosenzweigs Anspruch, ausdrücklich *ohne* vorprogrammiert, zugleich aber auch *ohne* beliebig zu sein. Genau diesem Anspruch nähern sich Gott, Welt und Mensch in der Offenbarung. Rosenzweig kennzeichnet sie als eine „zweite" Offenbarung. In der ersten, der Schöpfung, war Gott von einer Selbstverneinung des Nichts zu einer Weltbejahung gelangt. Diese Weltbejahung, so sagt Rosenzweig am Anfang des zweiten Buches, war aber nur eine abermalige Verneinung seiner eigenen Lebendigkeit, ein Nichts höherer Stufe, „Nichts nur mit Bezug auf das, was ihm entsprang, in sich aber ein Nichts voller Charakter, eben kein Nichts, sondern ein Etwas. Nichts war sie nur darin, dass sie, indem sie sich auftat, sofort in neue Gestalten auseinanderbrach" (SE 175). In diesem Zusammenhang nun redet Rosenzweig selbst von Gott als einem mütterlichen Wesen, dessen „innere ‚Natur', die unendliche Meeresstille seines Seins", auf Offenbarung drängt – oder ihrer bedarf.

Es fällt mir schwer, hier nicht entweder einfach nachzuerzählen – oder sehr kritisch zu kommentieren. Spekulationen über Seinsvorgänge in mystischen Urgründen haben der Rationalistin immer etwas Raunendes, Spökenkiekerisches, wenn sie *nicht* einfach nur eine sehr metaphorische Rede sein sollen. Hinter die Feststellung, dass Rosenzweig selbst die Notwendigkeit der inneren Umkehrung gesetzt hat, komme ich nicht zurück, auch dann nicht, wenn ich dreissig mal die Stellen lese, an denen er in der ersten Lebendigkeit Gottes den geometrischen Punkt bezeichnet sieht, aus dem nun der Hervortritt Gottes in die Offenbarung erfolgen müsse. Dies aber einmal gegeben, erkennt man an den Gegenüberstellungen zu Islam und Heidentum schnell, worauf dieses Umkehrungstheorem hinausläuft: Es versucht mit allen Mitteln der Theologie und der Philosophie, Gott und Mensch in eine lebendige Beziehung zu ziehen und dieses Lebendige selbst mehr zu *sagen* als nach dem Muster einer Begriffsreihe oder Kausalverknüpfung zu *erklären*. Dennoch soll die Rationalität in Geltung bleiben. Der „wahre Glaube" soll nicht nach Art der geheimnisvollen oder mythischen Religion funktionieren und einfach eine der Erklärung nicht weiter bedürftige Behauptung aufstellen, wie es die buntbebilderte Götterwelt der Heiden tue. Das Verborgene der Macht hinter der vorgefundenen Schöpfung soll dem wahren Glauben gerade stark bewusst und fühlbar sein. Die Feststellung, dass die Schöpfung gut war, „gar sehr", war am Ende von II.1

zugleich der Tod, denn es war eine Feststellung *über* ein ein für allemal Gegebenes. Rosenzweig nennt es dunkel oder verborgen. Licht nennt er die augenblickshaft hereinbrechende oder aus Gott hervorbrechende Offenbarung, und sie ist in seiner Metaphernwelt zuerst etwas Väterliches: „Das Mütterliche ist stets das, was schon da ist, das Väterliche kommt erst hinzu" (SE 177). Und als hätte er sämtliche spätere Lehrbücher der Psychoanalyse schon mal vorab gelesen, kommt dieses Spätere hinzu als Namengebung und Anrede. Wieder ist es ganz unmöglich, die Briefe zu übergehen, die Rosenzweig in diesem Zusammenhang schrieb. Etwa diesen Briefanfang vom 15.08.1918:

„Liebes Gritli,
—ich sitze ganz stumm vor den zwei Worten und möchte weiter gar nichts schreiben, habe auch eigentlich gar nichts weiter zu schreiben, – und habe ich dir denn eigentlich je etwas andres geschrieben?" (GB 118)

Ich werde nicht von Bewährung reden. Ich werde nicht die Briefe auf den *Stern* oder den *Stern* auf die Briefe zurückführen. Ich werde auch die Zeitproblematik nicht schärfer stellen als Rosenzweig selbst es im *Stern* tut (obwohl ich den Eindruck habe, man müsste das). Festgehalten sein soll nur: Die Erschaffung der Welt ist für Rosenzweig etwas, was Gott aus sich heraussetzt, was aber auch „in ihm selber als dem verborgenen vorgeht". Symptomatisch dafür ist ihm das göttliche Selbstgespräch des „lasst uns einen Menschen machen". Nun könnte er in die Dunkelheit seiner Verborgenheit oder des Nichts, aus dem heraus er die Welt erschaffen hat, zurücksinken. Dann wäre die Schöpfung da: als ein „Ding" und als insofern stummes Zeugnis der ersten, der noch fast uneigentlichen Offenbarung. Und Gott wäre wieder verborgen. (Übertragen auf die Situation zwischen einer Mutter und einem Kind könnten wir sagen: das Kind wäre geboren, könnte aber die Nähe zur Mutter jederzeit wieder verlieren, wie die Mutter mit dem Kind ihr Muttersein verlieren könnte). Eine Offenbarung, die ihn am hellen Licht hielte, wäre aber diejenige, die nicht durch Selbstverneinung des göttlichen „Wesens" ein „Ding" setzte. Sie müsste vielmehr eine Beziehung zu dem nun stumm vorhandenen Ding beginnen und also nicht wieder etwas Neues erzeugen, sondern „nichts sein als das Sichauftun eines Verschlossenen, nichts als die Selbstverneinung eines blossen stummen Wesens durch ein lautes Wort, einer still ruhenden Immerwährendheit durch einen bewegten Augenblick" (SE 179).

Mit diesen systemischen Anforderungen an das, was eine Offenbarung innerhalb des geometrischen Schemas und in ihrer Mitte zu leisten hätte, leitet Rosenzweig zu seinem persönlichen, philosophischen Hohelied der Liebe über.

2.3 Die Theodizee-Arbeit der geliebten Seele

Aus der in Gott selbst begründeten Notwendigkeit einer inneren Umkehr folgt nun eine weitere Umkehrung, die ich mit Bedacht nicht mehr unter der Überschrift der „inneren" Umkehr behandeln möchte. Es kommt nämlich in dem in eigentümlichen Tempi beschriebenen Verhältnis von Gott als dem Liebenden und der menschlichen Seele als der Geliebten zu eigenartigen Umkehrungen nicht nur der traditionellen Begriffe in sich, sondern der Verhältnisse selbst, innerhalb der Begriffe, innerhalb der Seelen der Beteiligten und zwischen ihnen. (Das wird in den folgenden Büchern dann auch Folgen haben für die Umkehrungen in den Verhältnissen der Religionen zueinander).

Es beginnt mit der Liebe des Liebenden. Diese muss augenblickshaft sein und bleiben. Sie ist treulos in ihrem Wesen, weil ihr Wesen der Augenblick ist, der allein sie zum Anderen für den bisherigen göttlichen Stillstand machen kann. Sie ist seine Verbindung zu Zeitlichkeit und Lebendigkeit. Der Liebesaugenblick kann aber (das ist die innere Umkehrung in der Idee der Liebe des Liebenden) aus dem Element der tiefsten Untreue zur Voraussetzung für die beständige Treue werden, mit der der Liebende die Geliebte täglich ein bisschen lieber hat. Die so verstandene Liebe steigert sich, weil sie immer neu sein will. Dennoch ist sie nicht nur eine flüchtige Wallung. Ich gehe nicht weiter in die Nacherzählung der Elemente. Es geht hier vor allem um die Konstruktion der Verbindung von stiller Ewigkeit und lebendiger Zeitlichkeit. Interessant daran ist, dass diese so sehr augenblickshafte, von Augenblick zu Augenblick sich wieder offenbarende Liebe des Liebenden eben die geliebte Seele braucht. Wenn auch nur, um etwas zum Lieben zu haben. Sie ist unberechenbar und punktuell, durchwandert aber das ganze All. Am Gegensatz zum Islam – wie er ihn sieht – erläutert Rosenzweig, wieso sie nun nach und nach ergreifen muss, aber jedes einzelne in dem jeweiligen Augenblick so, dass sie darüber alles andere vergisst. Der – systematische – Grund besteht in der besonderen Verbindung, die durch die Antwort der geliebten Seele erst zu einer Verbindung wird. Die Seele wird von dem Augenblick, in dem die Liebe des Liebenden sie ergreift, „überschauert", wie Rosenzweig schreibt. Was bisher Trotz war, wird nun dieselbe Eigenschaft, die sie befähigt, diesen Augenblick dauernd und gleichmässig festzuhalten. So dass sie – die sterbliche – vom Modus des zu sehr Bewegten in den Modus der Ruhe übergeht. Es ist, wenn man so will, ein Austausch der Elemente von Festigkeit und Bewegtheit. Wobei die geliebte Seele zunächst diejenige bleibt, die sich daran genügen lässt, das Geliebtwerden zu empfangen, sich für es zu öffnen und es festzuhalten als den Liebesglanz des eigenen Lebens, dessen Vergangenheit vor diesem Augenblick zu nichts wird.

Natürlich liegt in seinen wortreichen Schilderungen dieser Aspekte der Liebe zwischen dem liebenden Gott und der geliebten Seele die Metaphorik der erotischen Liebe zwischen Mann und Frau am nächsten. So sehr, dass Rosenzweig selbst sich genötigt sieht, einer zu direkten Übertragung eine Grenze zu setzen, indem er sagt, dass „die Rollen des Liebe Gebenden und Liebe Empfangenden hin und her [gehen], obwohl von den Wurzeln der Geschlechtlichkeit her sich immer wieder das eindeutige Verhältnis der Natur wiederherstellt" (SE 189). Dennoch glaube ich, man kann es fast anschaulicher machen, wenn man wieder die Situation zwischen der Mutter und dem sehr kleinen Kind ins Auge fasst. Dieses ist wirklich in sehr hohem Masse für sein Leben darauf angewiesen, dass die Eltern sich ihm immer wieder neu zuwenden, es beim Namen nennen, ihm überhaupt einen Namen geben, durch den sie es aus dem Diffusen ebenso herausrufen wie aus dem bloss Gegenständlichen. Auf das kleine Kind trifft zu, dass es wirklich nicht war, bevor es in die elterliche Liebe geholt wurde. Und auf das erste Ichsagen des kleinen Kindes trifft in besonderem Masse zu, was Rosenzweig über das Ich überhaupt sagt: dass es „stets ein laut gewordenes Nein", ein „Ich aber" ist.

Rosenzweig geht nun den Urdialog zwischen Gott als Liebendem und dem Menschen als geliebter Seele durch. Der Gott der Gebote sagt „Ich der Ewige" und redet als solcher den Menschen mit „Du" an. Das Grundgebot Gottes lautet aber: „Liebe mich." Und die geliebte Seele antwortet darauf: „Ich habe gesündigt." Von Rosenzweig übersetzt als das beschämte Eingeständnis, dass sie vor dem Hören dieses Anrufes durch den Liebenden ohne Liebe war. Sie bekennt aber nicht nur die Liebeleere der Vergangenheit, sondern vor allem, dass sie „auch in diesem gegenwärtigsten der Augenblicke noch lange nicht so liebt, wie sie sich geliebt weiss". Wieder erscheint mir die Analogie mit dem Selbstgefühl des von einem Schutz gebenden und bergenden Erwachsenen geliebten Kindes evident.

Mit diesem elementaren Dialog aber verändern sich die Verhältnisse. Das Bekenntnis der geliebten Seele zu dem, von dem sie sich geliebt weiss, ist schon ein Bekenntnis Gottes. Das Vertrauen der geliebten Seele gegenüber dem liebenden Gott macht diesen erst offenbar. Rosenzweig geht weiter: Durch das Bekenntnis holt die Seele Gott nicht nur ins „Diesseits seiner Verborgenheit", sondern: „Indem die Seele vor Gottes Antlitz bekennt und damit Gottes Sein bekennt und bezeugt, gewinnt auch Gott, der offenbare Gott, erst Sein: ‚wenn ihr mich bekennt, so bin ich.'" Dafür wiederum gibt Gott der Seele eine Vergangenheit: „Ich habe dich bei deinem Namen gerufen. Du bist mein." Damit gibt das grundlos als Beziehung in die Welt der Dinge hineingerufene Gotteswort der Seele ihrerseits einen Grund in der Beziehung. Wieder ist die Folge für „den Glauben" dieselbe wie in der gelingenden primären Bindung zwischen Mutter und Kind: „Gewiss, schon vorher konnte ihn nichts von Gott scheiden, aber doch nur, weil er in seiner Vertiefung in Gegenwärtiges nichts ausser sich sah. Jetzt darf er ruhig die Augen öffnen und um sich schauen in die Welt der Dinge…Die Seele kann mit offenen Augen und ohne zu träumen sich in der Welt umtun; immer bleibt sie nun in Gottes Nähe. Das ‚du bist mein', das ihr gesagt ist, zieht einen schützenden Kreis um ihre Schritte. Sie weiss nun, dass sie nur die Rechte auszustrecken braucht, um zu fühlen, dass Gottes Rechte ihr entgegenkommt. Sie kann nun sprechen: mein Gott, mein Gott. Sie kann nun beten." (SE 205). Für den Augenblick, den eigentlichen „Punkt" des Offenbarungsgeschehens ist das schon alles. Das Gebet selbst ist – wieder anders als in der heidnischen Vorstellung – die Erfüllung. „Sie betet um das Betenkönnen, das mit der Gewissheit der göttlichen Liebe ihr schon gegeben ist." So ist das in der Gegenwart des Offenbarungsaugenblick. Für die Beziehung der geliebten Seele zu Gott scheint nun alles geklärt. Aber noch geht es nur um

Betenkönnen und Betenmüssen – so wie es zuvor bei Gott um Liebenkönnen und Liebenmüssen gegangen war, das sich aber noch irgendwohin ergiessen musste, so geht es der Seele nun auch. Aus der passiven Aktivität Gottes und der aktiven Passivität der Seele kommt etwas Neues hervor, denn der Augenblick der Wechselrede mit Gott bleibt nicht stehen. Es gibt noch die Beziehung der menschlichen Seele zur Welt. In dieser gibt es Zukunft, und für diese hat die Seele einen Wunsch, eine Frage, einen Schrei. Hier scheint jetzt meine Veranschaulichung mit der seelischen Entwicklung des Kleinkindes in der Beziehung zur Elternperson nicht mehr aufzugehen.

Rosenzweig drückt sich da jedenfalls recht eindeutig erotisch aus: „Denn der Schrei, den die Seele im Augenblick der höchsten unmittelbaren Erfüllung stöhnt, tritt über die Schranken der Wechselrede hinaus; er kommt nicht mehr aus der seligen Gestilltheit des Geliebtseins, sondern steigt in neuer Unruhe aus einer uns noch unerkannten Tiefe der Seele und schluchzt über die ungesehene, doch gefühlte Nähe des Liebenden hinweg in den Dämmer der Unendlichkeit hinaus." (SE 206) Mit einer abermaligen konzentrierten Zusammenfassung des Sprachgeschehens, der Namengebung, des Gebots und der sich sagenden Annahme und mit einem Umweg über eine in sich ponderable Theorie des Genies, nähert sich Rosenzweig wieder dem Hohelied. Er paraphrasiert: „Die Geliebte fleht, der Liebende möge den Himmel seiner allzeitlichen Gegenwärtigkeit zerreissen, der ihrem Sehnen nach ewiger Liebe trotzt, und zu ihr herniederfahren, auf dass sie sich ihm wie ein ewiges aufs immerzuckende Herz legen kann und wie ein fest umschliessender Ring auf den nimmerrastenden Arm" (SE 228). So übersetzt er den Satz „O dass du mein Bruder wärest". Und in den letzten Absätzen scheint es sich zunächst wirklich fast 1:1 um eine Anrede an Gritli zu handeln: Das Reich der Brüderlichkeit, nach dem die Seele sich sehnt, „stiftet ihr nicht mehr die Liebe des Liebenden, von der sie bisher stets das Stichwort erwartet hatte, um Antwort zu geben. Soll dieser Sehnsucht Erfüllung werden, so muss die geliebte Seele den Zauberkreis der Geliebtheit überschreiten, des Liebenden vergessen und selber den Mund öffnen, nicht zur Antwort mehr, sondern zum eigenen Wort. Denn in der Welt gilt nicht das Geliebtsein, und das Geliebte darf es hier nicht anders wissen, als wäre es allein auf sich angewiesen und ungeliebt, und alle seine Liebe wäre nicht Geliebtheit, sondern ewig – Lieben. Und nur im geheimsten Herzen mag sie bei diesem ihrem Gang aus dem Wunder der göttlichen Liebe heraus in die irdische Welt der Alten Wort bewahren, das dem, was ihr zu tun bevorsteht, durch die Erinnerung des in jenem Zauberkreis Erlebten Kraft und Weihe gibt: Wie er dich liebt, so liebe Du." (SE 228)

Damit endet das zweite Buch. Im Kern machen Seele und Gott einander wirklich, indem sie diesen sehr dynamischen Urdialog, den Gott durch sein Beim-Namen-Nennen initiiert, miteinander führen, bei dem jeder sich verändert. Ohne diese Offenbarungsbeziehung zwischen Mensch und Gott wäre Gott ein Gott mit Eigenschaften, zu denen ein ihn selbst überwältigendes Verlangen nach Liebe zu seinen und von seinen Geschöpfen niemals gehören dürfte. Und der Mensch wäre ein Ding, das man unter Begriffe bringen könnte, die ihm aber kein Haus zum Wohnen sein würden, sondern, so schreibt Rosenzweig, sein zuständiges Gerichtsgebäude, zu dem er nur gerufen würde, um vernommen zu werden – was bei ihm zu den üblichen Ausreden, das Weib, die Schlange, der Apfel, führen würde. Durch die Liebe und das Geliebtsein werden beide lebendig und wirklich. Das als Mängelwesen nach Liebe dürstende Menschenwesen ist gerade in seiner Schwäche liebenswert, und auch Gott ist dem Menschen als Liebender gewiss, weil er selbst sich als liebender offenbaren muss, wenn er einmal bekannt wurde.

Vermutlich kann man so etwas nur schreiben, wenn man es erstens überhaupt kann, und wenn man zweitens – wie Rosenzweig es zur Zeit der Herstellung dieses Textes war – emotional so tief berührt ist, dass alle Akkorde aus der primären Bindung wieder anklingen, wo man selbst liebt. Nur dann ist das Buch selbst wie das Hohelied, von dem es handelt, Gleichnis und zugleich mehr als ein Gleichnis: ein Sichsprechen.

Damit, wie die so zuinnerst erfahrene Liebe nun in die Welt geht, beschäftigt sich das dritte Buch, und es geht allmählich vom unmittelbaren Glühen der sich sprechenden Begegnung wieder in ein Erklärendes über. Mein Beitrag aber endet hier.

Weiterführende Lektüre

Fricke, M., (2003), *Franz Rosenzweigs Philosophie der Offenbarung. Eine Interpretation des Sterns der Erlösung*, Würzburg, Königshausen und Neumann.
Joskowicz, A.A., (2008), *Rosenzweigs Konzept der Offenbarung und die Zeichen der Liebe*, in: Naharaim 12 (2008) 164–187.
Rühle, I., (2004), *Gott spricht die Sprache der Menschen: Franz Rosenzweig als jüdischer Theologie – eine Einführung*, Tübingen, Bilam Verlag.

Zweiter Teil, drittes Buch: Erlösung oder die ewige Zukunft des Reichs *und* Schwelle

Renate Schindler

Franz Rosenzweig (1886–1929) wurde in Kassel geboren. Er gehörte dem emanzipiert-liberalen deutschen Judentum an und war im Ersten Weltkrieg als Soldat in Mazedonien stationiert. Ab 1916 befand er sich an der Balkanfront und entwarf hier – teilweise auf Feldpostkarten und in den Schützengräben – sein philosophisches Jahrhundertwerk, den *Stern der Erlösung* (veröffentlicht 1921)[186]. Geprägt von traumatischen Erfahrungen schreibt er gegen Ende des Krieges an seine Mutter und an seinen engen Freund und Cousin Rudolf Ehrenberg:

[…]ich könnte einen ruhigen Winter gut brauchen, denn ich habe ein Buch […] angefangen, mein System, muss ich wohl sagen […] es hat drei Teile zu je drei Büchern […]. Es ist vor 14 Tagen plötzlich da gewesen und seitdem sitze ich unter einer Dusche von Gedanken.[187]

---

[186] Im Folgenden werden dem laufenden Text Stellen aus diesem Werk in Klammern eingefügt – Zitate gemäss Franz Rosenzweig, Der Stern der Erlösung, Frankfurt a.M. 1993.

[187] GS II, Brief vom 4.9. 1918 an Rudolf Ehrenberg und seine Mutter Adele Rosenzweig; vgl. auch Martin Buber, Franz Rosenzweig, in: ders., Der Jude und sein Judentum. Gesammelte Aufsätze und Reden, Gerlingen 1993, 801:

How to cite this book chapter:
Schindler, R. 2021. Zweiter Teil, drittes Buch: Erlösung oder die ewige Zukunft des Reichs *und* Schwelle. In: Brasser, M., Bojanić, P. and Ciglia, F. P. (eds.) The Star *for Beginners: Introductions to the Magnum Opus of Franz Rosenzweig.* Pp. 113–130. London: Ubiquity Press. DOI: https://doi.org/10.5334/bco.j. License: CC-BY

In der Endfassung einer der wichtigsten glaubensphilosophischen Abhandlungen des 20. Jahrhunderts befindet sich das Kapitel über die *Erlösung oder die ewige Zukunft des Reichs* als drittes Buch im zweiten Teil von Rosenzweigs Hauptwerk. Unter der Überschrift *Schwelle* markiert es zugleich den Übergang in den dritten Teil der Studie. Wie der Begriff der ‚ewigen Zukunft' auf das Thema der Erlösung verweist, so kündigen auch die Titel der drei anderen Teilbände das systematisch entfaltete Verhältnis zwischen Zeit und Ewigkeit an. Es zieht sich als roter Faden durch die gesamte Abhandlung hindurch. Denn die spekulative Kosmologie des *Stern der Erlösung* wendet sich vehement gegen die Tradition des kontinentalen Denkens „von Jonien bis Jena" (13) oder „von Thales bis Hegel" (15), in der die Zeiterfahrung des einzelnen sterblichen Menschen dem Herrschaftsanspruch eines allgegenwärtigen und zeitlosen Begriffsapparats ausgeliefert worden sei.[188]

Rosenzweigs Kritik am traditionellen Rationalitätsbegriff und dessen Auswirkungen auf die Krise der europäischen Kultur setzt dagegen einen Begriff von Philosophie voraus, der für den „Weltanschauungs-, ja Standpunktsphilosophen" charakteristisch ist (117). Auf den Spuren Schellings, Schopenhauers und Nietzsches verteidigt Rosenzweig das benannte einzelne Individuum gegen die zeitlose „Identität von Denken und Sein"[189]. Denn er zeigt, dass in der Geschichte Gottes, der Welt und des Menschen verschiedene Zeiten und Ewigkeiten ineinander spielen: Die Ewigkeit im ersten Teil, der von der immerwährenden Vorwelt des antiken Heidentums handelt, ist von der Dauer und der bleibenden Zeit geprägt. Der zweite Teil stellt die Ewigkeit des Allzeiterneuerten und Sich-Erneuernden dar. Hier ist es das komplexe Gefüge der Zeiten und Ewigkeiten der Schöpfung (oder des immerwährenden Grundes der Dinge), der Offenbarung (oder der allzeiterneuerten Geburt der Seele) und der Erlösung (oder der ewigen Zukunft des Reiches), das in den lebendigen Beziehungen zwischen Gott, Welt und Mensch gründet und den Beginn der Weltgeschichte markiert. Im letzten Band geht es schliesslich um die von der wahren und eigentlichen Ewigkeit Gottes geprägte Überwelt.

In jeder dieser Welten und ihrem zwischen Zeiten, Ewigkeiten und Geschichte ausgespannten Horizont diskutiert Rosenzweig die Tatsächlichkeiten ambivalenter Grunderfahrungen von Leben und Sterben, Tod und Liebe, Sprechen und Schweigen sowie Glauben und Wissen. Er reflektiert sie mit Bezug auf

---

Buber teilt uns im Jahre 1930 mit, dass er für die Darstellung der besonderen Art, in der die damalige Zeit „die Katastrophen der historischen Wirklichkeiten" als „Krisen des menschlichen Verhältnisses zur Wirklichkeit" erfahren hat, „kein grösseres und deutlicheres Beispiel als das Franz Rosenzweigs" gefunden habe.

[188] GS III, 139–161, insbesondere 149–152; vgl. auch Renate Schindler, Zeit, Geschichte, Ewigkeit in Franz Rosenzweigs *Stern der Erlösung*, Berlin 2007, 27–68.

[189] GS III, 151.

die existentielle Bedeutung der Zeitphänomene theoretischer Philosophie, praktischer Philosophie und Theologie, um unsere Aufmerksamkeit auf deren logische und sprachliche Verknüpfung untereinander zu lenken.

Die Bahn der Zeitdimensionen der Weltzeit im zweiten Teil des *Stern der Erlösung*, die in der ewigen und allzeiterneuerten Gegenwart des geschichtlichen Ereignisses der Offenbarung ihr Zentrum findet, strahlt nicht nur in die ‚erste Offenbarung' Gottes in der Vergangenheit der Schöpfung aus, sondern auch in die an der Zukunft ausgerichtete Welt der Erlösung. Hier rückt der „Zeiger der Weltuhr" „[…] wie bei der Gestaltwerdung Gottes von der Schöpfung zur Offenbarung […] bei der Gestaltwerdung der Seele von der Offenbarung zur Erlösung" weiter (236). Deren entscheidendes Merkmal besteht darin, dass die Welt als menschliche Mitwelt entdeckt wird.

Um die Struktur des Kapitels über die Erlösung und deren Einbettung in das gesamte System von Rosenzweigs Hauptwerk erschliessen zu können, geht es im Folgenden zunächst um Rosenzweigs fundamentale Frage, die sich auf eine Interpretation des Verhältnisses von der in der Offenbarung geäusserten Liebe Gottes zu den Menschen und deren Liebe untereinander bezieht. (1)

Im Anschluss hieran werden die zentralen Thesen aufgegriffen, die Rosenzweig zur Tat der (Nächsten)Liebe sowie zu den Unterschieden und Gemeinsamkeiten zwischen dem Reich Gottes und der säkularisierten Welt aufstellt. Sie sind in den Zusammenhang einer Analyse der für die Erlösungsproblematik charakteristischen Sprache eingebettet und stellen auch deren kritisch gegen den Deutschen Idealismus gewandte Implikationen in einer Theorie der Kunst dar. (2)

Ein weiterer Schritt führt uns in das Zentrum des Textes, das in der Entwicklung des Begriffs messianischer Zukunft besteht (3). Sie leitet zu Rosenzweigs Ausführungen im kurzen Kapitel *Schwelle* über, das zugleich den Beginn des dritten Teils markiert und Grundzüge der eigen Überwelt Gottes beschreibt. (4)

1. Die Schlüsselfrage: Wie hängt das Gebot der Nächstenliebe mit dem Gebot der Liebe zu Gott zusammen?

Die ersten Sätze des Buches über die Erlösung lauten

Liebe Deinen Nächsten. Das ist, so versichern Jud und Christ, der Inbegriff aller Gebote. Mit diesem Gebot verlässt die mündig gesprochene Seele das Vaterhaus der göttlichen Liebe und wandert hinaus in die Welt. (229)

Rosenzweig knüpft hier an das bereits in den Ausführungen zum Offenbarungsgeschehen hervorgehobene erste Moment der Erlösungserfahrung an. Denn er nimmt den Gedanken der absoluten Gegenwart der wechselseitigen Liebe zwischen Gott und Mensch wieder auf und bestimmt sie als den Grund für die Liebe zum Nächsten:

> Indem die Liebe zum Menschen von Gott geboten wird, wird sie, weil Liebe nicht geboten werden kann ausser von dem Liebenden selber, unmittelbar auf die Liebe zu Gott zurückgeführt. Die Liebe zu Gott soll sich **äu**ssern in der Liebe zum Nächsten [...]. Die gottgeliebte Seele allein kann das Gebot der Nächstenliebe zur Erfüllung empfangen. Gott muss sich erst zum Menschen gekehrt haben, ehe der Mensch sich zu Gottes Willen bekehren kann. (239f.)

Der Leser wird gleich zu Beginn der Ausführungen zum Thema der Erlösung mit der Frage konfrontiert, wie der im Deuteronomium (6,5) angeführte Imperativ[190], das in der Offenbarungsgegenwart Gottes zu vernehmende „Liebe mich", notwendigerweise zu einem weiteren Liebesgebot führt. Rosenzweig fasst hier die wichtigste These des Kapitels über die Offenbarung zusammen: Das „Urgebot" der Liebe zu Gott das „in allen einzelnen Geboten mittönt und sie erst aus der Starrheit von Gesetzen zu lebendigen Geboten schafft" (ebd.) sei „der Inbegriff, das worin alle [...] Gebote schliesslich münden" und „gebietet [...] die einzige Liebe [...], die geboten werden kann" (229).[191]

Emmanuel Lévinas hebt es als deutlich jüdischen Zug in Rosenzweigs Denken hervor, dass unter der Offenbarung Gottes nicht nur der Beginn des Werks der Erlösung verstanden wird. Denn sie ist zugleich ein Werk, dessen Vollendung davon abhängt, ob es dem Menschen gelingt, den ihm in der Nächstenliebe aufgegebenen sittlichen Auftrag zu verwirklichen:

> Das Judentum, in dem die Erlösung untrennbar mit den Geboten zusammenhängt, bedeutet keineswegs die Last des Gesetzes, sondern genauer gesagt Liebe. Dass das Judentum durch die Gebote gekennzeichnet wird, bezeugt die Erneuerung der Liebe Gottes zu jedem Menschen in jedem Augenblick. Ohne sie hätte die Liebe, die in den Geboten aufgetragen wird, dem Menschen überhaupt nicht aufgetragen werden können.[192]

Rosenzweigs entscheidende Frage lautet nun, wie sich das Urgebot der Liebe zu Gott, „damit [...] vereint" (229), dass die Liebe zum Nächsten ebenfalls

---

[190] Vgl. hierzu Robert Gibbs, The Grammar of the Laws, 3, 4 (zitiert nach dem Manuskript eines Vortrags auf dem Internationalen Rosenzweigkongress in Paris 2009). Gibbs widmet sich im Kontext der Bedeutung von Gesetz und Gebot im Judentum der Frage nach der Philologie in der Auszeichnung des Du im Gebot der Gottesliebe sowie dessen Übersetzungen in verschiedenen Ausgaben der Bibel.

[191] Vgl. Schindler, a.O., 289ff.

[192] Emmanuel Lévinas, Entre deux mondes. Biographie spirutuelle de Franz Rosenzweig, in: La Conscience Juive – Données et Débats, Paris 1963, 121–149. Hierzu kritisch Stéphane Mosès, La critique de la totalité dans la philosophie de Franz Rosenzweig, in: Les Études philosophiques 3 (1976), 351–366.

geboten werden kann. Die folgende programmatische Formulierung bildet den Rahmen um die ganze Problematik der Erlösung:

> Die Antwort auf dieses Bedenken könnte leicht in einem kurzen Wort vorweggenommen werden. Statt dessen sei ihr lieber das ganze Schlussbuch dieses Teils gewidmet. Denn sie enthält, so einfach sie ist, alles in sich, was die beiden vorangehenden Bücher noch offen lassen mussten. (ebd.)

Welche ‚kurze Antwort' meint Rosenzweig? Und was wurde bisher ‚offen' gelassen?

2. Gliederung des Erlösungskapitels und zentrale Thesen

Die Tat der Liebe und die Liebe zum Nächsten

Gemäss dem Verlauf von Rosenzweigs Argumenten im Blick auf sein gesamtes Buch wurde insbesondere das Thema der auf die Zukunft bezogenen Liebestat (229–243) noch nicht erschöpfend behandelt: Wenn sich der von Gott geliebte Mensch nun auf seinen Nächsten im Sinne des zu-nächst jeweils Nächsten als ‚rea', plesios, proximus (243, 262) richtet, so geht es letztlich um die Strukturen verantwortlichen Handelns, die die Lebenspraxis einer säkularisierten sowie eine der Erlösung bedürftigen Welt erfordern.

Die aus der Nächstenliebe resultierende Tat kommt an verschiedenen zentralen Stellen zur Sprache:

a) Rosenzweig erörtert sie im Kontext der Bestimmung des Freiheitsbegriffs, den er als Grundlage des Gebots der Liebe zum anderen auffasst und von Kants Konzeption des in Autonomie begründeten Moralgesetzes absetzt (287f.). Er knüpft hier an die gleich in der Einleitung zum *Stern der Erlösung* aufgestellte These an, dass „[d]as Gesetz […] dem Menschen, nicht der Mensch dem Gesetz gegeben […] ist. (15). Diese neue Grundwahrheit besagt, dass die Vernunft und ihre Selbstgesetzgebung nicht mehr – wie bei Kant – das wichtigste Fundament der Moral bilden, sondern das in der Freiheit des menschlichen Willens und im Begriff des Nächsten verankerte ‚Bedürfen des Anderen'. Der Andere ist für Rosenzweig ein ‚Du', insofern von ihm gesagt werden kann: „[E]r ist wie Du" (267). Einen kritischen Blick wirft er auch auf die Auslegung des Gebots in der neben Juden- und Christentum dritten monotheistischen Weltreligion, im Islam (240–243). Die Erfüllung von Gottes Gebot durch die „Welttat" erschöpfe sich bei den Anhängern dieser Glaubensgemeinschaft letztlich im reinen Gehorsam, dem Weg Allahs auch durch Glaubenskriege zu folgen. Die Vorschriften des islamischen Kriegs- und Eroberungsrechts weichen nach Rosenzweig grundsätzlich vom kanonischen und talmudischen Recht ab, weil sie den „Unterschied von Liebesgebot und Gesetzesgehorsam" nicht erkennen (242).[193]

b) Im Zusammenhang mit der Interpretation der Sprache der Liebestat spielt es eine wichtige Rolle, wie sich der je andere dem einzelnen Menschen in der Grammatik des Pathos (254f.) und im Lob-und Dankgesang der Gemeinde (262) erschliesst.

c) Das ‚Ich' öffnet sich dem ‚Du' des Nächsten, indem sich die zunächst verschlossene Seele einer anderen Seele bedingungslos zuwendet und sie als Repräsentanten ‚der Welt' wahrnimmt (267f.)

Welt und Reich

Es sind nach Rosenzweig folglich „zwei Seiten", von denen aus „an das verschlossene Tor der

Zukunft gepocht wird": Vonseiten der menschlichen Seele, deren Herz und Gemüt ihren Weg zum Wirken am Nächsten sucht, und vonseiten des Lebens der Welt (254).

Denn die Welttat der Liebe bezieht sich im Erlösungsgeschehen auch auf die Vorwegnahme des Reiches und damit weniger unmittelbar als im Gebot der Gottesliebe, aber indirekt ebenfalls auf Gott, der in der Schöpfung den *immerwährenden Grund der Dinge* gelegt hat (243–254). Das Wissen um die Vergangenheit der Schöpfung als der „Pforte, durch die die Philosophie ins Haus der Theologie eintritt" (104), spielt bereits in Rosenzweigs Ausführungen zum Begriff des gegen den Rationalismus der Aufklärung verteidigten Wahrheitsgehalts des Offenbarungswunders eine entscheidende Rolle.[194] Es ist die Schöpfung, die den Pfeiler bildet, der das gesamte System des zweiten Teils des *Stern der Erlösung* trägt. Auf der Bahn der allzeiterneuerten Welt in der Geschichte von Gott, Welt und Mensch werden die theologischen Kategorien Offenbarung und Erlösung ausdrücklich auf die Schöpfung zurückgeführt. Sie ist erst dann vollendet, wenn sich das Individuum der Welt und der menschlichen Mitwelt so

---

[193] Vgl. Martin Brasser, Rosenzweig und die Karikatur des Islam. Negative Konstruktionen im interreligiösen Dialog, Vortrag, in: ders. (Hg. u.a.), Rosenzweig Jahrbuch 2 / Rosenzweig Yearbook 2, Kritik am Islam / Criticism of Islam, Freiburg 2007, 128–151 (hier zitiert nach der Manuskriptvorlage). Brasser hat die Gründe für Rosenzweigs geostrategische (1–6) sowie interreligiöse Interpretationen des Islam methodisch dargestellt, die bewusst auf eine ‚Parodie' und Karikatur dieser Religionsgemeinschaft zielen (6–13); Vgl. zur Ausrichtung von Rosenzweigs Darstellung des Islam auf den Offenbarungsbegriff hin im *Stern der Erlösung* auch Gesine Palmer, Der verkannte Islam, in: Wolfdietrich Schmied-Kowarzik (Hg.), Franz Rosenzweigs „Neues Denken", Internationaler Kongress Kassel 2004, Band 2, Freiburg/München 2006, 1109–1118.

[194] Vgl. Schindler, a.O., 211ff.

zuwendet, dass er sie durch Taten der Liebe verändert, die sich an der Vorwegnahme des Reiches Gottes orientieren. Es gelte – so hiess es an früherer Stelle:

> die Offenbarung selbst und ihre Einbindung und Begründung in die Zuversicht auf das Kommen des sittlichen Reichs der endlichen Erlösung, diesen ganzen heut als den eigentlichen Kern des Glaubens empfundenen Zusammenhang, den die Hoffnung zwischen den Begriffen Offenbarung und Erlösung stiftet, selber wieder einzubauen in den Begriff der Schöpfung. Auch Offenbarung, auch Erlösung sind eben in gewisser, noch nicht auseinanderzusetzender Weise Schöpfung. (114)

Hierauf bezieht sich Rosenzweig, wenn er nun die „Sonderstellung der Welt" (244) hervorhebt, indem er sie als ‚unfertig' bezeichnet und als stets im Werden begriffenes lebendiges Reich Gottes, dessen Ewigkeit für alle Zukunft in der Gegenwart des Augenblicks vorweggenommen werden kann (244, 245, 248–251).[195]

Weiterhin geht er in seinen methodischen Erläuterungen (255–257) davon aus, dass in wahrem Sinne „nur Einer" der Erlöser sein kann (255), d.h. dass Gott „in viel stärkerem Sinn [...] der Erlöser [...] als er Schöpfer und Offenbarer ist". Denn Gott erlöst die Welt durch den Menschen, und diesen in der Welt. Er ist ein Dritter, der sich in der Erlösung von Mensch und Welt auch selbst erlöst (229–265).

Diese Welt der Erlösung ist nicht nur deutlich vom falschen Zauber abzugrenzen, der den plastischen Kosmos der Antike sowie seine Künste der Magie und Astrologie in der *immerwährenden Vorwelt* prägte (245–248). Die erlöste Welt unterscheidet sich auch grundsätzlich von der Entzauberung der Welt in der modernen Wissenschaft (246, 247) sowie vom Fortschrittsbegriff des Islam. Im Unterschied zum Judentum und Christentum verfügt er nach Rosenzweig über keine einheitliche Darstellung der Geschichte (251–253). Insbesondere sei „hier der Gedanke der Zukunft in der Wurzel vergiftet", da er auf einem ins Unendliche reichenden Fortschrittsbegriff beruht. Im Islam werde verkannt, dass die wahre Zeit der Ewigkeit eine von Gott verliehene Gabe ist, die den Menschen dazu befähigt, das Ende in der Gegenwart vorwegzunehmen. Der Gedanke, dass das Reich Gottes „heute" kommt, diese „Verewigung des Augenblicks" erlischt laut Rosenzweig „in dem islamischen wie im modernen Begriff der Zeitalter" (253).[196] Denn wir können darauf vertrauen, dass das Walten und Wachsen des Gottesreichs für menschliche Augen sichtbar ist und in uns „trotz aller Enttäuschungen" auch durch die Vermittlung der rabbinischen Lehre immer neue Hoffnung auf einen besseren Zustand der Welt erweckt (252).

---

[195] Vgl. Abschnitt 3 im vorliegenden Text.
[196] Dies scheint insbesondere darauf zurückzuführen zu sein, dass Rosenzweig den Islam als „Anti-Offenbarungsreligion" funktionalisiert – vgl. hierzu Brasser, a.O., 12.

Die Sprache der Erlösung

In menschlichen Handlungen, die sich auf den Nächsten richten, entdeckt Rosenzweig eine sprachliche und grammatikalische Struktur, in der „Mensch und Welt [...] in unauflösbarer Wechselwirkung aufeinander und miteinander [...] wirken" – das „Wirken entbindet die Tat aus dem Menschen, aber bindet die entbundene auch wieder hinein in die Welt". Gut könne die Welt nur „durch die Guten" werden, da Welt und Mensch „nicht voneinander zu lösen" sind und daher nur miteinander erlöst werden können (254, 255).

Wie Rosenzweig in seinem Aufsatz über *Das neue Denken* (1925) schreibt, der im Untertitel *Einige nachträgliche Bemerkungen zum ‚Stern der Erlösung'* ankündigt, herrscht in der Erlösung „die Sprache des Chors"[197]. In Analogie hierzu schreibt er in seinem Hauptwerk:

> [D]ie Erlösung der Seele an den Dingen, der Dinge durch die Seele geschieht im gleichatmenden Zwiegesang der beiden, im Satz, der aus den Stimmen der beiden Worte zusammenklingt. (255)

In der sprachlichen Struktur der Lob- und Dankgesänge, der Psalmen und im liturgischen Leben der jüdischen Gemeinde zeigt sich die Erwartungshaltung gegenüber dem zukünftigen Kommen des Reichs der Erlösung (255–281). Den Ausführungen Rosenzweigs zum Chor der Erlösung geht im ersten Teil seines Hauptwerks eine Theorie über den Chor der (antiken) Tragödie vorher, im dritten Teil greift er die Bedeutung des Chores in der Kirchenmusik auf (401ff.). Man kann geradezu davon sprechen, dass sich Rosenzweigs Ästhetik von der „Warte" des Chores wie von einer Festung aus erschließen lässt.[198] Das Wort „Chor" selbst kommt im *Stern der Erlösung* zwar nur elfmal vor.[199] Aber es steht jeweils in allen drei Teilen seines Systems der Philosophie im Kontext von Interpretationen der Kunst und des Schönen, in denen Rosenzweig seine Gegnerschaft zur idealistischen Ästhetik betont.

Auch in der Bestimmung der Bedeutung des gemeinsamen Gesangs der jüdischen Gemeinde und deren grammatikalischen Charakteristika bezieht sich Rosenzweig auf das wichtigste Merkmal seines *neuen Denkens* als eines Sprachdenkens. Die Sprache als Organon existentiell erfahrbarer Zeitlichkeit und sinnliches Medium der im Sprechen, Miteinander-sprechen und Hören zu erkennenden Wirklichkeit untergräbt den in der idealistischen Tradition der

---

[197] Rosenzweig, a.O., 151.
[198] Luca Bertolino, Die Rolle des Chors in Franz Rosenzweigs *Stern der Erlösung*, in: Martin Brasser, Hans Martin Dober (Hg.), Rosenzweig Jahrbuch 5 / Rosenzweig Yearbook 5, Wir und die Anderen / We and the Others, Beiträge zum Kongress der Internationalen Rosenzweig-Gesellschaft in Paris vom 17.-20.Mai 2009, Teil I, Freiburg 2010, 141–159, hier 141.
[199] Ebd.

Philosophie unbedacht vorausgesetzten Anspruch eines Apriori der Vernunft und ihrer sich selbst genügenden begrifflichen Logik.

Im Rekurs auf die beiden vorangegangenen Bücher des zweiten Teils erinnert Rosenzweig an die Sprachform der Erzählung, in der er auf den Spuren Schellings die „Sätze der Geschichte"[200] der Vergangenheit der Schöpfung in der dritten Person Singular dargestellt hat: „Er schuf, er sprach, er schied und so fort. Vergangenheit und ‚er'." So fasst Rosenzweig seine Analyse des Buches *Genesis* zusammen (168).[201] Die Offenbarung dagegen ist von der Präsenz des Dialogs in der Liebeserfahrung eines Ichs und eines Du geprägt und wird am Beispiel des Hohelieds veranschaulicht; Gott eröffnet das Wechselgespräch mit dem Menschen sowie dasjenige zwischen Mann und Frau, „das zwischen zweien hin und her geht". Im Ereignis der Erlösung jedoch „tritt die Grammatik […] als strophisch sich steigernder Gesang […]" in den Vordergrund und wird als Augenblick messianischer Zukunft erlebt (258). Es ist die Gemeinschaft der ‚Wir' als der Mitglieder der jüdischen Gemeinde, die an der Liturgie teilnehmen und gemeinsam ihre Stimme erheben (278–281). Der messianische Gehalt der Sprache der Erlösung kommt auch im Gebet zum Ausdruck, das „die Erfüllung all dessen ist, worum gemeinsam gebetet werden kann" und die Zukunft der Verheissung in die Gegenwart vorwegnimmt.[202]

Die beiden Nominative ‚Mensch' und ‚Welt' sowie die zu ihnen gehörenden Akkusative bilden das mächtige Unisono der „Wir alle"; Gott, dem der Gesang gewidmet ist, steht im Dativ (259f.). Die einzelnen singulären Stimmen des ‚Ich' und ‚Du' ermutigen sich gegenseitig und gelangen vom Sprachmodus des Dual in denjenigen der von der Pluralität zu unterscheidenden Allheit:

Im Wir also hebt die Schlussstrophe des Gesangs der Erlösung an; im Kohortativ hatte er mit dem Aufruf der Einzelnen, die aus dem Chor

---

[200] Vgl. hierzu Wolfdietrich Schmied-Kowarzik, Vom Totalexperiment des Glaubens. Kritisches zur positiven Philosophie Schellings und Rosenzweigs, in: ders. (Hg.), der Philosoph F. Rosenzweig (1886–1929), Internationaler Kongress Kassel 1986, Band 2, Freiburg/München 1988, 771–798; Rosenzweig konzipiert den Systembegriff im *Stern der Erlösung*, dem die Frage der Vereinbarkeit von ‚System und Offenbarung' zugrundeliegt, in steter Auseinandersetzung mit Schellings Begriff von ‚positiver' und ‚negativer' Philosophie; den Begriff der Erzählung entnimmt er Schellings Philosophie über die *Weltalter*, über die allgemeine Geschichte göttlichen Lebens – vgl. hierzu Schindler, a.O.,62–68, 229–246.

[201] Vgl. zur Analyse der Sprache Rosenzweigs im Horizont des hermeneutischen Prinzips im Umgang mit Bibel und Talmud Gérard Bensussan, Parole, langage et temporalités, in: J.E. Marquet (Hg.), Revue de Métaphysique et de Morale 4 (2000), 461–478.

[202] Donatella di Cesare, Die Messianität der Sprache, in: Wolfdietrich Schmied-Kowarzik, a.O., 862–871, hier 867.

hervortraten, und den Responsen des Chors darauf begonnen; im Dual ging es in einem zweistimmigen Fugato, an dem sich immer neue Instrumente beteiligten, fort; im Wir endlich sammelt sich alles zum choralmässig gleichen Takt des vielstimmigen Schlussgesangs. (264)[203]

Das Sprachdenken impliziert, wie Rosenzweig in seinen *nachträglichen Bemerkungen* schreibt, all diese Modalitäten der Sprache, weil es „überhaupt vom Leben des anderen" lebt, „mag der nun Hörer der Erzählung sein oder der Antwortende des Zwiegesprächs oder der Mitsprecher des Chors".[204]

Die „Chorform" der Erlösung vereint Mensch und Welt im Lobgesang auf Gott, der die Welt erschaffen hat und im Dank dafür, dass er seine Liebe offenbart hat. Der „Urgesang" der Erlösung gipfelt im „Stammsatz": „[E]r ist gut", der als ein „'denn er ist gut'" (258) zu verstehen ist (Ps 106,I, 118,I,29, 136,I) und die Stammworte der Schöpfung und Erlösung zusammenschliesst. Der Schöpfung wird ausschliesslich das Prädikat „gut" verliehen.[205] Am Beginn der Offenbarung steht das Ich Gottes, welches im Imperativ des Liebesgebots das Du des Menschen erweckt, indem er ihn bei seinem Namen anruft.[206] Nun jedoch geht es in der Gemeinschaft der Zweistimmigkeit von Welt und Mensch um den Namen Gottes. ‚Er ist gut' – dieser Satz der Erlösung bildet nach Rosenzweig

> das Dach über dem Hause der Sprache, der an sich wahre Satz, der Satz, der wahr bleibt, einerlei wie er gemeint ist und aus welchem Munde er kommt. (258)

Anschaulich erläutert er im Anschluss an die These von der herausragenden Bedeutung dieses Satzes:

> Dass zwei mal zwei vier ist, kann unwahr werden, etwa wenn man es einem Papagei gelehrt hat und der es nun „spricht"; denn was ist dem Papageien die Mathematik? Aber der Satz, dass Gott gut ist, kann selbst in diesem skurrilsten aller möglichen Fälle seines Lautwerdens keine Unwahrheit werden; denn auch den Papageien hat Gott geschaffen, und auch auf ihn geht schliesslich seine Liebe. (Ebd.)

---

[203] Bertolino, a.O., 151.
[204] GS III, 151.
[205] Wolfdietrich Schmied-Kowarzik hat herausgearbeitet, dass Rosenzweig die in Schellings Schöpfungsthematik der *Weltalter* angesprochenen negativen Aspekte kreatürlichen Daseins und deren politisch-gesellschaftliche Auswirkungen ausser acht lässt. Rosenzweig, der einerseits fundamentalethisch die Verantwortlichkeit des Einzelnen gegenüber der Geschichte stark macht, spricht mit Bezug auf die Schöpfung nicht vom Leid und den Verfehlungen der Menschen gegenüber sich selbst, gegenüber der Natur und mit Bezug auf den Glauben – vgl. ders., a.O., 795ff., 789.
[206] Vgl. hierzu Schindler, a.O., 288.

Die Theorie der Kunst

In der Vergötterung der Kunst und im Verwerfen des „geschaffenen Gottesgartens der Sprache" (162f.) zeigt sich nach Rosenzweig die Armut des idealistischen Denkens und seiner Logik, die daher ebenso wie die Ästhetik einer vollkommenen Erneuerung bedarf.[207]

Der wahre Reichtum lebendiger alltäglicher Erfahrungen und Erkenntnisse wurde im *Hortus conclusus* der Kunstauffassung des Idealismus ignoriert. Wenn Kultur an die Stelle der Natur trete und das Kunstwerk nur als „bewusstloses Erzeugnis des Geistes gilt",[208] so ist der Mensch dazu verurteilt, gegenüber der werdenden Welt der Offenbarung blind und taub zu sein.

Die Lehre von der Kunst,[209] die im zweiten Teil des *Stern der Erlösung* lediglich als notwendige „Episode" (213, 221) bezeichnet wird, nimmt jedoch in Rosenzweigs Werk einen beachtlichen Raum ein. Sie geht weit über die Darstellung der „klassischen" Kunst hinaus, da Rosenzweig ihre tiefreichende Verbindung zum lebendigen Dasein aufzeigt und ihr zutraut, den Menschen in den verlorenen Gottesgarten zurückzuführen. Diese These findet in der Soziologie der Kunst im dritten Teil des *Stern der Erlösung* ihre Bestätigung (393–397, 399–403, 412–415) und zeigt sich in der Bedeutung, die Rosenzweig der Kunst in der Liturgie zuspricht: Ihre gesellschaftliche Rolle besteht darin, das Bedürfnis nach Religiosität widerzuspiegeln, und sie stellt – so heisst es auf der „Schwelle" zum dritten Teil – die Nähe des Menschen zur „ewige[n] Überwelt" Gottes her (293).[210] Insofern kommt der Kunst im *neuen Denken* die entscheidende Aufgabe zu, als angewandte Kunst insbesondere der Liturgie die klassische und idealistische Auffassung vom reinen und „zweckfreien Wohlgefallen"[211] am Schönen zu bereichern und zu überwinden.

Im Kapitel über die Erlösung umfasst die Theorie der Kunst (270–277) deren wesentliche Elemente und Bereiche: Rosenzweig untersucht den Urheber als Künstler, Mensch, Genie oder Dichter (272f. vgl. 165f, 215), das Werk in seinen epischen, lyrischen oder dramatischen Ausdrucksformen (272f., vgl. 216f.) und das Publikum bzw. den Betrachter (270–272) in ihrer jeweiligen Rolle, die sie in der Systematik von Bildkunst, Tonkunst und Dichtung spielen (273–276; vgl. 217–221).[212]

---

[207] GS III, 140.
[208] Bertolino, a.O.,144.
[209] Ebd., 142.
[210] Ebd., 144, 145.
[211] Ebd., 142: Bertolino verweist darauf, dass sich Rosenzweig mit dem Begriff vom „zweckfreien Wohlgefallen" vermutlich auf Immanuel Kant bezieht – vgl. ders., Kritik der Urteilskraft (1790), Akademie-Ausgabe, Bd.5, 204f., 209f., 354.
[212] Umfassend wird Rosenzweigs Ästhetik u.a. in folgenden Beiträgen dargestellt: Stéphane Mosès, L'esthétique de Franz Rosenzweig, in: O. Mongin (Hg. u.a.), Franz Rosenzweig, Les Cahiers de la nuit surveillé 1 (1982), 119–135; Jules Simon, Rosenzweig's Messianic Aesthetics, in: Schmied-Kowarzik,

3. Das Zentrum des Textes: Messianische Erfahrung zukünftiger Ewigkeit

Wenn man sich Rosenzweigs Schlüsselfrage nach dem Zusammenhang zwischen dem Gebot der Gottesliebe und demjenigen der Liebe zum Nächsten noch einmal vor Augen hält, so besteht der Kern seiner Ausführungen in den Facetten der Entwicklung des im Horizont zukünftiger Ewigkeit bestimmten Erlösungsbegriffs: Das Wirken des Einzelnen als Nächstenliebe in einer stets im ‚Werden' zu verstehenden Welt in ihrer säkularisierten Form sowie in der jüdischen Liturgie, die sprachlichen Grundlagen der ‚Wechselwirkung' zwischen Mensch und Welt im allgemeinen sowie im Chorgesang – jeder dieser Themenbereiche bezieht sich auf die Vorwegnahme der Ankunft des Gottesreichs in der durch die Anwesenheit zukünftiger Ewigkeit erfüllten Gegenwart.

Wie geht Rosenzweig nun genauer betrachtet vor, um das Oszillieren zwischen Zeit und Ewigkeit, welches dem Aufbau seines ganzen Werkes das systematische Gerüst liefert, im Kontext des Erlösungsgeschehens verständlich zu machen?

Das Heute, der Augenblick und das ausserzeitliche ‚Wachstum' des Gottesreiches

Bereits in einer Passage des Kapitels über die Offenbarung setzt Rosenzweig die Welt und Mensch erlösende Liebe Gottes mit der Ewigkeit im ‚Heute' gleich und leitet daraus drei Thesen ab, die verschiedene Aspekte des Begriffs einer messianischen Zukunft zueinander in Beziehung setzen:

> [...] Gottes Liebe [...] ist immer im Heute und ganz im Heute, aber alles tote Gestern und Morgen wird in dieses sieghafte Heute einmal verschlungen, diese Liebe ist der ewige Sieg über den Tod; die Schöpfung, die der Tod krönt und schliesst, kann ihr nicht Stand halten; sie muss sich ihr ergeben in jedem Augenblick und darum schliesslich auch in der Fülle aller Augenblicke, in der Ewigkeit. (182)

Die als Ewigkeit zu verstehende Gegenwart wird hier positiv bewertet und von den zeitlichen Dimensionen der Vergangenheit und derjenigen leeren Zukunft abgegrenzt, welche nicht die des ankommenden Messias sind. Der „ewige Sieg über den Tod" bedeutet zweitens, dass der Erlösung insofern Vorrang vor der Schöpfung zukommt, als der in dieser ‚mitgeschaffene' Tod definitiv überwunden werden kann. Und drittens spricht Rosenzweig von der Ewigkeit als der

---

a.O., 407–418; Annemarie Meyer, Die Bedeutung der Kunst in Franz Rosenzweigs Werk, in: Werner Licharz (Hg. u.a.), Franz Rosenzweig und Hans Ehrenberg. Bericht einer Beziehung, Frankfurt a.M. 1986, 35–54.

„Fülle aller Augenblicke", also von einer im umfassenden Sinn erfüllten Lebenszeit, die auf eine andere Zukunftsdimension als die des ‚toten Morgen' anspielt.

In der im Titel der Erlösungstheorie angesprochenen *ewigen Zukunft* des *Reichs* überschneiden sich diese drei Aspekte und werden im Verlauf der Argumentation durch folgende Gedankengänge ergänzt: Rosenzweig holt zunächst die ewige Zukunft in die Gegenwart ein und bezeichnet sie als Dauer, in der alle lebendige Kreatur „dem Tode [...] widersteht [...]". Als ‚kreatürlich' werden nicht „bloss Lebewesen, sondern auch Institutionen, Gemeinschaften, Gefühle, Dinge, Werke – alles" bestimmt. (248). Hier scheint der Autor auf die natürliche oder physikalische Erfahrung gegenwärtiger Zeit anzuspielen. Sie besteht jeden Augenblick auf der ständigen Spannung zwischen Leben und Tod, die einem immer gleichen Wechsel von Veränderungen unterliegt. Der Focus liegt jedoch auf der von der ewigen Zukunft durchdrungenen Gegenwart, welche dem tödlichen sukzessiven Zeitfluss des Lebens abgerungen wird. Nach Gershom Scholem begegnen wir hier dem Moment der immer, d.h. der ewig gegenwärtigen Zukunft der Erlösung, die auch die Kabbalisten als „„die immer kommende Welt"", als den „olam haba", gedeutet haben.[213] Es ist dieser Zukunftsbegriff, der die Bedeutung der messianischen Erfahrung zeitlicher Ewigkeit am deutlichsten zum Ausdruck bringt. Denn er verweist unmittelbar auf die geschichtsphilosophische Idee, dass die diesseitige Welt mit dem Anbruch des Reiches „ganz lebendig werden" kann, da „das Lebendige [...] nach Ewigkeit [...] verlangt [...]" (249). Die für Rosenzweigs Zukunftsbegriff aufschlussreichste Passage schliesst sich direkt an die These von der Ewigkeit alles Lebendigen an:

> [...] das Reich, die Verlebendigung des Daseins, kommt von Anfang an, es ist immer im Kommen. So ist sein Wachstum notwendig. Es ist immer zukünftig, aber zukünftig ist es immer. Es ist ebenso schon da wie zukünftig. Es ist einfürallemal noch nicht da. Es kommt ewig. Ewigkeit ist nicht eine sehr lange Zeit, sondern ein Morgen, das ebensogut heute sein könnte. Ewigkeit ist eine Zukunft, die, ohne aufzuhören Zukunft zu sein, dennoch gegenwärtig ist. Ewigkeit ist ein Heute, das aber sich bewusst ist, mehr als Heute zu sein. Und wenn also das Reich ewig kommt, so bedeutet das, dass zwar sein Wachstum notwendig ist, aber dass das Zeitmass dieses Wachstums nicht bestimmt ist, ja genauer: dass das Wachstum gar kein Verhältnis zur Zeit hat. Ein Dasein, das einmal ins Reich eingegangen ist, kann nicht wieder herausfallen, es ist unter das Einfürallemal getreten, es ist ewig geworden. (250)

Hervorzuheben ist demnach vor allem derjenige Zukunftsbegriff, der die Ewigkeit des Reiches als in der Gegenwart anwesende Zukunft so bestimmt, dass sie noch etwas qualitativ anderes ist als die Ewigkeit des Augenblicks, welche den

---

[213] Gershom Scholem, Franz Rosenzweig und sein Buch *Der Stern der Erlösung*, Nachwort, in: SE, 525–549, hier 544.

natürlichen Zeitfluss sprengt. Denn das Wachstum des Reiches Gottes geschieht zwar notwendigerweise, hat jedoch kein ‚Zeitmass'. Dies expliziert Rosenzweig in den drei Sätzen, welche die Zeitlichkeit der Ewigkeit bestimmen: Sie ist nicht die leere Unendlichkeit der ‚sehr langen' Zeit, sondern die Möglichkeit des Morgen im Heute. Trotz dieser potentiellen Gegenwärtigkeit bleibt die Ewigkeit zukünftig; sie durchsetzt zwar die Gegenwart, geht aber nicht in ihr auf. Und obwohl die Ewigkeit in der Zukunft ist, welche nie aufhört, ist sie in einem über die Unmittelbarkeit des Augenblicks hinausweisenden Heute erfassbar.

Es ist diese Form der Ewigkeit, die Rosenzweig meint, wenn er über „das geniale Kapitel" in der *Ethik des reinen Willens* (1904) seines Lehrers Hermann Cohen schreibt, „das vom Ideal handelt". Hier betont er, dass Cohens Messianismus „eben keine Ausflucht der Trägheit" sei, „die das Ziel ins Unendliche rückt, um sich inzwischen im Endlichen in zielloser Behaglichkeit einzurichten". Vielmehr sei „Ewigkeit für Cohen „grade nicht die Summe aller Zeit", sondern die „auf den Augenblick bezogene, in seiner ‚Nussschale' [...] vollzogene fernste Zukunft".[214]

Gegenwart und das Warten auf das Ende der Zeit

In der zweiten und dritten Bestimmung der Ewigkeit kommt ein für Rosenzweigs Erlösungstheorie grundlegendes Paradox zum Ausdruck, das im Spannungsfeld zwischen Theologie und Existenzphilosophie anzusiedeln ist: Aus der Sicht des immer kommenden, ausserzeitlichen Reiches Gottes wird die ewige Zukunft der Ewigkeit betont, vom Standpunkt des sterblichen Menschen dagegen deren Gegenwart.[215] Zukünftig kann die Ewigkeit für die menschliche Erfahrung nur sein, wenn sie in der Gegenwart erwartet, und als Ende der Zeit in ihr vorweggenommen wird:

> [...] zur Zukunft gehört vor allem das Vorwegnehmen, dies, dass das Ende jeden Augenblick erwartet werden muss. Erst dadurch wird sie zur Zeit der Ewigkeit [...]. Dass jeder Augenblick der letzte sein kann, macht ihn ewig. Und eben dass jeder Augenblick der letzte sein kann, macht ihn zum Ursprung der Zukunft als einer Reihe, von der jedes Glied durch das erste vorweggenommen wird. Dieser Gedanke der Zukunft nun, dies, dass das Reich „mitten unter euch" ist, dass es „heute" kommt, diese Verewigung des Augenblicks erlischt im islamischen wie

---

[214] GS III, 196f. Rosenzweig bezieht sich hier auf folgenden Satz Cohens in der Ethik des reinen Willens. Werke, Bd.7 (hg. H. Holzhey), Hildesheim/New York 1981, 424: „In jeder Nussschale liegt die Unendlichkeit; sie liegt nicht in ihr; aber sie vollzieht sich in ihr".

[215] Vgl. hierzu Eva Birkenstock, Heisst philosophieren sterben lernen? Antworten der Existenzphilosophie: Kierkegaard, Heidegger, Sartre, Rosenzweig, Freiburg/München 1997, 270f.

im modernen Begriff der Zeitalter. Hier bilden die Zeiten zwar eine unendliche Reihe, aber unendlich ist nicht ewig, unendlich ist nur „immerzu". (252f.)

Mit Bezug auf die Welt bedeutet dies, dass sie aus jeglichem starren Vergangenheitsbezug herausgelöst ist; durch die in die Gegenwart vorgezogene ewige Zukunft des Reiches Gottes betrachten wir sie als immer ‚unfertig', da sie sich in einem ständigen Zustand des ‚Werdens' befindet.

Stéphane Mosès stellt im Zuge der Ausarbeitung einer Phänomenologie des Wartens fest, dass Rosenzweigs Zukunftsbegriff insofern auf die religiöse Grunderfahrung zurückzuführen ist, dass die Menschen im Einbruch der mit Ewigkeit aufgeladenen Zukunft des Reiches Gottes „auf etwas radikal Neues" warten.[216] Dieses ragt aus dem Verlauf des natürlichen Zeitflusses heraus, es kann in dessen Binnenhorizont nicht erlebt werden. Denn die religiöse Zukunftserfahrung sei von der Vorstellung der berechtigten Hoffnung auf einen Zustand der Welt dominiert, der völlig anders als der jetzige ist und sofort eintreten kann. Während die Utopie das bezeichnet, was „was ganz am Schluss der Zeit" und am Ende eines Weges mit ungewissem Ziel liege, beziehe sich die spezifisch menschliche messianische Hoffnung auf eine erlöste Welt, die durch die Vorwegnahme der Ankunft des Endes „schon jetzt eintreten kann".[217]

‚Messianische Ungeduld'

Die menschliche Erfahrung der Zukunft wird für Rosenzweig also wesentlich durch die Erlösungssehnsucht bestimmt, die er in einem Brief an Gertrud Oppenheimer aus dem Jahre 1917 als messianische Ungeduld bezeichnet. Er erläutert anhand von zwei Beispielen, was darunter zu verstehen ist. Zuerst gibt er eine talmudische Legende wieder:

> Ein Rabbi trifft am Eingang einer Höhle den Profeten Elias (bekanntlich Vorläufer des Messias, nach Maleachi, Schlussvers) und fragt ihn: Wo ist Messias? Drinnen in der Höhle. Da geht er hinein und findet Messias da sitzen. Da fragt er: wann kommst du, Herr? Messias antwortet: Heute. Da geht er fröhlich heraus und wartet bis zum Abend. Als aber Messias immer noch nicht kommt, sagt der Rabbi zu Elias: Messias hat gelogen; er sagte, er käme heute. Antwortet Elias: er meinte: [...] ‚heute, wenn ihr auf meine Stimme hört' (Zitat Psalm 95,7).[218]

---

[216] Stéphane Mosès, Von der Zeit zur Ewigkeit. Erlösung – eine problematische Kategorie bei Franz Rosenzweig, in: Gotthardt Fuchs (Hg. u.a.), Zeitgewinn. Messianisches Denken nach Franz Rosenzweig, Frankfurt a.M. 1987, 154.
[217] Ebd., 155.
[218] GS I, 344f. – Vgl. auch Hermann Cohen, Die Messiasidee, in: Jüdische Schriften (Hg. B.Strauss), Bd.1, Berlin 1924, 105–124, insbesondere 120.

Danach erzählt Rosenzweig eine kleine Geschichte über seinen Lehrer Hermann Cohen und die messianische Hoffnung bei den Juden: Er habe Cohen einmal gefragt: „Glauben Sie, Herr Professor, dass das messianische Zeitalter in den nächsten 50 Jahren anbrechen wird?" Darauf antwortete dieser: ‚Nein, aber in den nächsten hundert' – eine Geschichte", fährt Rosenzweig fort, „die doch fast ebenso schön ist wie die ‚Heute'-Geschichte".

Und er unterscheidet anschliessend zwischen „dem Heute, das nur die Brücke zum Morgen sein will, und dem andern Heute, das das Sprungbrett zur Ewigkeit ist [...]". Es stehe „keinem Tage an der Stirn geschrieben, ob er dieses oder jenes Heute ist. ‚Man kann nie wissen'".[219] Das ‚Man kann nie wissen' drückt nach Rosenzweig die wesentliche, aus der Ungewissheit im jüdischen Messianismus resultierende Ungeduld in der Erwartung eines gänzlich anderen Weltzustandes aus.

Im Unterschied hierzu ist sei die Erfahrung des linearen Fortschreitens der Zeit von Trostlosigkeit, ja Verzweiflung geprägt, weil es zwischen zwei Augenblicken keinen qualitativen Unterschied geben kann, und jedes Heute dem Morgen und Gestern ähnlich ist:

> Ohne diese Vorwegnahme und den inneren Zwang dazu, ohne das „Herbeiführenwollen des Messias vor seiner Zeit" und die Versuchung, das „Himmelreich zu vergewaltigen", ist die Zukunft keine Zukunft, sondern nur eine in unendliche Länge hingezogene, nach vorwärts projizierte Vergangenheit. Denn ohne solche Vorwegnahme ist der Augenblick nicht ewig, sondern ein sich immerwährend Weiterschleppendes auf der langen Heerstrasse der Zeit (253f.).

Michael Löwy ist der Überzeugung, dass Rosenzweig hier die radikale Kritik am linearen Fortschrittsbegriff vorwegnimmt, die Walter Benjamin in seinen Thesen *Über den Begriff der Geschichte* (1940) formuliert hat.[220]

---

[219] GS I, 344f.

[220] Michael Löwy, Erlösung und Utopie, Jüdischer Messianismus und anarchistisches Denken, Berlin 1994, 83. Löwy stellt fest, dass Rosenzweig wie Benjamin die Idee eines unendlichen Fortschritts in der Geschichte durch die jüdische Idee ersetzen wolle, dass jeder Augenblick die Fülle der Ewigkeit in sich aufnehmen könne. Dies stimme fast wörtlich mit der im Anhang der geschichtsphilosophischen Thesen vertretenen Ansicht Benjamins überein. Er führt folgende Stellen bei Walter Benjamin an: Ders., Über den Begriff der Geschichte, in: Sprache und Geschichte, Philosophische Essays, Stuttgart 1992, 141–154, hier 153, These A: „dass für die Juden in der Gegenwart der "‚Jetztzeit' [...] Splitter der messianischen" Zeit „eingesprengt" sind, und dass die Zukunft gemäss jüdischer Auffassung keine homogene und leere Zeit meint, sondern „jede Sekunde" als „ kleine Pforte" betrachtet, „durch die der Messias treten könnte". (These B, ebd., 154.)

4. Auf der Schwelle zum zeitlosen Werden Gottes in der Ewigkeit der Überwelt

Im Übergang zum dritten und letzten Teil von Rosenzweigs Hauptwerk, in einem kurzen Kapitel mit dem Titel *Schwelle*, wird die im letzten Buch des zweiten Teils bestimmte Ewigkeit der Zukunft in diejenige Ewigkeit überführt, die vollkommen ausserhalb der Zeit ist.

Bereits im Buch über die Erlösung heisst es, dass das ‚Wachstum' des Gottesreichs kein ‚Zeitmass' habe. Aber der Schwerpunkt von Rosenzweigs Ausführungen liegt, wie wir gesehen haben, auf einem Begriff von Geschichte, der im Zeichen der Zukunft steht. Es geht um die Bestimmung des vom Anspruch der Nächstenliebe geleiteten Handelns und Wirkens in der Welt, die noch kommen soll. Dennoch spielt bereits hier der Begriff der Ewigkeit Gottes, auf dessen Explikation der dritte Teil des *Stern der Erlösung* abhebt, eine entscheidende Rolle:

> Von Gott also nimmt die Erlösung ihren Ursprung, und der Mensch weiss weder Tag noch Stunde. Er weiss nur, dass er lieben soll und stets das Nächste und den Nächsten; und die Welt, sie wächst in sich nach scheinbar eigenem Gesetz; und ob sich Welt und Mensch nun heute finden oder morgen oder wann – die Zeiten sind unberechenbar, sie weiss nicht Mensch noch Welt; die Stunde weiss allein ER, der das Heute jeden Augenblick erlöst zur Ewigkeit. Die Erlösung ist also Ende, vor dem alles Angefangene in seinen Anfang zurücksinkt. Nur dadurch ist sie Voll-endung. (269)

Auf der *Schwelle* zum dritten Teil des *Stern der Erlösung* geht es Rosenzweig nun vorwiegend darum, die Ewigkeit Gottes, die auf den Augenblick bezogen und dabei stets im Werden begriffen ist, vom ‚Immerwährenden' der als ‚zeitlos' attackierten Vorwelt des ersten Teils seines Hauptwerkes abzugrenzen und zugleich in Beziehung zu setzen. Das ‚Immerwährende' wird quasi im Sinne Hegels ‚aufgehoben', d.h. zugleich ‚bewahrt' und unter neuen Gesichtspunkten auf einer qualitativ anderen Erkenntnisstufe betrachtet. Gott sei

> von Anfang an und [...] in jedem Augenblick und [...] immer im Kommen; und nur wegen dieses Zugleichs seines Immerwährend-, Allzeit- und Ewigseins muss man das Ganze als ein Werden bezeichnen. (287f.)

Die auf die Bahn des Beziehungsreichtums in Schöpfung, Offenbarung und Erlösung geratenen Elemente traten, so lautet nun Rosenzweigs Zusammenfassung, „in die Form der Zeitlichkeit" ein, die für sie selber „den Weg zur Ewigkeit bedeutet" (288). Dieser Weg führt sie von der Einheit der traditionellen All-Philosophie zu einer neuen Einheit, zur Einheit Gottes, die den Punkt bezeichnet, „der schon so jenseits der ‚Bahn' liegt wie ihr göttlicher Ursprung jenseits ihres Anfangs". Die all-umfassende Einheit der Ewigkeit Gottes im neuen Denken, die mit der Tradition herkömmlicher Metaphysik und Ontologie bricht, ist Einheit nicht, indem sie „ist", sondern „nur indem sie wird" (287).

Rosenzweig erläutert hier den letzten Schritt seiner existentiell-religionsphilosophischen Umdeutung der ‚Zeitlosigkeit' des griechisch-idealistischen All-Denkens in die wahre Ewigkeit Gottes. Er grenzt sich von Hegels Dialektik ab, die das ‚Sein' als ‚Kugel' auffasst. Und er prangert die ‚schlechte', da „in sich selber zurückgekrümmte Unendlichkeit des Idealismus" an (283f.), um ihr die Wahrheit des im *Stern der Erlösung* entwickelten Ewigkeitsbegriffs entgegen zu halten. Dieser führt uns in die Überwelt, deren Ewigkeit – wie das Immerwährende der dunklen Vorwelt – von „Schweigen" erfüllt ist. Aber nun handelt es sich nicht um die Lautlosigkeit der mathematischen Sprache, um das stumme Selbst oder um die Einsamkeit des Helden in der griechischen Götterwelt. Das Schweigen der Überwelt ist vielmehr erleuchtet, weil sie über das Wunder des geschichtlichen Ereignisses der Offenbarung hinausweist in die Vollendung einer erlösten Welt. Wir stehen nach Rosenzweig an der „Schwelle vom Wunder zur Erleuchtung", die nur in der ‚Schau' erfassbar ist (291).

Weiterführende Lektüre

Bertolino, L., (2020), *Bach in die Synagogen!". Erlösende Noten in Franz Rosenzweig*, in: Naharaim 14 (2020) 209–223.

Dubbels, E., (2011), *Figuren des Messianischen in Schriften deutsch-jüdischer Intellektueller 1900–1933*, Berlin, De Gruyter.

Scharf, O., (2019), *Thinking in Translation: Scripure and Redemption in the Thought of Franz Rosenzweig*, Berlin, De Gruyter.

Dritter Teil. Die Gestalt Oder Die Ewige Überwelt

/

Part Three. The Structure, Or The Eternal Over-World

Part Three, Introduction: On the Possibility of Entreating the Kingdom

Gabriella Caponigro

On reaching the threshold of Part Three of *The Star*, the reader might be tempted to think that the path of reflection undertaken so far might well be concluded, with Redemption, as expounded at the end of Part Two. But the redemptive space, formally considered within the horizon of revelation, does not substitute the final goal. The real world neither attains to the fullness of meaning nor does it contain the ultimate truth, so that the path experienced in it cannot but account for a dimension essentially incomplete.

If, on one hand, the cognitive dynamics of Parts One and Two are expressed by the figure of the Star by superimposing the two triangles[221], on the other, the figure that comes across to us alludes to a supreme and ultimate truth, to a final port of call that forever remains beyond this world and which, as such, stays programmatically unfulfilled and postponed to futurity. However, the sense of such incompleteness needs to be understood, properly, as a "need for time"[222] or rather as a "need of eternity". In other words, the figure of the Star still has to find its fulfilment and reveal itself in its truth, that is in its eternity.

---

[221] That of the elements God–Man–World (Part One) and that of the relational movements Creation–Revelation–Redemption (Part Two).
[222] Cf. *Das neue Denke*n, GS III, 151.

Certainly, the real cosmos does maintain in itself the tension towards this hyper-cosmos, an intentionality directed to the ultimate consummation. Divine love poured upon man and the world demands substantiation in that eschatological dimension which Rosenzweig defines as "the eternal hyper-cosmos of the truth". For the philosopher, truth is not what is true but what longs to be confirmed as the truth[223]. It demands the sacrifice of life, the ethical, political and religious commitment of all generations; it longs to be anticipated in time. It is, therefore, understandable why in this part of the *Star* the function of the *organon* is taken on by the *liturgy*, being the system of visible signs typical of collective religious life that have the power to anticipate eternal reality.

Moreover, the truth longs to be beseeched, implored. For Rosenzweig the problem of truth is, evidently, the problem of desiring truth. What is at stake is redemption but, ever more so, the *desire* for redemption. Hence, the entire *Introduction* is dedicated to *prayer*[224]. That is the essential notion in the great shift from "the always-renewed-cosmos" to "the eternal-hyper-cosmos". It denotes a new temporality between the redeemer and the redeemed, just as it happens under forms of religious life, and indicates a new configuration of being, beyond-knowledge (erkennen) and beyond-experience (erleben)[225].

Prayer implores the Kingdom of God, a reality to come which comprises the fulfilment of redemption. While redemption is already part of the real world as much as it is of creation and revelation, the Kingdom of God is present in

---

[223] Cf. GS III, 158. On the pragmatism of the truth, see our paper: G. Caponigro, *Phenomenology of religious pragmatism. Truth and testimony in Franz Rosenzweig*, in: «Archivio di filosofia/Archive of philosophy», LXXXIII, 2015, n.3, pp. 85–95.

[224] See also Part Two of *The Star*, which contains a number of significant reflections on prayer. It is defined as the greatest gift that is given unto man in revelation; however, a gift that comes across only as a possibility, as a "being able to pray", which must seek its fulfilment in the prayer for the coming of the Kingdom. See: GS II, 205–206, 260–261. For a comprehensive elaboration on the relationship between prayer and temporality, cf. Bernhard Casper, *Über das Gebet. Betrachtungen zu Franz Rosenzweig im Hinblick auf Emmanuel Levinas*, in: *Philosophisch Theologische Grenzfragen. Festschrift für Richard Schaeffler*, Essen 1986, 35–43; *Das Gebet stiftet die menschliche Weltordnung. Zum Verständnis der Erlösung im Werk Franz Rosenzweigs*, in: Gotthard Fuchs and Hermann Henrix (eds.), *Zeitgewinn. Messianisches Denken nach Franz Rosenzweig*, Frankfurt 1987, 127–150; *Das Ereignis des Betens. Grundlinien einer Hermeneutik des religiösen Geschehens*, Freiburg i.B., 1998.

[225] Cf. titles of the introductions to the three parts of *The Star*: *Über die Möglichkeit das All zu erkennen, Über die Möglichkeit das Wunder zu erleben, Über die Möglichkeit das Reich zu erbeten* (GS II, 3, 103, 295).

the history of the world only – as Rosenzweig clarifies – as a *growing reality*[226]. This is a temporality completely different from that which can be intentionally calculated, a temporality that has no relation whatsoever with time[227]. Such growing reality is rather characterized by an intrinsic and unavoidable temporal disproportion between the messianic action of man, called to act and to sacrifice his own life for the coming of the kingdom, and the growth of the latter. The disproportion between man and world may only be removed with the advent of the Kingdom, when God, man and world become a unity[228]. However, the guarantee of the "becoming unity" lies in man's action. The cosmos *becomes* a redeemed hyper-cosmos awaiting man's action to become *one* with God's action.

The temporality on which human action is founded consists of distinct efforts to love one's fellow man, where every movement towards exteriority is always a new beginning[229], as such inadequate in creating a continuous sequence and shaping a history. The world, however, has a history that develops independently of man, according to a continuous progression. This temporal disproportion explains why it is impossible for man to grasp any progress in the history of redemption and, as an immediate consequence, grasp any *telos*. The redemptive space brings about a true and proper "eschatological drama", an eschatology that never takes on the form of a teleology. In consequence, man's action is marked by its non-coincidence with respect to the worldly order and it cannot but proceed casually. The attainment of redemption, however, depends on the above coincidence. How then to reconcile, within the categories of the "new thinking", man's being in time with the worldly horizon and with God's being eternal and one?

The unknowability of the *telos* drives man to the fullness of being. Since man cannot predict the scheme of history, nothing remains unto man except to trustingly await, without any constriction, the fulfilment of God's work, which, in turn, needs man's free action to become true (*bewähren*). The concept of *Bewährung* thus turns into the cornerstone of the entire Part Three of *The Star*.

The non-teleological form of this "eschatological drama" underpins the absolute freedom and the space of *human action*. What kind of action can be considered effective, capable of activating the redemption process? In Rosenzweig's view, the knowledge must abandon the will in order to be able to transform itself

---

[226] Cf. GS II, 250–251.
[227] «The tempo of this growth is not fixed, nay, more exactly: the growth has no relationship at all to time» (GS II, 250/ SH, 224). For an in-depth analysis on the special comprehension of temporality in Rosenzweig's thought, cf. F.P. Ciglia, *Nel labirinto del tempo. Storia ed escatologia nel confronto fra Rosenzweig e Agostino*, in: R. Panattoni, G. Sciolla (ed.), «Teologia Politica», 2, 2006, 144–185.
[228] Cf. GS II, 288.
[229] Cf. GS II, 239–240.

into desire, which is essential to the coming of the Kingdom at the end of time. The redemptive action is the prayer, capable of reconciliating the temporality of man and the one of the world, and to project desires and intentions far in the future. Despite his cognitive defect and the limited horizon that surrounds him, man can resort to the prayer, the «utopian modality»[230] of his action.

However, this projection of desires opens up a problematic horizon. As Stéphane Mosès asserts[231], prayer projects us undoubtedly beyond our immediate horizon, but then, if it aims too far and demands the unattainable, it misses its appointment with the most attainable desire—the redemption. The latter does not let itself be taken arbitrarily at any moment in time, nor to be reduced to a simple actualization of desires. Redemption does not allow itself to be "ravished" by overbearing prayer, that demands the unattainable, instead of awaiting with *trust* and imploring that "ever possible" that makes up the very statute of redemption.

Therefore, now we may better understand why, in the caption to the *Introduction*, we find the motto *In tyrannos!* Beside the mottoes found in Parts One (*In philosophos!*) and Two (*In theologos!*), *In tyrannos!* bears testimony to the main preoccupation that animates Part Three and all of *The Star*: the risk of a relapse into subjectivism, in the infinite desire to embrace the fullness of history, to constitute oneself overlord of the heavens and of the last things. Prayer is certainly an itinerary directed to the last things but in an incomplete and non-teleological way. It is the possibility to put oneself at stake in the *eschata*, but the impossibility to avail of it.

The unknowability of the *telos* and of the rhythm that guides history establishes the free space of human action, but also the unavoidable possibility of missing the mark, of being led into *temptation*. One may miss the target because one is tempted. The idea of temptation emerges right from the *Introduction*. This is an essential category that explains the major peril inherent in man's action, that is man's will to replace God in the redemptive process. Hence, Rosenzweig writes: «Temptation will be as fundamental for the passage to Part Three as miracle for Part Two»[232]. Only before God the Redeemer does one have the unlimited liberty to decide and to tempt God; a liberty that would not be possible were it not God first to tempt man, that is to hide Himself, so that the individual may have the possibility to freely choose whether to believe and confide in Him or to replace Him with himself.

As emphasized above, redemption opens unto man a problematic horizon, not only with regard to what has just been said about its utopian peculiarity but also because it is not God's direct work. It is rather an indirect work of

---

[230] Cf. Stéphane Mosès, *Système et Révélation. La philosophie de Franz Rosenzweig*, Paris, 1982, 158ff.
[231] Ibid., 161.
[232] Letter to Margrit Rosenstock-Huessy, dated 13 October 1918, in: GB, 169, our translation.

His, which takes place wherever the freedom poured forth in the act of love joins the mutable life of the world in a relationship. Only in this relationship does the real possibility of tempting God occur and it is prayer that institutes such a rapport.

Without the enlightenment of prayer love's action would be blind, it would not see the history of the world, neither a *telos*, nor the world itself. It would only be directed to those who happen to be the fellow man from time to time. Prayer thus enlightens the world that, otherwise, love alone would not be able to see.

However, in instituting the human order of the world, the prayer runs the risk to overcome the act of love and tyrannically move towards the last things. Because it is impatient, the tyrannical prayer is ineffective: «True, the man enlightened in prayer would like to adduce the kingdom of heaven forcibly, before its appointed time. But the kingdom of heaven will not be coerced: it grows. And thus, the magic power of the individual suppliant falls into the void if it strays beyond the nearest»[233]. There is a desirable time—a time of grace — for praying. Not only does the tyrannical prayer miss its appointment with that time—coming too early—but also with the fellow being. The act of love, which does not know *telos* nor history, becomes, in the tyrant's prayer, an act aimed at an unattainable utopia. Whereas the desirable time is one in which human will accords perfectly with the objective state of the things of the world. Hence, Rosenzweig affirms, there is no wrongful content of prayer, but only a wrong moment.

The time in which redemption grows is that of the life of the world, whose rhythm and laws it is not given to man to know. However, despite this unknowability, the possibility is conceded to man to see his prayers answered, if such prayer takes place precisely in the acceptable time of grace.

This time demands a further effort on the part of man, a trust[234] that drives actions and intentions towards achievable objectives. The experience of the future must always be able to find support in the natural time of the world, because the redemption is precisely the most realistic desire.

But if man does not have the realistic wisdom to understand his creatural limits, his prayer cannot but be tyrannical. The fanatic, the sectarian, the mystic, all

---

[233] GS II, 302; SH 271.

[234] The notion of *Vertrauen* takes on a fundamental role in various passages of *The Star*. It is not only what animates faith in revelation, in the man who awaits the Kingdom (cf. the introduction to Part Two), but also it is the essential attitude that unites Jews and Christians in their common task to bear witness to the truth. The proof whereof is that the word recurs in the crucial portions that conclude *The Star* (GS II, 472). For an in-depth analysis of the argument, see: Irene Kajon, *Il concetto di* Vertrauen *nella Stella della Redenzione*, in: *Il futuro del nuovo pensiero. In dialogo con Franz Rosenzweig*, «Teoria», 28, 2008. 1, 159–173.

of heaven's tyrants, end up exhausting the act of love, thus delaying the coming of the Kingdom which they impatiently wanted to accelerate.

Apart from the visionary, Rosenzweig also identifies another equally barren attitude to the future, that of the sinner, that is of the man who does not trust God's redemption and wastes the time of grace in praying for something—one's own being—which he already possesses right from the creation. His is an egoistic prayer, he prays for his Own self, so that the fellow man eternally remains a "he", an object amongst the many in the world of creation. Thus, by breaking the bond with the world and the fellow man, the sinner denies the work of redemption which, by contrast, consists in orienting oneself towards a "he" as if he were one other "I". Hence, Rosenzweig's definition: «For what is redemption other than that the I learn to say Thou to the He?»[235]. Thus, the sinner who remains within the limits of "his Own self", anchored to what he already possesses, that is to his past, misses the encounter with the fellow man thereby delaying, again, the coming of the Kingdom.

On the other hand, effective prayer is one that keeps abreast of love, raised at the opportune time. But, asks Rosenzweig, how and when is this prayer raised?

At this point, Rosenzweig surprisingly introduces the figure of Goethe[236], «the man of life», «the pure son of this earth»—as he describes the poet—the fulfilment of paganism, the incarnation of earthly and natural wisdom. Effective prayer is the one recited by Goethe, who has managed to fully reconcile his intentionality with the mutable life of the world: «Labour of my hands that I / finish, grant, oh Fortune high!»[237]. It is the prayer of a solitary individual, addressing neither the future of the Kingdom nor his own self, but his personal destiny. The notion of "destiny" is a decisive one. It designates the fulfilment, in the overall course of life, of the true and proper essence of man; this is what makes man one and indivisible in his singularity, a microcosm, which, at the same time, unites him with the world, roots him and makes him grow in it. Man is in the world in so far as he has a *destiny*. This intimate bond that ties the part to the whole, human life to the entire life of the world, is precisely what destiny is. And it is this intimate bond, corresponding to a segment, to an *hour*, that which has to be implored in prayer. «And, that being so, this prayer is always fulfilled. Even as it is prayed, it insinuates itself into the face of the world; it never misses its mark, is never too late nor too early […] it occurs in the

---

[235] GS II, 305; SH, 274.

[236] *The Star* is full of references, some of which implicit, to Goethe's work. Most of those references are contained in the *Introduction* hereby examined. To Rosenzweig, Goethe's life represented a synthesis of classical harmony, the only possible reconciliation of the duality between the objective and the subjective, between world and self, which constituted the great theoretical problem of the initial period of his speculative work. Cf. notes dated 11.1.06, 19.2.06, 16.03.06, 27.4.06, 6.5.06, 4.9.06, in: GS I.1.

[237] GS II, 306; SH, 274.

personal hour [...] Accordingly, it is ever in the desirable time»[238]. To Rosenzweig, all of this signifies nothing but entering upon what has always existed in the world – in creation – and thereby come into redemption, since the latter consists in the union of the object of the revelation – man – with that of the creation – world – which is to say in the coming together of a *plan* and a *history*.

The prominent reference to Goethe throws a new light on the reality of paganism, as a reality that opens up the possibility of man's reconciliation with the world's time, that is the very object of redemption. Rosenzweig writes: «Goethe is really at the same time the great pagan and the great Christian»[239]. If the statement about Goethe's paganism may easily be understood—he represents the unbelief of the creaturely being—the one regarding Christianity is less comprehensible. Even Goethe describes himself as the only remaining Christian. Such a claim may be understood if what is meant by Christian is someone who longs to live like Christ binding himself to the destiny of the world. Goethe is one who, with his concrete life, has brought to fulfilment the spirit of Christianity—it being the exaltation and sanctification of creation.

At this juncture, in order to account for Goethe's uniqueness, Rosenzweig develops the history of Christianity as one of paganism. *Die Nachfolge Christi* is a decisive passage in the *Introduction*, since it sheds light on Rosenzweig's conception of the secularisation of Christianity. Taking a leaf out of Schelling's *Philosophie der Offenbarung*[240], Rosenzweig subdivides the history of Christianity into three fundamental stages, each corresponding to an apostle and a theological virtue, each reflecting a certain relation of the Church with the life of the world.

The Church of Peter, risen out of the ruins of the Roman Empire, was the one that turned to the whole world as a missionary, transcending the borders of the nations. It built churches throughout the world, and organised itself as a visible body. The individual, and with him the Church itself, finds himself immediately inserted, by way of love, in the life of the world. However, what was tied to the destiny of the world was only «the destiny of his act, not, however, the destiny of his thought»[241]. Therefore, although the Petrine Church was able to

---

[238] GS II, 308; SH, 277.
[239] GS II, 315; SH, 283.
[240] Friedrich Schelling, *Philosophie der Offenbarung*, 1854. On the importance of Shelling's philosophy in Rosenzweig's thought, see: Xavier Tilliette, *Rosenzweig et Schelling*, in: «Archivio di filosofia», LIII, 1985, n. 2-3, 141–152; Wolfdietrich Schmied-Kowarzic, *Vom Totalexperiment des Glaubens. Kritisches zur positiven Philosophie Schellings und Rosenzweig*, in: Id. (ed.), *Der Philosoph Franz Rosenzweig* (1886-1929), Internationaler Kongress Kassel 1986, Vol. 2, Freiburg/München 1988, 771–799; Robert Gibbs, *The Limits of Thought: Rosenzweig, Schelling and Cohen*, in: «Zeitschrift für Forschung», 43 (1989), 614–640.
[241] GS II, 311; SH, 280.

convert the external visible paganism, it could do nothing about the internal paganism, which was remembered and survived in a Christianised world. The power of love, which always acts towards a corporeal exterior, could not fight such a paganism. A different instrument was needed in order to divert the eyes from the world «which acted within the soul itself and upon the soul»[242], freeing it of its paganism.

Faith was this instrument that acted with power in the Pauline centuries, which, in Rosenzweig's reconstruction, correspond to the centuries of the Protestant Reform. The Church of Paul certainly converted the soul, but dearly paid for such an internalisation of the faith with the loss of the unity of the visible body. Having become the invisible Church of a religion reduced exclusively to the ambit of interiority and subjectivity, it soon showed its weakness: if the Petrine Church had been too bound up with the body, the Pauline Church was too focused on the soul to the extent that, at the end of the Pauline centuries, it was from such a weakness that German Idealism with its idea of a self-producing spirit, unmindful of the body, drew its energies. Faith, in regaining the soul, had lost the body and the world. Protestant theology and Idealist philosophy marked the triumph of subjectivity, but, conversely, they paved the way for secularism.

However, Rosenzweig asserts, man is an indivisible microcosm. His essence lies neither in the body nor in the soul, but *becomes* so fulfilling itself in the world through his destiny, which is at once body and soul. Since this destiny may be prayed for, this is where such dualism is transcended, a new time is inaugurated: that of the consummation of Christianity. Hence, the pagan prayer, that of a non-religious but creaturely faith, can become the prayer of all Christian peoples, who, like Goethe in his singularity, would be able to access the destiny of the world and grow with it. Growth and fulfilment ought to be able to coincide in life.

Thus, the new future Church will not be one of the exterior or interiorised pagan, but that of the living pagan, who sacrifices his own life in the trusting expectation of fulfilment. Hope will be the greatest virtue, which comprises in itself love and faith, and leads it back neither to the external nor to the internal, but, on an axis of temporality, towards the future. As in the *Gritlianum* dialogue, from their separation body and soul join together in the cry of hope: «*O dass du den Himmel zerrissest und führest hernieder!*»[243]. This is the age of the living pagan, of Johannine completion, which, being the fulfilment of the preceding figures, does not take on any specific form and does not become visible as a third Church. And since such a Church is not built, in Rosenzweig's view, it can only grow. Underlying here is a veiled critique of Rosenstock's vision of

---

[242] GS II, 312; SH, 281.
[243] GB, 826–831. Cf. GS II, 206; SH, 191. For an in-depth analysis of the text, see: Francesco Paolo Ciglia (ed.), *Il grido*, Morcelliana, Brescia 2003.

Christianity as *Ecclesia triumphans*[244]. The Kingdom of Heaven must not be identified with the reign of the Church, nor with any other visible institution. Instead, it is an invisible community that is to bring to fulfilment the time, the community of a religion of humanity.

It is at this point that Rosenzweig introduces the Jewish people as the constituent element of this new Christian age. However, it is not an emancipated Judaism that enters political reality as a visible character, participating in the history of peoples and nations, but the Judaism of the Holy Covenant, which becomes, beside and within Christianity itself, the element of the Johannine civilisation. Rosenzweig writes: «Accordingly, in this incipient fulfilment of the ages it is rather the Jew, accepted into the Christian world, who must convert the pagan within the Christian. For hope […] lives as a matter of blood-inheritance only in Jewish blood»[245].

The father of this Johannine Church is none other than Goethe, who, in his prayer to destiny, has created a time that is alive, a current in which could *grow* the vitality of the creaturely life of the man. But his prayer, which must certainly be given credit for having brought temporality back to life, is not a prayer for the advent of the Kingdom, rather it interrupts its growth. It is its unavoidable precondition, as it leads man back to the singularity of the creaturely life, but not a sufficient condition, since such pure temporality needs to access eternity. More appropriately, an accelerative power must be added to life's pure temporality in order to anticipate the future in Today, to transform eternity into an "Infinite Now". Such prayer which accelerates the coming of the Kingdom is the one pronounced by the believer: completion and not abolition of the unbeliever's prayer. Such prayer demands much more than the fulfilment of destiny, it desires eternity here and now.

This is perhaps one of the key passages to understand the heart of the problem of redemption. Rosenzweig introduces the notion of "hour" as metaphor of eternity. It represents the cyclic recurrence of the identical, the projection of the immutable in perceived time. Certainly, not the hour as a temporal, transient, fluid projection, but as an abiding moment, as a *nunc stans*, like «a circle returning in upon itself»[246]. In order to redeem himself from the transient, man transforms into "hour" the natural rhythm of the times of the sun and the moon. Thus, year, month and day become "hours" in human life. Through such a human institution, man gives time an immutability that becomes the projection of eternity.

The week, in particular, a purely human time, marked by the alternation of work and rest is, as such, a "true hour". It represents the point in which human

---

[244] Cf. the second book (GS II, 390–392) and the third book of Part Three (GS II, 445–447). Cf. also the correspondence between Rosenzweig and Rosenstock in particular the letters dated 7.11.16, 30.11.16, in GS I.1.
[245] GS II, 317; SH, 285.
[246] GS II, 322; SH, 290.

and sacred time converge by intertwining. This is even more evident on the day of rest, which is the day consecrated not only to the contemplation of the work done by man in the preceding six days, but also to the blessing of God's work, that is of creation. The week articulates and regulates the cultural service of the earth, but, in its infinite repetition, it is also the earthly representation of the eternal. This passage takes place through the fundamental mediation of the liturgical rite. Natural time transformed, through cultural repetition of the earth, into human-social time, is in turn transformed through liturgical repetition into time suited to the reception of eternity. Thus, Rosenzweig writes, the week is «the kernel of the cult», «temporal abodes into which the eternal is invited»[247]. In other words, sacred time stands on and is understood on the basis of profane time.

Returning to prayer: what does it really comprise, and where does the power of this prayer lie that makes it capable of extending such an appealing invitation to the eternal as to be indeclinable? Precisely in liturgical time, that is in the time that belongs to everyone.

The believer's prayer is the prayer of the entire community and what is highlighted to all its members is not a personal destiny but the shared reality: the end of all things, that which is the farthest, the Kingdom. Since the self-same reality to come is highlighted in the experience of an entire community, the individual may now really raise himself above his own horizon of finiteness. The believer's prayer is the consummation of the unbeliever's prayer: it is indeed necessary for life to come alive with unbelieving prayer in order to be able to receive the gift of the eternal in time. Therefore, Goethe's "May *I* fulfil the work of *my* hands" can no longer suffice, but "May *thou* fulfil the work of *our* hands". Hence, it becomes clear why the prayer to the Kingdom marks the threshold point between the manifest cosmos and the hyper-cosmos. It mediates between revelation and redemption and its concrete form in the religious community, the liturgy, with its power to anticipate, cannot but be the *organon* of Part Three of *The Star*.

The figure with the two superimposed triangles, may now shine as a star and become fully visible. This bright figure will not be revealed by way of language, as in Part Two, but it will do without words in order to become pure liturgical gesture, the gesture of arms raised to the heavens, «which is eloquent without the lips having to move»[248].

In the liturgical gesture the pagan's prayer fuses with that of the believer: the intention turned to one's own action in history now becomes one and the same with the intention turned to the eternity of the Kingdom. Here lies the heart of Rosenzweig's vision of history: the relation between human action and the last things, which is the core of Part Three of *The Star*. The history of salvation takes place each time anew amongst free intentions oriented to the Kingdom

---

[247] GS II, 324; SH, 292.
[248] GS II, 328; SH, 295.

and the consummation of time. If it were not so, human action would only be able either to remain ineffective, bringing about acceleration or delay in the advent of the Kingdom, or, on the contrary, be effective but interrupt its growth in history.

Men himself becomes the request, the cry addressed to the eternal Kingdom, because what is at stake is the relation between love and the world, human action and the last things, the finite possession of time and the eternal reality. Redemption is thus possible only in the yearning that it be fulfilled, recognising its ever being beyond anything containable within knowledge or experience. Man may only act oriented by the desire to become-one with God and the world, according to a modality that he can never fully embrace.

All of Part Three of *The Star* may thus be understood only in the light of that motto, *In tyrannos!*: against all totalitarianisms of heavens, all presumption to embrace all of history and the entire truth, against radical subjectivism that overcomes creatural limits [249].

Unbelief and faith become one: «God's truth wants to be entreated with both hands»[250], with the hands of the believer and the unbeliever. Truth demands that the incessant and eternal quest for realisation join the quest oriented by the hope of the Kingdom towards a common goal; the intentionality must fuse with the historical experience of a calling to the eternal. The unbeliever's hand has to rise together with that of the believer, with the hand – we might add – of Judaism and Christianity, as will be seen in the following books of *The Star*.

---

[249] Expanding this issue to collective tyranny, the motto "*in tyrannos!*" acquires significance within Rosenzweig's polemic against the tyrannical power of the State and Hegel's universal history (see Book One, Part Three of the *Star*). For further elaborations of Rosenzweig's view on politics, see: Stephane Mosès, *Politique et réligion chez Franz Rosenzweig*, in: Jean Halpérin (ed.), *Politique et réligion*, Paris 1981, 283–311; Gérard Bensussan, *Etat et éternité chez Franz Rosenzweig*, in: Arno Münster (ed.), *La penseé de Franz Rosenzweig*, Paris 1994, 137–148; Id., *Instant éthique et raison politique*, in: Wolfdietrich Schmied-Kowarzik (ed.), *Franz Rosenzweigs »neues Denken«*, Internationaler Kongress Kassel 2004, Vol. 1, Freiburg/München 1988, 459–469; Marc Crépon, *Politiques de Rosenzweig*, in: Ibid., 516–537; Guy Petitdemange, *Hegel et Rosenzweig, la différence se faisant*, in: Olivier Mongin (ed.), *Franz Rosenzweig*, "Les Cahiers de la nuit surveillée" 1 (1982), 157–170; Jörg Kohr, *«Gott selbst muss das letzte Wort sprechen». Religion und Politik im Denken Franz Rosenzweigs*, Freiburg/München, 2008. For further elaborations on "tyranny" as it appears in different ways along the various stage of Rosenzweig's thought, see: Irene Kajon, *La critica della tirannia in Franz Rosenzweig*, "Archivio di Filosofia" 59, 1991, n. 1-3, 219–241. See also our work: G. Caponigro, *Unde Malum? Libertà e tirannia in Franz Rosenzweig*, preface by Bernhard Casper, Ets, Pisa 2015.

[250] GS II, 330; SH, 297.

Further readings

Bernhard Casper, *Das Gebet stiftet die menschliche Weltordnung. Zum Verständnis der Erlösung im Werk Franz Rosenzweigs*, in: Gotthard Fuchs and Hermann Henrix (eds.), *Zeitgewinn. Messianisches Denken nach Franz Rosenzweig*, Frankfurt 1987, 127–150.

Sax, B., (2011), Das geflügelte Wort: Franz Rosenzweig as Post-Goethekenner, in: Naharaim 5 (2011) 115–149, [https://www.degruyter.com/journal/key/NAHA/5/1-2/html]

Stéphane Mosès, *Système et Révélation. La philosophie de Franz Rosenzweig*, Paris 1982.

Part Three, Book One: The Fire or The Eternal Life

Petar Bojanić

In the first book of the third part of the *Star of Redemption* (*Stern der Erösung*), entitled "The Fire or The Eternal Life," we find, similar to the rest of the books, the problem of a difference between the 1921 and later editions. The first was published during Rosenzweig's lifetime, whereas Nahum D. Galtzer published the second edition, allegedly in accordance with Rosenzweig's instructions, in 1930, shortly after his death, complete with appendices and chapter titles. It would appear that of all the translations into various languages (the most recent was into Russian, appearing in 2017), only the second English translation follows the first edition, although the translator, Barbara E. Galli, retains the titles and subtitles in the margins, so as to facilitate reading. In the first publication of *Stern*, the book here in question is 47 pages long [SE1, 375–421] and is divided into 60 chapters. Eight of the 60 are capitalized, with the first letter of the book, 'G' ("*Gepriesen sei…*"), larger than the other seven (E, W, W, D, I, E, U). Overall *Stern* has only 76 capitalized chapters, each book usually having one, seven or eight. Considered in the context of the whole volume, it might appear as if Rosenzweig's careful calculation yields the word GEWW (Hebraic for 'from within' or 'inside', or else 'from the community' or 'from the home') or DIEU, but this is rather wrongheaded. Of the eight capitalized units in this part[251]

---

[251] The eight are: Die Verheisung der Ewigkeit (The Promise of Eternity) [SE1 375; SE 331; SG 317]; Das Ewige Volk: jüdisches Schicksal (The Eternal

---

How to cite this book chapter:
Bojanić, P. 2021. Part Three, Book One: The Fire or The Eternal Life. In: Brasser, M., Bojanić, P. and Ciglia, F. P. (eds.) *The Star for Beginners: Introductions to the Magnum Opus of Franz Rosenzweig*. Pp. 145–158. London: Ubiquity Press. DOI: https://doi.org/10.5334/bco.l. License: CC-BY

(the longest of which is a page and a half long), the first and last play the role of introduction, that is, conclusion to the book. Meaning that six are particularly emphasized in Glatzer-Rosenzweig's intervention. But two units, numbers 5 and 6, capitalized in the first edition have 'reduced significance' in the second: "Soziologie der Gemeinschaft: das Mahl" and "Soziologie des Ganzen: der Gruss" – without the same emphasis as the other six.

How should we read this complicated book? To begin with, what does Rosenzweig wish to achieve with the book and its title, what does he introduce in his introduction? The practice of Judaism in eternity or in eternal life is supposed to be described as a blaze. Yet, the flame (*Flamme*) or "the heart of the fire" (*das Kernfeuer*) is special indeed, since it has to burn such that it is never extinguished but always fueled of itself (it needs nothing, it burns nothing other than itself). This pure flame is outside time, regenerates itself and overcomes all forms of time, above all the past and future – in the name of the eternal now. Rosenzweig thematizes time within Judaism several times in the book; the formulation at the top of this chapter, which begins with "*Indem so die heilige Gesetzeslehre*" (Since teaching of the Holy Law) [SE1 382; SG 323], is not specially marked in the second edition [SE 338] yet is probably the most precise. "The Jewish people does not calculate the years of its own chronology." Life in time is forbidden to the Jewish or holy people, for the sake of eternal life in the eternal now. This is life beyond time or life that does not pass.

To all the better explain these complex structures comprising several rather complicated terms (time, eternity, life, and on the side, self-sustaining fire), throughout the book Rosenzweig distinguishes everything concerning what is 'Jewish' (people, law, language, war, time, etc.) from everyone else (Christianity, other peoples, peoples of the world, etc.). The book, "The Fire or The Eternal Life" is above all a "book of distinctions," helping to clarify often complicated constructions. Thus, Rosenzweig differentiates a community based on blood from one grounded in spirit, will and hope [SE1 376; SE 332; SG 317]. In contrast with Christian peoples, the Jewish people never finds its roots in the land on which it stands [SE1 376; SE 332; SG 318]. As opposed to others, it

---

People: Jewish Destiny) [SE1 375–383; SE 331–339; SG 317–324]; Das eine Volk: jüdisches Wesen (The One People: Jewish Essence) [SE1 384–387; SE 339–342; SG 324–327]; Das heilige Volk: das jüdisches Jahr (The Holy People: The Jewish Year) [SE1 388–395; SE 342–349; SG 327–334]; Soziologie der Gemeinschaft: das Mahl (Sociology of The Community: The Meal) [SE1 395–403; SE 349–357; SG 334–341]; Soziologie des Ganzen: der Gruss (Sociology of The Whole: The Greeting) [SE1 404–412; SE 357–364; SG 341–347]; Die Völker der Welt: Messianische Politik (The Peoples of The World: Messianic Politics) [SE1 412–420; SE 364–371; SG 348–354]; Der Ewigkeit der Verheisung (The Eternity of The Promise) [SE1 420–421; SE 371–372; SG 354–355].

never identifies itself with the language it speaks [SE1 379; SE 334; SG 324].[252] Rosenzweig poses the problem of borders, since the Jewish people "can then no longer enclose itself within borders, but it must include the borders within itself" [SE1 384; SE 339; SG 325]. Finally, in contrast with the peoples of the world [*die Völker der Welt*], the reality of the Jewish people is already realized [SE1 413; SE 365; SG 348], etc.

The entire construction of this book and its meaning could really be an answer to two questions at the beginning of the third unit: "But what does that mean – rooting in ourselves (*Verwurzelung im eigenen Selbst*)? What does it mean that here an individual or a people seeks the guarantee of its survival (*seines Bestehens*) in nothing external, and precisely here, precisely in its absence of relationship (*Beziehungslosigkeit*), wants to be what is eternal" [SE1 384; SE 339; SG 324]? How, then, is an entity constructed or self-constructed? By what means and deploying which strategy, can it be made to be beyond all connection with anything else, yet still last forever and surpass all else? Rosenzweig is here trying to constitute an entirely new "social ontology," in opposition to Hegel's institutionalism and his state-grounding project in general.[253] Simultaneously working on *Stern* and his doctoral thesis on Hegel, while also being a participant in one of the most terrible wars in history – thus, Hegel (philosophy), Judaism, and war are the first three elements of Rosenzweig's project, which intertwine, sometimes entirely chaotically, in the book – his intention is to systematize a few concepts that could explain the eternal life of a community. Yet, before that, is it possible to quickly formulate the nature of Rosenzweig's

---

[252] Rosenzweig brings the second unit to a triumphant close thus: "We alone cannot imagine this sort of time; for everything in which the existence of peoples takes root, has long ago been taken away from us; land language, custom and law long ago departed from the sphere of the living and for us is raised from the living to the holy; but we, we are still living and live eternally. Our life is no longer interwoven with anything external, we have taken root in ourselves, without roots in the earth, eternal wanderers therefore, yet deeply rooted in ourselves, in our own body and blood. And this rooting in ourselves and only in ourselves guarantees our eternity for us" (*in uns selbst schlugen wir Wurzel, wurzellos in der Erde, ewige Wanderer darum, doch tief verwurzelt in uns selbst, in unserm eignen Leib und Blut. Und diese Verwurzelung in uns selbst und allein in uns selbst verbürgt uns unsre Ewigkeit*). [SE1 383; SE 338–339; SG 324].

[253] Later, in a letter to Martin Buber of 3 July 1925, Rosenzweig pens a complicated sentences that describes the terrible travails of the struggle against institutions in which he condenses his efforts to remain consistent and uncover all the dangers of institutionalism contained in the Jewish heritage. "The struggle against institutions takes all too breath-drainingly long for the tempestuous breath of the prophet" (*Kampf gegen Institutionen ist eine viel zu langatmige Sache für den Sturmatem des Profeten*). [GS2 1050].

institutionalism and its novelty? What is it that he does? I think that the first premise could be that Rosenzweig opposes the institution and state[254] (Hegel's state, but not only his) with the house. "The chamber of the Jewish heart is at home" [SE1 410; SE 362; SG 346], and it is in the home that begins and ends "the struggle against death" (in the previous section he speaks about marriage and sexual difference).[255]

Franz Rosenzweig speaks of institutions in which there is no life. In two different places in his texts (from the second half of 1919), he presents the confrontation between life and the institution, the house and the institution, all the while (pro)claiming a new institution that is to be an alternative to the university. (He founded his 'counter-institution', "Lehrhaus Forschungsinstitut" in Frankfurt in 1920.) What, then, is a house for Rosenzweig? It ought to protect life and be separated from the city, just as dwelling out to be separated from other city activities.

> We can no longer wish to remain naked people. We look 'backward', but not in a way for us to sacrifice our living life to the image of the holy institution that destroys life. No, the institution may only be house, we must know and render true that we are more than an institution, a living Jewish people. (*Wir können heute nicht mehr nackte Menschen bleiben wollen. Wir sehen "zurück" aber nicht so, dass wir unser lebendiges Leben wieder dem lebenzerstörenden Bild einer heiligen Institution opfern würden. Nein, die Institution darf uns nur Haus sein, wir müssen es wissen und wahrmachen, dass wir mehr sind als die Institution, lebendige jüdische Menschen*).[256]

This passage – from a lecture note – appears as the reconstruction of a fragment from a letter to Rudolf Ehrenberg (of 17 August 1919). In both the letter and the lecture, Rosenzweig goes back and forth. In the letter, he writes:

> I do not understand how someone can persist in petrifying people into institutions. We are otherwise happy when able to revive the institution. Here too is real, living, true life good enough to be built into the corner stone of the institution, yet for which no one knows when or even whether it will be built (*Ich begreife nicht wie man daran hängen kann,*

---

[254] In his 1920 lecture, "Der Jude im Staat," complete with his reservations towards Zionism, Rosenzweig insists that the state in or for Jews was "*nicht lebendig.*" "*Der Jude muss im Staat sein, weil der Staat nicht im Juden sein kann.*" [GS3 554].

[255] In the following, third, book of *Stern*, "Die Strahlen oder der ewiger Weg," Rosenzweig is even more precise: "*Das ewige Volk ruht schon im Hause des Lebens; die Völker der Welt bleiben auf dem Weg*" [SE1 471; SE 397; SG 346].

[256] This is a note for the lecture "Lessings Nathan" Rosenzweig held at the end of December 1919. [GS3 450].

Menschen zu Institutionen zu versteinern. Sonst ist man froh, wenn man Institutionen menschlich beleben kann. Und hier ist ein wirkliches, lebendiges, tatsächliches Leben grade gut genug dazu, in den Grundstein einer Institution eingemauert zu werden, von der keiner weiss, ob überhaupt und wenn, wie sie gebaut werden wird).[257]

The institution stands in opposition to life (Rosenzweig first separates them, speaking of the 'naked' Institution and naked man), turns life to stone; yet this simultaneously announces the possibility of life not only capable of reviving the institution, but also able to *a priori* be in the background and in the foundation of some institutions which do not yet exist, which are yet to come, which we await. "We are otherwise happy when able to revive the institution" (*Sonst ist man froh, wenn man Institutionen menschlich beleben kann*). The institution is not only capable of preserving life (not only ought it protect life), but the reverse is also true: we are the ones capable of preserving the life of the institution, to announce its new life and revive it, to expect it entirely new and alive.

It seems to me that the idea that *we alone* (*Wir allein*), our very own common life can constitute a home or an entirely new institution that has all the characteristics of a new and living house (one that does not petrify us, nor that we petrify and move away from). This is the beginning of Rosenzweig's engagement in whose service are all the concepts he uses.[258] At the very beginning of this book, Rosenzweig anticipate the first person plural, 'We' (a pronoun almost never thematized in the history of Western thought), and this is the introduction into the construction of a community or reconstruction of an eternal community. Indeed, this is the basic theme of this book. Rosenzweig needs to show what it is that holds this community together or what binds us all into one entity, which as such is *a priori* outside time. The pronoun '*Wir*' appears at the beginning of the book in quotations marks, as part of the phrase '*Wir sind ewig*', referring to generational transmission, from grandparent to grandson. 'We' thus refers to a blood community, to eternity, common language, and a future that affirms the present. Later in the text, Rosenzweig uses '*Wir allein*' several times. In unit six, in which he writes about sin, *Wir* transforms into a very compact community equated with humanity or mankind (*Manschheit*), that is, Israel.[259]

---

[257] [GS2 640].

[258] Life is actually the unconditional condition of all that exists, the first concept and the concept that holds all other concepts in order as it constructs it. There is no better sentence about life than the one Rosenzweig writes in the conclusion of the third unit dedicated to "Jewish Essence:" "*Aber das lebendige Leben fragt ja nicht nach dem Wesen. Es lebt. Und indem es lebt, beantwortet es sich selbst alle Fragen, noch ehe es sie stellen kann.*" [SE1 387; SE 342; SG 327].

[259] In his 1922 lectures, published as "*Die Wissenschaft vom Menschen,*" Rosenzweig returns to the *Wir*. "*Mein Ich wird Wir. Im Wir sehe ich mich gleichzeitig von aussen und von innen*" [GS3 650].

This shift from a speech act to sin that closely binds the individuals of a community into Israel is entirely new and surprising.

Constructing 'Wir' or the phrase "*Wir sind ewig*" is the axle that holds all other concepts together, giving place to all concepts in a stable order. The various concepts could be divided into a few groups. The first set would include the already mentioned first and crucial articles that determine the difference between Judaism and Christianity. They eminently determine what is Judaism: it is a 'people' ('chosen', 'holy', 'first' – these attributes have complementary function), it is 'blood', always opposed to 'will' and 'spirit', it is (holy) 'language' and writing, it is (holy) 'law', and finally, 'land' or 'territory', which implies "Israel." Everything Rosenzweig wrote at the time with regard to land and territory would today certainly demand complete revision, in the context of the newly-formed state of Israel. Nevertheless, however much the contemporary reader finds Rosenzweig's anti-Zionism hard to understand and perhaps too aggressive and decadent, a hundred years or even seventy years since the founding of Israel, I find his conclusions and arguments still inspiring indeed.

The following group of terms simultaneously directs and revises all the terms, and in a particular way confirms the self-construction of the 'We-axle' or pure flame: this is 'time' or the uses of time and understanding of time always in harmony with eternity. (Rosenzweig insists on an annual cycle that ensures Judaism its eternity; he then further processes all the crucial holy days that regenerate and hold the people together; finally, he constantly mentions the 'present' and 'now', which reflect eternity by excluding the temporality of time.) The group further includes the term 'border', thematized ingeniously in only one place in the book, but further developed in his geopolitical texts from the last period of the war. (A sort of theory of the border in Rosenzweig is a combination of three different sources: Hegel – whose variations on *Schranke* and *Grenze* are crucial for understanding his logic and his system in general; Rosenzweig's experience as soldier studying maps and thinks borders in the context of crossing, shifting, fluidity; and Rosenzweig the Talmudist, translator and reader of the world text, always distinguishing and separating significance and meaning.) Finally, the last term in this unit is 'Messiah' ("the future of the Messiah, which is surely drawing near"[260]) and 'messianism', named in the second to last unit of this book as "*messianische Politik*," implying the existence of something we might call 'messianic action'.

At the beginning of this unit, Rosenzweig attempts to explain the 'messianic protocol' as such, through an important explanation about the Jewish people, finally "at its goal" (*am Ziel*): "In the cycle of its year the future is the motive power; the circular movement does not give birth as it were by push (*durch*

---

[260] "*Und die Gesänge des „dritten Mahls", zu dem sich im Dämmer des versinkenden Tages Greise und Kinder am langen gedeckten Tische vereinen, sind ganz trunken von dem Rausch der gewißlich nahenden Zukunft des Messias*" [SE1 393; SE 347; SG 332].

Stoß), but by tug (*sondern durch Zug*); the present elapses, not because the past shoves it forward, but because the future drags it along."[261] Rosenzweig additionally explains the difference between the words *Stoß* and *Zug*, both carrying multiple meanings, in the second part of the sentence: the present elapses primarily because the future drags it along (*die Zukunft sie [die Gegenwart] heranreißt*). The future being strength (the future does not contain strength, but is strength, says Rosenzweig) *pulls out* the present. The construction of this sentence, in which the 'messianic topology', and in general 'messianic action' or 'messianic movement', is 'most clearly' described, can perhaps be part of an ideal introduction into the theory of messianic time. Rosenzweig's contribution and decisive turn is not achieved by simply opposing the strength of the future to that of the past, nor by the substitution of two forms of movement ('pushing' with 'pulling'), but by the use of the word *Zug* (*sondern durch Zug*). Rosenzweig's *durch Zug* assumes a sudden and surprising pulling out of something hidden, something from a hole. 'The messianic' is double: it is always present as hidden in the now ("today is not yet the true 'Today'"), and it appears suddenly and from a spasm.

The third and fourth group of concepts is particularly interesting. Rosenzweig incorporates them into the 'We axle' as two dimensions that are new and crucial for the ontology of the eternal flame that constitutes itself. The third group refers to the 'community', and comprises three passages subsequently entitled with 'sociology'. In it, the community is elaborated in detail. (Three other sections of the second book of the third part of *Stern* are entitled 'sociology.) The fourth group of terms could be reduced to the name 'state' or potentially 'of the world', rather than politics or 'messianic politics'.

Three chapters of the second edition carry titles containing the word 'sociology': "Soziologie der Menge: das Hören" (Sociology of The Crowd: Listening – not capitalized in the original edition), "Soziologie der Gemeinschaft: das Mahl" (Sociology of The Community), and finally "Soziologie des Ganzen: der Gruss" (Sociology of The Whole: The Greeting). These last two have a reduced status in comparison to the other six units of the book. With these three, Rosenzweig is attempting to reconstruct the community (or 'Jewish community') by way of a few sub-concepts. These are 'silence', 'listening', 'meal', 'greeting', 'rest', and 'discipline'. (I believe these terms to be more significant over all the others that occur more than once.) All these protocols produce a network that constitutes a community, connect individuals into a 'We'. Rosenzweig's originality in this respect is to introduce into social ontology something entirely new and surprising, which he has drawn from living Jewish tradition, its laws and mandates.

---

[261] "*In dem Kreislauf seines Jahres ist die Zukunft die bewegende Kraft; die kreisende Bewegung entsteht gewissermaßen nicht durch Stoß, sondern durch Zug; die Gegenwart verstreicht, nicht weil die Vergangenheit sie weiterschiebt, sondern weil die Zukunft sie heranreißt.*" [SE1 412; SE 364; SG 348]

'Silence'. Even when speaking of holy language, Rosenzweig insists on "the power of silence" (*Macht des Schweigens*). "With his brother he therefore cannot speak at all; with him the glance informs him better than the word, and there is nothing more deeply Jewish than a final suspicion of the power of the word and a heart-felt confidence in the power of silence." [SE1 380; SE 335; SG 321]. What is the function of the word or of dialogue, and what is role of "mutual silence (*das gemeinsame Schweigen*)? At the beginning of unit 5, he writes: "Because in eternity the word ceases to exist in the silence of the harmonious gathering (*im Schweigen des einträchtigen Beisammenseins*) – for we are united only in silence; the word unites, but those who are united grow silent (*denn nur im Schweigen ist man vereint, das Wort vereinigt, aber die Vereinigten schweigen*) – therefore the burning mirror that collects the sunbeams of eternity in the tiny cycle of the year, the liturgy, must introduce man into this silence" [SE1 388; SE 343; SG 327].

'Listening'. The brief chapter "Soziologie der Menge: das Hören" sketches a theory of listening that leads to the community of all who listen a written text. Rosenzweig presents his own experience of lecturing: "The sermon like the text read aloud is itself there to produce the mutual silence of the gathered community (*Die Predigt wie der verlesene Text selber ist dazu da, das gemeinsame Schweigen der versammelten Gemeinde zu schaffen*). And its essence is therefore not that it is a speech but exegesis; the reading out of the written word is the main thing (*die Verlesung des Schriftworts ist die Hauptsache*); in it alone the mutuality of the listening (*die Gemeinsamkeit des Hörens*) and hence the firm ground of all the mutuality of those gathered (*Gemeinsamkeit der Versammelten*) is produced" [SE1 389; SE 344; SG 329]. Learning how to listen means learning in a way that does not stimulate speaking or the speech of one speaking; rather, listening such that the answer is relinquished while simultaneously encouraging all to listen (each other). "The silent listening (*Das schweigende Hören*) was only the beginning of the mutual participation" [SE1 395; SE 349; SG 334].

'Rest'. The chapter that speaks of rest (*Ruhe*) (which also unifies) is specific in that Rosenzweig uses the word '*Einsetzung*' to mean Sabbat three times (the word is usually translated with 'institution'), and only on the fourth occasion insisting that in the house "the day of rest instituted" (*der Ruhetag eingesetzt*) [SE1 395; SE 348; SG 333]. Rest means to reacquaint oneself once again with silence and listening, eschewing idle chatter.

'Meal'. Each of these terms align and gather into a community of all. In the unit entitled "*Soziologie der Gemeinschaft: das Mahl*" (Sociology of the Community: The Meal) all these terms finally combine to participate equally in the order of the house: "The mutual life (*Das gemeinsame Leben*) that is thus born is to be a silent life (*ein schweigendes Leben*), living silence (*lebendiges Schweigen*); so we can only wait to find it in bodily life (*leiblichen Leben*). The creation in another way, the exchanging of the out-dated material takes place in the meal. For the individual, eating and drinking are already the new birth of the bodily man (*leiblichen Menschen*). For the community, the meal together (*gemeinsame Mahl*) is also the treatment in which it is born again to conscious life (*bewußten Leben*). The silent mutuality of listening and obeying already founds the smallest of communities, that of the home" (*Die schweigende Gemeinsamkeit des Hörens und Gehorchens stiftet schon die kleinste Gemeinschaft, die des Hauses*). This addition and new term appearing in the home simultaneously with the appearance of the meal and common feast – 'obeying' – is immediately deconstructed, with Rosenzweig insisting that all are equal at the table, that "the mutual life of the home does not live in the mutual obeying." Most importantly, however, at the table, there is no conversation. "Speaking can be done in the street and marketplace with chance meetings; in comparison, a meal together always means a real, realized and active community (*eine wirkliche, bewirkte und wirkende Gemeinschaft*). In this wordless mutuality in itself of the meal is taken mutually, the mutuality is presented as a real mutual participation animated in life (*Gemeinschaft als eine wirkliche im Leben lebendige dargestellt*). Where a meal is taken together, there such mutual participation exists. It is so in the home, but so too in monasteries, lodges, casinos, associations. And where mutual participation is lacking, as in classrooms or even in just university lectures, or even seminar practices, it does not exist, although the foundation of mutual participation (*das wirkliche Gemeinschaftsleben*), the mutual listening is indeed by all means here" [SE1 396; SE 349–350; SG 334].

'Greeting'. In the conclusion of the fifth unit, in which he states that during holidays the community celebrates itself at mealtime, Rosenzweig also warns that "mans has as little stopped at the inn of the mutuality of the last silence as in the holidays of the mutual listening" (*der Mensch schon in die Gemeinsamkeit des letzten Schweigens eingekehrt*). There is something higher, he adds, "and this that is higher may even be located at the outermost border of the mutual participation and be mutuality beyond the mutual life" (*und sei dies Höhere auch an der* äußersten *Grenze der Gemeinschaft gelegen und eine Gemeinsamkeit jenseits des gemeinsamen Lebens*) [SE1 403; SE 357; SG 340–341]. What is this 'higher', and what is at the border of the community? Rosenzweig differentiates the silence of listeners to lectures, which is the silence of each individual separately, from the silence during mealtime, in which others cease to be others. "One is greeted when encountered (*Man grüßt sich, wenn man sich begegnet*). The greeting is the supreme sign of silence (*höchste Zeichen des Schweigens*): they are silent because they know each other (*man schweigt, weil man einander kennt*). (…) Only if everything were silent would the silence be perfect and the mutual participation all-mutual (*die Gemeinschaft all-gemein*). The greeting of all to all (*Aller an Alle*), wherein this fully mutual silence would show itself, would have, like every greeting would have at least one's announcement and the exchange of a few words, the mutual listening and the mutual meal as the supposition. But how is this greeting of all to all supposed to happen?" (*Wie aber soll dieser Gruß Aller an Alle geschehen?*) [SE1 403; SE 357–358; SG 341].

'Discipline'. Rosenzweig's example of a higher order, disciplined community, one containing "the greeting of all to all" (*Aller an Alle*) is the military. Soldiers or "comrades" ought to achieve the greatest unity in discipline. This is Rosenzweig's introduction "into the universal mutual participation (*Allgemeinschaft*) where everyone knows everyone and greets him without words – face to face" (*von Angesicht zu Angesicht*) [SE1 406; SE 359; SG 343]. 'Discipline' is here a new and auxiliary term that first appears at the moment where Rosenzweig needs to explain what is obedience, mentioning "*die Zucht des gemeinsamen Gehorchens geben*" (the discipline of mutual obeying).[262] "But what it does not give is the feeling of freedom that only a mutual life conjures up before the never dwindling background of this mutual discipline (*das vor dem nie schwindenden Hintergrunde jener gemeinsamen Zucht: erst ein gemeinsames Leben hervorzaubert*). Such a mutual life as it is presented in the meal together is also not yet that which is last, as little as is the listening together (*gemeinsame Hören*). But on the road of education toward this last, the mutual silence (*gemeinsamen Schweigen*), this is the second halting-place (*die zweite Station*), while the listening is the first one" [SE1 397; SE 351; SG 335]. Discipline or a disciplined military as a new and higher constitution of a people as an armed group or a people as an army is condition upon Rosenzweig's remark that common meal determines a people to be free, which instantly opens up the danger of begin destroyed. The community achieved in common mealtime as a symbol of freedom and independence necessarily implies danger. "Not only today have there been rebellions against us to annihilate us, but in each generation back to that first one that migrated from Egypt—and in each generation God has saved us" [SE1 400; SE 353; SG 337].

The fourth group of terms appears in the finale of this book, unit seven, "Die Völker der Welt: Messianische Politik" (The Peoples of The World: Messianic Politics). These are: '(holy) war', 'pacifist' or 'pacifism', 'people', 'peace', 'world', 'state', 'right', 'violence'. Rosenzweig's great project on the war is here condensed and abandoned for good in favor of a form of pacifism or a "messianic dilemma" with regard to pacifism that decisively orients the holy people. The war project – let us call it "war" and accept that it was nothing but an ingenious project – was given different code names by Rosenzweig: "*Kriegsopera*," "*Putzianum*," "*Hansiaca*," "*Kriegsausgang*," and "*Kriegsgrund*," as well as "*Theatrum Europaeum. Ein Versuch über den Schauplatz der Weltgeschichte.*"[263] After many

---

[262] I have modified the English translation here, replacing the word 'cultivation' with 'discipline'.

[263] In the three letters sent to three different address in the first half of 1917, Rosenzweig explains in detail the origin of his idea for a big book on the war and says he has begun writing, aware that he would be unable to finish the whole project during his time on the front. For us it is certainly important to notice that "Globus," conspicuously longer than the other ten, is the basic part of the first projected book, and that the other texts are miniature

twists and turns, and many attempts – lest we forget, in August and September 1916, Rosenzweig is convinced that pacifism ought to be abandoned because "ultimate peace" (*Endfrieden*) is not man's work (*Menschenwerk*) but a direct act of God (*Einwirkung Gottes*) [GS1 204], while in December of 1922 he still mentions the inadequacy of believing in pacifism and the power of "spiritual arms" [GS1 874] – perhaps it is now possible to insist on two of Rosenzweig's suggestions. Both suggestions about the role of pacifism in war ("messianic and world war") are based in his acceptance of violence, and the belief that it is really possible to achieve by means of war something not otherwise achievable by peaceful means (based on his theory of two peaces or two kinds of pacifism). Hence, Rosenzweig is completely certain, as is Walter Benjamin for example, that violence can make something (that violence makes a new right or justice, or that by way of violence an old justice becomes some new justice) [SE1 418; SE 370; SG 352–353]. Also, the geopolitical construction helps Rosenzweig claim that only by means of war could the transition of national states and Europe be completed into the planet and the world (war as transition). It also allows him to claim war as a sort of subject (God), deciding on its own beginning, duration and end ("*Der Krieg ist der große Entscheider*").[264] In an unusually important and detailed letter to his parents from 1 September 1916 [GS1 210–214], he writes about peace before (on the brink) of a possible war, that is of peace that exists in paradise (*paradiesischen*) and of the peace after the war

---

pieces and portions of that same big book. He tells us that in 1910 or 1911, while writing his thesis on Hegel and the state, he intended to write the history of grounds for war (*Kriegsgrund*). He hastens to finish his doctorate so as to dedicate himself to this task, since on 25 November 1910, Carnegie established a foundation financing projects that deal with the causes and origins of war. In the three letters of January, March and May of 1917 [GS1 334–335, 375, 395] Rosenzweig offers a few more details: that he wished to analyze wars from 1494 until today, that he is particularly interested in the relationship between the grounds for war (*Kriegsgründen*) and beginning of war (*Kriegsanfängen*). He adds that he writes primarily about what is currently taking place, that previously he wished to work in diplomatic archives and examine everything that grounds war, that is, the reasoning that would lead to the beginning of wars. Yet, he also says that he could never write such a book at present, that if he were to write it now, it would be part of some larger book, which demands even more time. Ultimately, this is why he must 'abort' the book…

[264] Cf. Rosenzweig often speaks of war that decides and judges, mostly in the texts "Globus" and "Vox Dei," "Die Gewissensfrage der Demokratie." [GS3 279] "*Der Krieg ist ein "göttliches Gericht", aber kein einfaches Strafgericht, sondern "Krisis," Scheidung, Böcke und Schafe*" [GS1 350]. In *Stern* he writes: "*Der Krieg allein, der über das Bewußtsein der Einzelnen hinwegrast, entscheidet.*" [SE1 416; SE 367–368; SG 351].

(or wars) that exists in the time of the Messiah and the thousand year reign. The first peace (the natural state or natural peace), taken care of by the so-called materialist pacifism, is a peace between creations and things that have no connection among themselves, where the frictions and tears are brought to a minimum, and identities and entities are completely separated one from another. In international relations, such a peace is founded on a tolerance of all peoples. The second peace, or the second world peace, the idealistic, messianic (*idealistischen, messianischen*), around which idealistic pacifism is organized, arrives after the last war. (Rosenzweig notes that it is advocated by German thinkers.) Such peace means a close connection of people and peoples, questions the reasons behind wars, and tries to transform them into reasons for peace and a new life of togetherness. The condition of this new peace and the stake of idealistic pacifism, according to Rosenzweig, is the last war.

This also shows, continues Rosenzweig, that the national and liberal states are in their beginnings (*in ihren Anfängen*) *einen pazifistischen Zug*. Both of these formulations, the pessimistic – that pacifism does not achieve true world peace and freedom, but only imperial peace determined by borders and governments, and the optimistic, whereby ("idealistic") pacifism is the part of the war machine that tears down state borders – alter the meaning of the phrase "*pazifistischer Zug*." The idea (of the national or liberal state) does not contain the *Zug*, but is the *Zug*. And it is the *Zug* at its very beginning, at the moment of its constituting. However, that which is at the beginning of its constitution is also really the beginning of its future end. To be or to have "*pazifistischer Zug*" means at the end to cease to be or cease having sovereignty – not being a national state. Thus, in a different register, Rosenzweig finds within (the main characteristics of) the state – violence, war, and revolution – precisely those elements that will completely destroy the state. "*Pazifistischer Zug*," as a deconstructive or affirmative element found within the construction and foundation of the national state itself, is foreshadowed in several places in "The Peoples of the World: Messianic Politics." This is done as Rosenzweig, with surprising inspiration, speaks of the state and of the Jewish people's resistance to having their own state, as well of the Jews (potentially) belonging to the peoples of the world due to this state. He reveals that there is something which contradicts the Jewish people within the state, something alternative, which, paradoxically, has the power to take away eternity from the eternal people. And he confirms the potential of the state to achieve something new and alternative ("if the State could get what it is reaching for"), and as a result "the people have become master over its enemy" [SE1 420; SE 371; SG 354]. Is a possible "*Pazifistischer Zug*" of the state of Israel not indicated by this?

But who reveals world peace and who is the ideal subject of pacifism? Who should be the agent of this process, according to Rosenzweig?

> Opposite this constant life in the war of faith (*Glaubenskrieg*), the Jewish people has its war of faith behind it in a mythic past. Therefore, all

wars that is still experiences are purely political wars (*rein politische Kriege*) for it. And since it does possess the concept of the war of faith, it therefore cannot take them seriously, like the ancient peoples for whom this concept was foreign (*fremd*). Of course, the Jew is really the only man in the Cristian world who cannot take war seriously, and therefore is the only genuine "pacifist." (...) by living the eternal peace, the Jewish people stands outside of a warlike temporality (*kriegerischen Zeitlichkeit*); by resting at the goal that it anticipates in hope, it is separated from the march of those who draw near to it in the toil of centuries.[265]

"Der Jude ist der einzige echte 'Pazifist'." "Ja der Jude ist eigentlich der einzige Mensch in der christlichen Welt, der den Krieg nicht ernst nehmen kann, und so ist er der einzige echte 'Pazifist'." The Jew is the real or the authentic "pacifist," because he cannot take seriously the wars Christian states lead one with another. Twice Rosenzweig underscores that the Jew "cannot" accept or give meaning to these political wars. They are foreign to him because they do not belong to the register or notion (*Begriff*) of religious wars. Regardless of the fact that in the chapter "War of Faith," which precedes this fragment, he says that as opposed to Christians, the Jewish people knows both types of war, and is the guardian of the knowledge of difference between them, and regardless of the fact that Rosenzweig unveils the possibility of existence of a another, "third" type of war (in which the religious and political are mixed) – the Jewish people remains completely outside the world, and outside "war temporality" (*kriegerischen Zeitlichkeit*). There are wars between states and peoples (in which peoples risk being annihilated. This is the main characteristic of so-called "political" wars: they are decided in a miraculous, completely mysterious way, by "God's will" or "war alone," and are beyond the consciousness of individuals. Is it really possible that such wars are completely without relevance for Rosenzweig, for a Jew? Did Rosenzweig's entire effort not precisely consist of the attempt to bridge the strict distinction between two kinds of wars within the Jewish political tradition, and to construct or renew the idea of last, messianic wars? If we leave aside his doubts, the dissatisfaction with the end of World War I and his abandonment of the *Kriegsgrund* project, what does it even mean to disregard political wars and to be the only genuine "pacifist?"

It seems to me that the correct answers to these difficult questions could justify not only the relevance of Rosenzweig's "argumentations" in favor of war (they are rather "argument sketches," intuitions, suggestions), but could also explain another epoch in the history of the Jewish people, which Rosenzweig did not have in mind – the Holocaust, forming of the state of Israel, its wars, new (preventive, asymmetrical) wars for world governance, etc. Although his political manifesto "The Peoples of the World: Messianic Politics" places the Jewish people beyond any state or conflict among states of the world, perhaps it

---

[265] [SE1 416; SE 368; SG 351].

may be possible to defend the consistency and logic of his project by "inscribing" the existence of the state of Israel into it. In the same vein, it seems important to espouse the paradoxical harmony of his project with the changes in the world that happened after his death.

The defense of Rosenzweig's engagement within a complex Jewish political tradition could move in three steps. The first step looks at the statement "*Der Jude ist der einzige echte 'Pazifist'.*" Purified of Rosenzweig's ambiguous use of quotation marks over the word pacifist and the controversial proximity of the words genuine and pacifist – is the Jew the only true and authentic pacifist or the only true and authentic "pacifist" (in the latter case, he is the only true pseudo-pacifist, or the real pacifist who is not a pacifist, a "militant pacifist")? – brings us back to the key word *der einzige*. Only the Jew is the true idealistic pacifist. In that context, the Jew is not interested in purely political wars, but what follows: true "Peace at all cost" which interrupts them. God (war) decides on its end, that is, the Messiah turns political wars into last wars, finally bringing about eternal peace.

Second step: Rosenzweig *de facto* guards the difference between religious war and ordinary war (*gewöhnlichen Kriegs*) [SE1 416; SE 367; SG 350]. Nevertheless, he very carefully opens up an uncertain field where this difference could be reduced. The existence of a large world war allows Rosenzweig to construct the idea of a political war or wars that cannot be interrupted before they become last and messianic wars. Only the last war can ever stop, and only when God's will brings it to an end or when the enemy unconditionally accepts peace. This is a novelty in the history of thought and justification of war.

Third step: A new world war, and the existence of the state of Israel and its wars, does not necessarily have to degrade Rosenzweig's project, nor the greatness of a people that was once "its goal." The issue is neither the closing nor the expansion of a particular state, but primarily a new speeding up of world history…the renewal of what Rosenzweig once, a long time ago, called *pazifistischer Zug*.

Further readings

Fisher, C., (2012), *Contemplative nation. A philosophical account of Jewish theological language*, Stanford Univ. Press, Stanford Calif.

Losch, A., (2015), Der Ewige" als „Synthese" des Stern. Der Gebrauch des Gottesnamens „der Ewige" bei Franz Rosenzweig, in: Naharaim 9 (2015) 195–215 [https://boris.unibe.ch/73752/1/naha-2015–0008.pdf]

Rubinstein, E., (1999), *An Episode of Jewish Romanticism. Franz Rosenzweig's The Star of Redemption*, State University of New York Press, Albany N.Y.

Part Three, Book Two: The Rays, or the Eternal Way

Ephraim Meir

In Part III of the *Star*, which discusses redemption as the relationship between man and the world, Rosenzweig creates a parallel between Jews (III.1) and Christians (III.2) before concluding that God is the "truth" above them (III.3). The two communities take part in this truth, which is higher than the truth experienced by either of these communities separately. Rosenzweig used older material in order to write III.1 and III.2. He was less excited about writing these sections, but curious about the outcome of III.3, which speaks of God as the "truth".

Rosenzweig describes how each community lives redemption differently: the intimate Jewish community lives eternity now, while the Christian missionary community involves itself in history and strives for eternity. Rosenzweig bases his thinking on Judaism with Christianity as its "antipodic child" not by analysing their respective faiths, but by using a quasi-sociological description of both communities. He writes on the Jewish people and on Christian individuals. The introverted Jewish life, which is, so to speak, not of this world, constitutes the "fire" of the *Star*. The "rays" of the *Star* are Christianity, involved in the world and working in history in order to bring people to the Father through the mediation of the crucified.

In Rosenzweig's view, Christians are eternally on the way, whereas Jews are the eternal people. They are related in a critical-complementary relationship.

How to cite this book chapter:
Meir, E. 2021. Part Three, Book Two: The Rays, or the Eternal Way. In: Brasser, M., Bojanić, P. and Ciglia, F. P. (eds.) The Star *for Beginners: Introductions to the Magnum Opus of Franz Rosenzweig*. Pp. 159–165. London: Ubiquity Press. DOI: https://doi.org/10.5334/bco.m. License: CC-BY

The relationship is unequal, because of the supremacy of Judaism over Christianity. Rosenzweig developed a rather positive attitude towards Christianity, but clearly favours Judaism. Jews anticipate the *eschaton*, whereas Christians strive to reach it by bringing the orientation of revelation in history. Judaism is rooted in itself, freed from time and history, whereas Christians work in the world and in history in order to vanquish paganism. Eternity is in the blood of the Jewish people, who transmit it from generation to generation. They have a land, a tongue and a law, all of which are eternal. The Jewish people are meta-historic, whereas other nations strive in vain for eternity in their respective States. Only the community of Christians represents an eternal way.

Throughout the *Star*, one finds philosophical reflections on politics and on aesthetics, both of which according to Rosenzweig represent a false striving for eternity. Also in III.2 it is clear that art and politics are not about real life. The plastic arts are mute and music is blind. Poetry is seen as the highest form of art, which is not surprising given Rosenzweig's predilection for language. In his philosophy of art, the applied arts of speech and gestures in liturgy receive special attention. In III.2 there is an ascending order of architecture, church music and dance. In III.2, he also develops a "messianic politics", in which he criticizes Hegel's problematic exaltation of the State and its inherent violence. In the midst of the collapse of the *Kaiserreich*, Rosenzweig becomes aware of eternity as a life outside the State and outside political life. Jews and Christians are associated with eternity; they are the "nevertheless" in the world against the world, beyond dominion and war.

As in I and II, Rosenzweig continues talking about the world (as in I.1), man (as in I.2) and God (as in I.3), as well as about creation (as in II.1), revelation (II.2) and redemption (II.3). III.1 and III.2 present old, known things, and Book Three (III.3) produces a thrill in him. III.1 on the Jewish people and III.2 on Christians are parallel responses to the revelation. III.3 is above them, like a lintel above doorposts.

At the start of Book Two, Rosenzweig brings Maimonides's characterization of Christianity as a "great error" ("*große Irreleitung*") and a "delusion" ("*Wahn*"). Christianity worships another beside God, but it paves the way for the Messiah to come. At the end of Book Two, in a kind of inclusion, he quotes Yehuda Halevi, who also gave a function to Christianity in the bringing of the Messiah. He uses Halevi's parable of the seed-kernel (Judaism) that falls in the earth: seemingly nothing remains of it, yet it becomes a big tree (Christianity and Islam) that brings forth the fruit (the Messiah) like the one out of which its seed once came. Maimonides's and Halevi's view on Christianity (not that on Islam) fit Rosenzweig's vision on Christianity as the "eternal path", complementary to Judaism as the "eternal way". Jews are the heart, the fire of the *Star*, Christians are the rays which shoot out. With this simile, Rosenzweig made it clear that the rays are nothing without the fire, whereas the fire needs to recognize the rays.

Immediately after Maimonides's evaluation of Christianity, Rosenzweig reflects on the relationship of Christians to time. Whereas the "eternal people" creates its own time, being on the bridge over the river of time, Christianity as the "eternal way" leads through time. Christians take up the contest with the river, they view the river as the flow of time from the steel tracks and the river is for them only a sign that they are on their way. They come from a place and go to a place "beyond" the river and so, they get power over time. Christians live always in the present, since what is before Christ is the past, whereas the future is Christ's expected return and the last judgment.

Rosenzweig depicts eternal life and the eternal way as both eternal. Yet, in his geometrical thought, they are as different as the infinity of a point and of a line. The point in its infinity is never wiped away, it is self-preserved. The infinity of the line consists in its unlimited extension. In non-figurative language: Christianity must always spread further, it must be missionary, just as it is necessary for Judaism to seal itself off. Begetting (*Erzeugen*) in Judaism is bearing witness (*Zeugnis*) for eternity; in Christianity one bears witness in faith, which is faith in the way. The Christian faith is faith in something, while the Jew does not have faith in something, he himself incarnates faith; the Jewish faith is the product of begetting. Rosenzweig explains that, on the eternal way, individuals are united to mutual action in the world. *Ecclesia* is the assembly of individuals, who bear testimony to Christ. A bond of brotherliness "in the Lord" unites people beyond differences of sex, age, class and race.

In III.2 Rosenzweig points to many other differences between Jews and Christians. Whereas the Christian experiences his Christianity in the brother who stands nearest, the Jew lives eternity in the oldest and the youngest, in the grandfather who is blessing and the grandchild who receives the blessing. The Christian in his faith goes back to the first Christian, the Jew in hope looks forward to the last days, to the Davidic Messiah. The Jew is rooted in himself, the Christian looks for expansion and mission. Another great difference between the twin religions lies in the fact that Judaism is the one people and the eternal people that carries oppositions in itself, whereas the peoples of the world meet the oppositions where they are separated the one against the other.

Rosenzweig specifies how God, man and the world are conceived differently in both responses to the divine revelation. In the elucidation of the different views on God, man and the world, Rosenzweig develops a hierarchical thinking: he has a clear preference for the oneness in Judaism that contrasts with the duality in Christianity. The Christian way makes man, world and God into Christian man, Christian world and Christian God: the way of the Christian is through the world, along the river of time. In the Jewish view, God, man and the world are conceived differently.

For the Jew, God is just and loving, creator and revealer; divine love and divine justice go together. The Christian has a twofold approach to God. There is the Father and the Son: only through the Son, who is a man, does one dare to approach the Father. With God who became man in Christianity, Rosenzweig sees a piece of paganism. With this God who must be man, the Christian walks with trust through life, as a brother in the Lord. Yet, he also goes another way, the way with the Father in the sphere of truth. This twofold way to God is not existent in Judaism. Both God and man are approached differently in Judaism and Christianity. A Jew is human and Jewish, loving God and beloved by God, but these oppositions come together in one person. In the Christian, these oppositions or separated ways clash. The same is true for the approach to the world. For the Jew, the world is full of slippery transitions between this world and the future world, whereas the Christian lives the twofold order of State and Church.

Before analyzing the spiritual year of Christians as parallel to that of Jews, Rosenzweig brings his reflections on art and its relation to the community of faith. Whereas III.1 dealt with the Jewish yearly circle in which mutuality is lived, III.2 discusses the Christian yearly circle that prepares the individual soul for mutuality. It is in this perspective that art, more specifically applied art, plays an enormous role in Christianity. Rosenzweig compares art with an attentive woman who takes care of her household through daily services and gives her husband strength for the great hours of public life. Many buildings serve multiple purposes; the house of God, however, has only one aim: one lingers in it in order to stay in mutuality with others in one room. Architecture and painting are helpful in realizing this goal. The garment of the priest is strictly for worship. The activity of the priest can only take place with specific clothing. His garment, strictly for worship, hides his personality, but brings a beyond.

After these preparatory remarks, Rosenzweig proceeds to depict the Christian yearly cycle. In his analysis of the Jewish and Christian calendars, he was influenced heavily by Rosenstock's calendar thinking: time was linked to calendars. The word had a great role in the different liturgies. Whereas in Jewish liturgy, the word is a symbol of the already established mutuality, in Christian services the word takes the individual by the hand and leads him to mutuality. We meet here again Rosenzweig's basic idea that the Jewish collective is a fact and that Christians are individuals who are still on their way to the aim that Jews have already reached. Augustine and Luther made the word into a sacrament that prepares the individual. As in Judaism, Christianity has a holiday of mutual listening. Significantly, the seventh day became in Christianity the first day. For Christians as eternal beginners and people with eternal youth, Sunday is the day of spiritual refreshment, the beginning of the week. Jews on Sabbath commemorate the divine rest on the seventh day and the freedom from the house of slavery in Egypt.

Rosenzweig parallels the first Sunday of Advent somehow with the Day of Atonement. However, Yom Kippur celebrates redemption and does not fall as a rule on a Sabbath, although it has an increasingly Sabbath–like character. Also the first Sunday of Advent has increasing Sunday-like radiance and announces the beginning revelation.

Like in Judaism, Christians have three holiday periods. Again Rosenzweig makes some remarks on art, this time on church music, inserted in the three festivals. Ecclesiastic music soars out of the artificial frame of "ideal time", just as ecclesiastical architecture and painting soar out of the artificial frame of "ideal space". In the Church application of music, music functions within the Christian chronology that is characterized by the central, epoch-making event of Christ's birth, with times before and after this event. It creates "real time". As architecture and painting, music prepares the individual soul onto the mutual way, it awakens each individual to the same feelings.

The sacrament of Holy Communion is distinguished from the Seder, from which it originates. Whereas the Seder is the festival of commemoration, Holy Communion belongs to the holiday of the way. In the Seder, mutual life becomes visible; in Holy Communion, each individual participates in the meal. The entire Seder is pervaded with hope for redemption, while Holy Communion is the sacrament of revelation.

The three Christian holiday periods start with Christmas at the beginning of the liturgical year. In Judaism, Pesach as the holiday of freedom of the people starts the liturgical year; in Christianity it is the birth of Christ, as the creation of revelation. Before Christmas, Advent brings the prophecies of the "Old" Covenant. After Christmas, the New Year and the holiday of the Three Kings bring secular life and faith together; redemption rings out. The Epiphany anticipates the future adoration of the divine child by all.

The Easter holidays are the real holidays of revelation. Parallel to the miracle at Sinai with the gift of the Torah after the Exodus (that has to be remembered), the Cross and not the manger are permanently before Christian eyes. The Christian greets the head full of blood and wounds: he is face to face with Christ. The entire holiday time, from fasting during Lent through Good Friday until the Pascha, prepares him for the central event in Christian life: the holiday of the revelation of redemption.

Pentecost, the third holiday, is dedicated to redemption. Just as Succot recalls the final rest only in the provisional one, Pentecost recalls the beginning of redemption. In Pentecost, the Church mastering all tongues acts in the world. Using a Jewish phraseology, Rosenzweig writes that God speaks everywhere with the words of man. However, Pentecost remains merely a first glance up to redemption. Rosenzweig notes that Christians do not have a special holiday of redemption, they do not have something similar to the Days of Awe. These days are lacking in the Christian calendar. Christmas celebrates the beginning, Yom Kippur the completion. In a sentence that encapsulates Rosenzweig's entire view on Christianity, he writes that in the Christian consciousness, the difference between revelation and redemption is blurred. The distinction between revelation and redemption is the eminently Jewish element in the *Star*.

Rosenzweig also pays attention to the commemorative holidays of Tisha be-Av, Purim and Hanukkah, which are extraneous to the Torah. These historical holidays became fixed, like the entire Jewish history. The historical memorial days of Christians are different: birthdays of kings or holidays for liberation last as long as the State lasts, they satisfy people as a sign of their permanence through their temporality and alteration.

The Church, Rosenzweig concludes, is a kind of mission to the pagans. It casts its transfiguring light upon nations, sowing eternity into the living. The Church participates in the life of the nations, but brings also its own history, for instance in the holiday of the reformation or the holidays of the saints.

Rosenzweig resumes his position towards Christianity again when writing on mutual kneeling. Mutual kneeling characterizes the Christian festivals: one kneels in front of the manger, in front of the Cross and before the transubstantiation in the Mass. Yet, only in Judaism, Rosenzweig maintains, the bending of every knee is celebrated in special holidays, the holidays of redemption. Only Jews with mutual kneeling live the eternity of redemption. Genuflection as the final redemption remains foreign to Christianity. Christians are on the way, they celebrate redemption in holidays of time.

At this point, Rosenzweig again discusses art, this time the art of poetry, but also gestures, dance and glance. As architecture and music, poetry had to leave its "ideal world" in favor of the "real world". Finally, poetry had to learn to be silent. Gestures, most of all kneeling, concern the whole man and are beyond action and speech. Again Rosenzweig jumps to the Jewish world in order to explain the importance of gestures. In the Jerusalem Temple, there was not even the smallest open place in the crowd that gathered in the forecourt, but when they fell face down, there was plenty of space.

Also outside the churches, in parades and processions and in plays such as Oberammergau, Christianity manifests itself. Rosenzweig discusses dance, collective dance, but also the dance of the individual, which is the first gesture. The simplest gesture is the glance: one may forget a word, but an eye that has glanced at us once, he writes, beholds us as long as we live. In his description of the Christian liturgy, Rosenzweig constantly returns to his basic scheme in which the Jews live eternal life, whereas Christians are the eternal way. Dance, for instance, is not performed in the Church, the procession goes out into the city. In Judaism, that celebrates redemption in the closed circle of the community, dance takes place on Simhat Torah, inside the house of God. And the Hasid dances, praising God "with all his bones". Christians are on their way: in the Christian mindset, baptism brings the individual on his way towards redemption. Of the five other sacraments that accompany a person through the events of his life and bring him towards redemption (the Eucharist being the sacrament of revelation), baptism is the central one.

Christianity, Rosenzweig repeats in conclusion, is young. The eternal people rests in the house of life; the nations remain on the way, and their way is the way of the Cross. The State with its incessant goals and war cry competes with Jewish life that has reached the goal. Art competes with the Christian way of the Cross. It is under the Cross that the Christian knows himself one with all souls.

Instead of artistic concentration upon the own suffering, it is the incomparable suffering on the Cross that unites souls who, on their way, experience eternity.

In a somewhat problematic phrasing, Rosenzweig writes that the Christian focuses upon the blood that flows from the Cross; it runs from the Cross into his veins, but the blood does not circulate in his veins themselves. The Christian feels the refreshment of the circulation of the blood from the Cross running in his veins and from there, it flows downward in the ocean of history. Continuing his metaphoric language, Rosenzweig closes III.2 by returning to the Jewish people: only one single water on earth circles within itself, without inflow or outflow, not flowing into the sea. This wonder and scandal for others is the eternal people.

Though Rosenzweig greatly respected Christianity, his view as formulated in the *Star* starts with a certain superiority of Judaism in comparison with Christianity. In view of the attempt of his Christian friends to convert him, he considered his own Judaism as "the unutterable happiness of being a Jew". He saw Christianity as an important lifestyle next to the Jewish one and noted many parallels and differences between the two ways of life. Jews had a special function towards Christians, which consists in reminding Christians that they must not revert again to their previous pagan stage. Christianity illuminates the entire world; Jews with their unity between nation and religion remind the Christians that they are on their way. The synagogue looks prophetically into the future. The Church also wants eternity, and yet Christians are much more linked to history. They have the task of bringing pagans in history to the one God and to vanquish their own paganism. Rosenzweig could not conceive of his own self as separate from the image of the other. He strove for a critical complementary relationship: Christians need Jews as their source, and Jews need Christians as the "rays" of their "fire".

Further readings

Bowler, M. G., (1997), The Reconciliation of Church and Synagogue in Franz Rosenzweig, Ann Arbor Mich.

Dober, H. M., (1990), Die Zeit ernst nehmen. Studien zu Franz Rosenzweigs «Der Stern der Erlösung», Würzburg, Königshausen & Neumann.

Surall, F., (2003), Juden und Christen – Toleranz in neuer Perspektive: Der Denkweg Franz Rosenzweigs in seinen Bezügen zu Lessing, Harnack, Baeck und Rosenstock-Huessy, Gütersloh, Chr. Kaiser Gütersloher Verlagshaus.

Dritter Teil, Drittes Buch: Der Stern oder die ewige Wahrheit *und* Tor

Caspar Battegay

1. Fragestellung

Der letzte Teil des *Stern der Erlösung* ist nicht etwa mit „Epilog" oder „Schlusswort" überschrieben, sondern mit dem konkreten Wort *Tor*. Mit dieser architektonischen Metapher ist das Ende als Ausgang konstruiert. Dementsprechend lauten die letzten Worte von Franz Rosenzweigs Text: „Ins Leben" (SE 472). Auch typographisch wird diese Konstruktion mit dem Ausdünnen des Drucksatzes nachgeahmt. Das Ende verweist auf das Jenseits des Buches, das durch dieses „Tor" zu erreichen sei: Das bunte Leben. Das Ende bedeutet Anfang. Doch was bedeutet dieses Paradox?

Dieser Beitrag zum dritten Buch des dritten Teils des *Sterns* geht von dessen formaler Position als letztem Kapitel aus. Das heisst, es wird zu zeigen versucht, dass es in diesem Buch eine Rhetorik des Finalen, des Letzten, des Schliessens und Über-das-Ende-hinausgehens gibt, die mit Rosenzweigs inhaltlichen Thesen eng verbunden ist. Inhaltlich ist das letzte Kapitel ausdrücklich dem klassischen philosophischen und theologischen Thema der Wahrheit gewidmet. Die Grundfrage „Was ist Wahrheit?" (SE 429) bildet die Leitfrage des letzten Kapitels des *Sterns* und des *Tors*. In gewisser Weise ist das Thema der Wahrheit schon von Anfang an im *Stern* präsent. Dessen

---

How to cite this book chapter:
Battegay, C. 2021. Dritter Teil, Drittes Buch: Der Stern oder die ewige Wahrheit *und* Tor. In: Brasser, M., Bojanić, P. and Ciglia, F. P. (eds.) The Star *for Beginners: Introductions to the Magnum Opus of Franz Rosenzweig*. Pp. 167–183. London: Ubiquity Press. DOI: https://doi.org/10.5334/bco.n. License: CC-BY

Motto bildet der hebräische Vers aus Psalm 45,5, den Luther mit „Zieh einher der Wahrheit zugut" und Martin Buber mit „Reite für die Sache der Treue" übersetzt haben. Die Differenz zwischen den Übersetzungen liegt am unterschiedlichen Verständnis des hebräischen Wortes *emeth*, das üblicherweise mit Wahrheit übersetzt wird, aber eben auch Festigkeit, Beständigkeit oder Treue bedeuten kann. Am Ende des *Sterns* nimmt Rosenzweig sein biblisches Motto wieder auf und versucht nun, es auch philosophisch einzubetten. Während die erkenntnistheoretische Frage, ob und wie der menschliche Geist zu sicheren Wahrheiten gelangen kann, in philosophischen Systemen klassischerweise am Anfang steht, beschäftigt sich Rosenzweig erst am Schluss damit. Er bemerkt: „Die Wahrheit aber erscheint immer erst am Ende. Das Ende ist ihr Ort" (SE 443). Aber was heisst das? Geht es in Rosenzweigs Rede vom Ende um ein Ziel, sei es der Philosophie, der Moral, des Glaubens oder gar des Lebens selbst? Oder ist dieses Ende vielmehr formal auf seine Argumentation bezogen und meint ein Abschliessen des im Text Dargelegten, das Einsetzen eines finalen Schlusssteins im System? Was soll es heissen, dass der „Ort" der Wahrheit das Ende ist? Und was bedeutet schliesslich Rosenzweigs Emphase des Lebens am Schluss dieses philosophischen Werks, in dessen erstem Satz es heisst, dass jede Erkenntnis mit dem Tod beginnt? („Vom Tode, von der Furcht des Todes, hebt alles Erkennen des All an" (SE 3)). Was heisst „Leben" hier eigentlich? Was ist die Stellung dieses Begriffs im System des *Sterns* und wie sind die Begriffe „Leben" und „Wahrheit" mit einander verbunden?

Bevor es hier um diese Fragen gehen kann, also darum, was Rosenzweig über und von der Wahrheit denkt und wie die Wahrheit mit dem zentralen Begriff des Lebens verbunden ist, sollen in einem ersten Teil einige Überlegungen und Verweise zum literarischen und philosophischen Topos des Anfangs im Ende gemacht werden. Diese verschlungene Struktur hat eine lange geistesgeschichtliche Tradition. „Wenn immer auch im philosophischen oder wissenschaftlichen Diskurs von einem Ende die Rede ist […], markiert diese Rhetorik des Endens zugleich einen weiteren Anfang. Das Wort *Finis* weist auf diesen ambivalenten Status des Endes hin: das Ende schliesst nicht nur etwas ab (eine Geste, eine Inszenierung, eine Erzählung), es markiert zugleich eine Grenze, einen Übergang."[266] Ähnlich wie das Wort „Finis", mit dem Johann Wolfgang Goethe das Ende des *Faust* bezeichnet, bezeichnet auch die Überschrift *Tor* dieses Oszillieren zwischen Ende und Anfang und in gewisser Weise „das Ende als Modus des Überlebens"[267]. Das heisst, dass erst im Enden ein Autor sich seiner Unsterblichkeit und ein Text sich seines immer wieder aufs Neue zu bewährenden Sinns versichert.

---

[266] Peter Brandes/Burkhardt Lindner, Einleitung, in: dies. (Hg.), Finis. Paradoxien des Endens, Würzburg 2009, 7–17, hier 9.

[267] Peter Brandes, Rhetorik der Vollendung (Ovid, Goethe), in: Finis. Paradoxien des Endens, 35–50, hier 50.

Anschaulich wird das, wenn man sich zum Beispiel den sprichwörtlich gewordenen letzten Satz eines berühmten Märchens, des in den *Kinder- und Hausmärchen* von Jacob und Wilhelm Grimm enthaltenen *Dornröschens*, in Erinnerung ruft: „ [...] und sie lebten vergnügt bis an ihr Ende."[268] Das Ende der Erzählung stellt kein absolutes Ende dar, sondern den Übergang in das Leben, das nun die in der Geschichte gelernte Moral bei jedem Erzählen neu bewähren muss. Nicht umsonst enden so viele Märchen mit einer Hochzeit, ein Übergangsritual, das Sinn stiftet und in dem gleichzeitig etwas zu einem Ende kommt (das ledige Leben von Braut und Bräutigam) und immer wieder etwas Neues beginnt (das Leben als Paar und die neue Familie).

Letzte Sätze nehmen in vielerlei Hinsicht eine spezielle Position in einem Werk ein. Sie können als Pointe einem Text eine letzte Wendung geben, Sinn festlegen oder problematisch werden lassen. Sie bilden einen Abschied, mit dem ein Autor sich der Nachwelt ins Gedächtnis schreibt, sie besiegeln ein Werk und erklären damit dessen Vollendung oder auch dessen potentielle Unabschliessbarkeit. Jedoch: Einmal *ist* Schluss. Und auch wenn dieser Schluss ein Abbruch ist, der Linearität des geschriebenen Textes entkommt er kaum. Gerade über die Richtung dieser Linearität hat Rosenzweig nachgedacht und eine landläufige Vorstellung von Aufbau und Entwicklung eines Sinns in einem Text umgekehrt. Im selbstauslegenden Essay *Das neue Denken* von 1925 bemerkt er, dass in philosophischen Büchern „ein Satz nicht aus seinem Vorgänger" folge, sondern „viel eher aus seinem Nachfolger" (GS III, 143). Die Schlusssätze nicht nur literarischer, sondern in besonderem Masse philosophischer Werke müssten also besondere Prägnanz aufweisen, vielleicht sogar alles zuvor Stehende fassen, abschliessen, es erklären. Denn wenn sich jeder Satz eines philosophischen Werkes aus seinem nachfolgenden Satz erklären liesse, dann wäre der letzte Satz eben der, bei dem die Erklärungskette stehen bleiben müsste. Der letzte Satz ist der erste, zu dem es keinen nachfolgenden mehr gibt. Das heisst, der letzte Satz würde nicht nur alles Vorherstehende erklären, sondern auch sich selbst.

2. Vom Ende her denken: Letzte Sätze

„Als ihm nun schon der Unterleib fast ganz kalt war [sagte er] und das waren seine letzten Worte: O Kriton, wir sind dem Asklepios einen Hahn schuldig, entrichtet ihm den, und versäumt es ja nicht."[269] So gibt am Schluss von Platons Beschreibung der letzten Stunden des athenischen Philosophen Sokrates dessen Freund und philosophischer Gesprächspartner Phaidon Sokrates' letzte

---

[268] Jacob und Wilhelm Grimm, Kinder- und Hausmärchen, Ausgabe letzter Hand, München 1977, 284.
[269] Platon, Phaidon, übersetzt von Friedrich Schleiermacher und mit einem Nachwort von Andreas Graeser, Stuttgart 1986, 96.

Worte wieder. Asklepios, dem Gott der Medizin und Heilung, opferte man im antiken Griechenland, wenn man von einer Krankheit genesen war. Sokrates' durch Phaidon und Platon vermitteltes Testament besagt also, dass das Leben selbst eine (vielleicht *die*) Krankheit darstelle, von der der Tod die Erlösung wäre. In den Tod bedeutet für Sokrates ins Leben. Denn gemäss der im *Phaidon* dargelegten Philosophie liegt der wahre Grund der Dinge in den Ideen, die ewig sind und dem irdischen Leben nicht unterworfen. Verkürzt argumentiert Platon so: Keine Idee lässt die Verbindung mit dem ihr Entgegengesetzten zu. Auch können Gegenstände, die einen wesentlichen Anteil an einer Idee haben, nicht einen wesentlichen Anteil an einer entgegengesetzten Idee haben. Die Seele ist mit der Idee des Lebens aber wesentlich verbunden, deshalb kann sie nicht teilhaben an der Idee des Todes. Sie ist demnach unsterblich und unvergänglich. Dass Platon am Schluss des *Phaidon* Sokrates sterben und ihn seinen eigenen Tod als eine Art Genesung kommentieren lässt, besiegelt ähnlich wie die Hochzeit am Schluss des Märchens die philosophische Erzählung mit einer Geste der Bewährung.

Dieses Behaupten der Unsterblichkeit und die Standfestigkeit vor dem Tod begleiten die Philosophiegeschichte, wie es Rosenzweig formuliert, „von Jonien bis Jena" (SE 13), und damit ausdrücklich zu Georg Wilhelm Friedrich Hegels *Phänomenologie des Geistes*, die in Jena verfasst wurde und 1808 erschien. In der Vorrede zu diesem zentralen Werk des deutschen Idealismus wird der Tod als „jene Unwirklichkeit" bezeichnet, der das „Leben des Geistes" trotzt.[270] Die letzten Worte von Hegels *Phänomenologie* bringen dieses Überleben des Geistes als Ziel des Philosophierens überhaupt zum Ausdruck:

> Das Ziel, das absolute Wissen, oder der sich als Geist wissende Geist hat zu seinem Wege die Erinnerung der Geister, wie sie an ihnen selbst sind und die Organisation ihres Reiches vollbringen. Ihre Aufbewahrung nach der Seite ihres freien in der Form der Zufälligkeit erscheinenden Daseins ist die Geschichte, nach der Seite ihrer begriffnen Organisation aber die Wissenschaft des erscheinenden Wissens; beide zusammen, die begriffne Geschichte, bilden die Erinnerung und die Schädelstätte des absoluten Geistes, die Wirklichkeit, Wahrheit und Gewissheit seines Throns, ohne den er das leblose Erinnern wäre; nur – aus dem Kelche dieses Geisterreiches schäumt ihm seine Unendlichkeit.[271]

Rein rhetorisch betrachtet, greift Hegel um abzuschliessen zu einem beliebten Trick, nämlich zu einem Zitat, um damit in der Rede eines anderen die eigene zu bestätigen. Hegel formuliert Friedrich Schillers *Die Freundschaft* jedoch

---

[270] Georg Wilhelm Friedrich Hegel, Phänomenologie des Geistes, neu hg. von Hans-Friedrich Wessels und Heinrich Clairmont, mit einer Einleitung von Wolfgang Bonsiepen, Hamburg 1988, 26.
[271] Ebd., 530–531.

leicht um. Bei Schiller heisst es in der letzten Strophe dieses Gedichts: „Freundlos war der grosse Weltenmeister, / Fühlte Mangel – darum schuf er Geister, / Sel'ge Spiegel seiner Seligkeit! – / Fand das höchste Wesen schon kein Gleiches, / Aus dem Kelch des ganzen Seelenreiches / Schäumt ihm – die Unendlichkeit."[272] Den schönen Gedanken, dass Gott sich die Welt erschuf um endlich Freunde zu finden, säkularisiert Hegel zu einem System, in dem das Abstraktum des „absoluten Geistes" auftritt, eine Figur, die als Geist sich selbst und seine Geschichte integral begreift und in sich vollständig absorbiert, aufhebt. In Hegels System ist das individuelle Leben und Sterben unwesentlich. Es ist eben das Wesen des Systems, dass seine „Wirklichkeit, Wahrheit und Gewissheit" darin bestehen, dass jegliche Individualität in der Arbeit am Begriff überwunden werden muss, bis sich das Denken in seiner Gewordenheit selbst begreifend gegenüber steht.

Der Erste Weltkrieg mit all seinen Schrecken und die mit ihm verbundene welthistorische Zäsur leiten den endgültigen Abschied von einer solchen idealistischen Philosophie ein. Den Zeitgenossen erschien es zunehmend absurd, dass angesichts des millionenfachen Abschlachtens mit Giftgas und Maschinengewehr, aber auch angesichts der zunehmenden Globalisierung und Partikularisierung der Gesellschaft so etwas wie ein absoluter Geist sich in „begriffner Geschichte" spiegeln könnte. Die Geschichte erschien zunehmend nicht als etwas zu Begreifendes, sondern als labyrinthisches Trümmerfeld, dem es irgendwie zu entfliehen gilt. So formuliert Thomas Mann im letzten Satz des 1924 erschienenen Romans *Der Zauberberg* den Ausgang aus der innerweltlichen Totalität des Todes nur noch als rhetorische Frage nach dessen Möglichkeit: „Wird auch aus diesem Weltfest des Todes, auch aus der schlimmen Fieberbrunst, die rings den regnerischen Abendhimmel entzündet, einmal die Liebe steigen?"[273] Doch auch die „Liebe" als Schlagwort, das Weltversöhnung und Transzendenz andeutet, vermag es nicht, den Tod des modernen Menschen zu überdauern. Paradigmatisch bringt diese Skepsis das Werk Franz Kafkas zum Ausdruck. Mit dem vielleicht berühmtesten letzten Satz der deutschen Literatur endet[274] *Der Process*, ein Romanfragment, an

---

[272] Friedrich Schiller, Werke. Nationalausgabe, Band 1, 111.
[273] Thomas Mann, Der Zauberberg, Berlin 1924, 938.
[274] Auf dem Deckblatt des Heftes, in das Kafka dieses Kapitel eintrug, schrieb er das Wort „Ende". Verkompliziert wird für den *Process* die Rede vom Schluss oder vom letzten Satz allerdings dadurch, dass Kafka nachweislich in seinem Schreibprozess *zuerst* den Anfang und das Ende geschrieben hatte, um *nachher* die anderen Kapitel, die teilweise nicht abgeschlossen sind, einzufügen. Die Reihenfolge dieser Kapitel ist bis heute philologisch nicht eindeutig festzulegen, wenn es denn überhaupt je eine gegeben haben sollte. Kafkas Schluss schliesst also nichts ab, sondern legt vielmehr einen Endpunkt fest, zu dem und von dem aus sich verschiedene Textstränge ziehen lassen. Vgl. Roland Reuss, Zur kritischen Edition von „Der Process" im Rah-

dem Kafka zwischen 1914 und 1915 geschrieben hat: „Wie ein Hund!' sagte er, es war, als sollte die Scham ihn überleben."[275]

Wenn man es genau nimmt, endet also Kafkas *Process*, obwohl er mit dem Tod des Protagonisten aufhört, mit dem Wort „leben".[276] Nur ist dieses *Über*leben, von dem hier die Rede ist, ein gänzlich anderes als das Überleben des Geistes angesichts des individuellen Todes bei Hegel – und sicher auch ein anderes Leben als das im *Stern der Erlösung* beschworene. Während bei Hegel das Wahre das Ganze ist, „und zwar das Ganze als ein Prozess"[277], wie sich Theodor W. Adorno prägnant ausdrückt, präsentiert sich bei Kafka dieses Ganze, dieser Prozess, als dunkle Erfahrung der absoluten, geschlossenen Kontingenz. Denken erlaubt keinen Ausweg aus dieser Krise. Denn der Begriff wird angesichts der Ungeheuerlichkeit der Welt als immer ungemäss empfunden, die Sprache wird auf sich selbst zurückgeworfen. Die Scham ist das Symptom des universellen Scheiterns an Gesetzen, die den Anschein machen, sie seien bloss für den Protagonisten im Augenblick ihres Übertretens geschaffen worden.

Kann es Philosophie so überhaupt noch geben? Ist die Liebe zur Weisheit – und das heisst ja Philosophie – nicht ebenfalls zu einem Ende gekommen, wenn Transzendenz vollkommen von Tod und Scham negiert werden? Diese Frage deutet Thedor W. Adorno an, wenn er sein 1945 erschienenes, bewusst unsystematisches Buch *Minima Moralia* mit „Reflexionen aus dem beschädigten Leben" untertitelt. In dem kurzen Text mit dem Titel „Zum Ende", der als 153. Reflexion Adornos Sammlung von Denkbruchstücken abschliesst, heisst es: „Philosophie, wie sie im Angesicht der Verzweiflung einzig noch zu verantworten ist, wäre der Versuch, alle Dinge so zu betrachten, wie sie vom Standpunkt der Erlösung aus sich darstellten."[278] Gemäss Adorno kann der Gedanke sich nicht von seiner Bedingtheit, der „Entstelltheit und Bedürftigkeit" lösen, muss jedoch trotzdem den immer scheiternden Versuch unternehmen, diese Unmöglichkeit zu begreifen. „Gegenüber der Forderung, die damit an ihn ergeht" so lautet der letzte Satz der *Minima Moralia*, „ist aber die Frage nach der Wirklichkeit oder Unwirklichkeit der Erlösung selber fast gleichgültig."[279]

---

men der Historisch-Kritischen Franz Kafka-Ausgabe, in: Franz Kafka-Hefte 1, Beilage zur Faksimileausgabe des „Process" in der Historisch-kritischen Ausgabe sämtlicher Handschriften, Drucke und Typoskripte von Franz Kafka, hg. von Roland Reuss und Peter Staengle, Basel/Frankfurt a.M. 1997, 3–25, hier 10.

[275] Franz Kafka, Der Process, Historisch-kritische Ausgabe, Heft „Ende", 25.

[276] Und ein Blick ins Manuskript des *Process* zeigt, dass Kafka über-leben trennt, so dass das Wort „leben" als einziges Wort auf der neuen, letzten Zeile steht.

[277] Theodor W. Adorno, Philosophische Terminologie. Zur Einleitung. Band 2, hg. von Rudolf zur Lippe, Frankfurt a.M. 1974, 128.

[278] Theodor W. Adorno, Minima Moralia. Reflexionen aus dem beschädigten Leben, Frankfurt a.M. 1980, 333.

[279] Ebd., 334.

Philosophie vom „Standpunkt der Erlösung" aus – bietet *Der Stern der Erlösung* vielleicht eine solche Philosophie an? Wie soll eine solche Philosophie nach dem Zerbrechen des Idealismus beschaffen sein? Und ist auch für Rosenzweig wie für Adorno „die Frage nach der Wirklichkeit oder Unwirklichkeit der Erlösung fast gleichgültig"? Was würde das überhaupt bedeuten? Mit diesen Fragen soll nun zum Schlusskapitel des *Sterns* und zum Thema der Wahrheit übergeleitet werden.

3. Wahrheit und Offenbarung

Rosenzweig ist ebenfalls – wie die erwähnten, genuin modernen Autoren Thomas Mann, Franz Kafka oder Theodor W. Adorno – an jener „Trauerarbeit der Moderne"[280] beteiligt, die darin besteht, nicht mehr mit dem Ganzen schliessen zu können, zu gar keinem schlüssigen Ende eines philosophischen Nachdenkens zu gelangen. Doch gibt er den Anspruch auf dieses Ganze am Ende nicht auf, wenn er auch ganz anders formuliert wird, indem religiöse Kategorien einbezogen werden. Wie Stéphane Mosès festhält, definiert auch Rosenzweig die Wahrheit als das Allumfassende, als das „Ganze des Systems"[281]. Aber dieses ist nicht als Logos eines Universal-Ichs verstanden. Die konkrete einzelne Person öffnet sich einer Exteriorität in einer Erfahrung von Passivität, die nichts mit Philosophie und ihrer rationalen Praktiken zu tun hat. Das All, das „einst zerschmettert", aber „wieder zusammengewachsen" durch den „Kitt" der Offenbarung (SE 434). Weiter heisst es:

> Das All, das sowohl alles wie ganz wäre, kann weder ehrlich erkannt, noch klar erlebt werden, nur das unehrliche Erkennen des Idealismus, nur das unklare Erleben der Mystik kann sich einreden, es zu erfassen. Das All muss jenseits von Erkenntnis und Erlebnis erfasst werden, wenn es unmittelbar erfasst werden soll. Eben dies Erfassen geschieht in der Erleuchtung des Gebets. (SE 434)

Der Schlussstein des Systems muss somit aus einem Jenseits des philosophischen Diskurses kommen, nämlich aus dem Diskurs der Religion. Dieser Diskurs bildet eine dritte Kategorie neben der rationalen Wissenschaft („Erkenntnis") und der irrationalen Mystik („Erleben"). Das System übersteigt sich selbst, nicht im Hegelschen Sinn, indem es sich selbst in einer gewaltigen Umstülpungsbewegung begreifen und selbst begründen würde, sondern in einem individuellen Augenblick des Sich-Selbst-Vorfindens in einem Geschaffenen, das Rosenzweig als „Erfassen" beschreibt. Dieser Moment des Erfassen

---

[280] Mischa Brumlik, Trauerarbeit der Moderne und melancholischer Messianismus, in: Ludger Heidbrink (Hg.), Entzauberte Zeit. Der melancholische Geist der Moderne, München/Wien: 1997, 210–230.

[281] Stéphane Mosès, System und Offenbarung. Die Philosophie Franz Rosenzweigs, München 1985, 210f.

verortet er immer als Moment der religiösen Tradition. Es besteht in Rosenzweigs Buch eine schwierige Ambivalenz zwischen einem allegorische und einem konkreten Verständnis: Ist diese religiöse Tradition mit ihren Ritualen, Sprachformeln und -beständen, ihren Narrativen und Feiern, allegorisch, als letztlich doch arbiträre Analogie zu verstehen – oder ist sie ein ontologisch zwangsläufiger Ausdruck eines irgendwo real existierenden Wahren? Diese Frage kann in diesem Beitrag nicht gelöst werden, es kann bloss auf die problematische Stellung des Religiösen im *Stern* aufmerksam gemacht werden. Auf jeden Fall sind es nun die Möglichkeiten und Grenzen einer Rede über und von Gott, und das Verhältnis von Gott und absoluter Wahrheit, die Rosenzweig am Schluss des *Sterns* auslotet. Im Hintergrund dieser schwierigen Auslotung stehen die Begriffe der Wahrheit und der Wahrhaftigkeit in Hermann Cohens 1919 ein Jahr nach dessen Tod publiziertem Hauptwerk *Religion der Vernunft aus den Quellen des Judentums*, auf das sich Rosenzweig immer wieder in ganz unterschiedlicher Weise bezieht. Auf einige dieser Bezüge soll im Folgenden verwiesen werden, wenn auch die Komplexität des Verhältnisses von Rosenzweig zu Cohen es nicht erlaubt, sie hier auszuarbeiten.[282]

Wahrheit wird im letzten Kapitel des *Stern der Erlösung* in dreifacher Hinsicht verstanden. Erstens entspricht die Wahrheit einer sichtbaren Form, durch die sich das Wesen Gottes offenbart, wie es auch die jüdische Tradition darstellt. Zu zitieren ist paradigmatisch das Talmudwort, nach dem „das Siegel des Heiligen" die Wahrheit [hebr. *emeth*] sei.[283] Rosenzweig thematisiert hier noch einmal die Kategorie Offenbarung, die für ihn das Verhältnis von Glauben und Wissen, Glauben und Ratio grundlegend verfasst. In der Offenbarung wird die Erfahrung Gottes besiegelt und bewährt – mit Wahrheit versehen. Sie erweist sich als philosophischer *und* theologischer Begriff, der eine prinzipielle erkenntnistheoretische Stellung und Dignität erhält. Zweitens spricht Rosenzweig damit verbunden von der Wahrheit als einer letzten Wahrhaftigkeit, also dem epistemologischen (=erkenntnistheoretischen) Problem eines letztgültigen Wahrheitskriteriums. Dieses Kriterium ist für Rosenzweig, wie sich zeigen wird, die Faktizität der Wahrheit selbst, die erfahrene oder erfasste Tatsache der Wahrheit. Drittens geht es um die menschliche Erfahrung von Wahrheit in den Religionen. Die Wahrheit ist ein Absolutes, an dem der Mensch immer

---

[282] Franz Rosenzweig besuchte vor dem Ersten Weltkrieg Kurse bei Cohen an der Hochschule für die Wissenschaft des Judentums in Berlin. Die Beziehung zum 44 Jahre älteren Lehrer war persönlich geprägt, Rosenzweig beschreibt sie in einem Brief als Vater-Sohn-Beziehung. Während er verschiedentlich sehr harsche Kritik an Positionen Cohens übte, bildet doch die Figur Cohens mit der Wendung zur jüdischen Tradition eine fundamentale Bezugsgrösse Rosenzweigs, vgl. Myriam Bienenstock, Cohen face à Rosenzweig. Débat sur la Pensée Allemande, Paris 2009.

[283] Vgl. Sabbat 55a (Der Babylonische Talmud, hg. und übersetzt von Lazarus Goldschmidt, Berlin/Wien 1925, Bd. I, 445.)

nur Anteil haben kann. Rosenzweig skizziert Judentum und Christentum in ihrem je eigenen anteilmässigen Verhältnis zur Wahrheit. Diese beiden Religionen sind im *Stern* nicht bloss Religionen. Sie werden vielmehr als die beiden grundsätzlichen Modalitäten menschlicher Existenz verstanden und in ihrem jeweils anderen Verhältnis zur Wahrheit als paradigmatische Seinskategorien beschrieben.[284] Diese drei verschiedenen Verständnisse von Wahrheit sollen nun eingehend diskutiert werden, bevor zum Schluss auf das Ende und die Bedeutung des Endes für den *Stern* zurückzukommen ist.

4. Drei Kontexte von Wahrheit

A) Gott und Wahrheit. Ist es überhaupt sinnvoll, über Gott zu sprechen? Wer an einen Gott glaubt, bedarf keiner Worte. Gerade das, was sich dem Diskurs entzieht, ist für ihn durch Gott besetzt. Wer aber nicht an Gott glaubt, also wie heute zahlreiche Menschen, für den ist eine solche Rede vorn vorneherein absurd. Es mag darum für viele heutige Leserinnen und Leser die Lektüre des *Sterns* erschweren, wenn Rosenzweig sich um etwaige Zweifel an der Existenz eines Gottes gar nicht zu kümmern scheint. Doch Rosenzweig nimmt zunächst eine entscheidende Differenzierung vor, die es nicht zu überlesen gilt: Er unterscheidet das Wesen Gottes an sich, und das, was dieses Wesen *für uns* sein *könnte*. Zu beachten gilt es den Konjunktiv: „Was Gott, der wahre Gott, vor der Schöpfung gewesen wäre, entzieht sich so jedem Gedanken. Nicht so, was er nach der Erlösung sein würde" (SE 426). Eine Rede von Gott ohne die Menschen, vor der Entstehung der Welt, ist also auch für Rosenzweig sinnlos. Vielmehr möchte er darüber nachdenken, was denn Gott potentiell für uns wäre, wenn eine Erlösung und eine Erlösbarkeit der Welt angenommen wird. Es geht also um eine Rede der Möglichkeit Gottes in einem virtuellen Zustand der Erlösung, gleichsam nach dem Ende der Welt.

Zunächst ist diese Erlösung bloss als eine Art Vorschein, als „Schimmer jenes Augenblicks der göttlichen Liebe" (SE 424) in der gegenwärtigen Welt präsent. Die allgemein erfahrene „Liebe" verbürge das Sein Gottes: „Dass Gott liebt, erfahren wir, nicht dass Gott die Liebe ist. In der Liebe kommt er uns zu nah, als dass wir noch sagen könnten: dies oder das ist er. Nur dass er Gott ist, erfahren wir in der Liebe, aber nicht, was er ist" (SE 424). Es ist nicht die Prämisse Rosenzweigs, dass aus dem „Weltfest des Todes" (um nochmals Thomas Mann zu zitieren) die Liebe steigt. Vielmehr macht sich Gott als Herr über Leben und Tod – der weder tot noch lebendig ist, sondern diesen Gegensatz in sich aufhebt – *in* der Liebe erfahrbar. Der *Stern* liefert in dem Sinn keine Theodizee (also keine Lösung der Frage, warum das Böse in einer von Gott geschaffenen Welt existiert). Die Grundan-

---

[284] Vgl. dazu ebenfalls Mosès, System und Offenbarung, 216–220.

nahme ist vielmehr, dass die Existenz Gottes in der ganz konkreten zwischenmenschlichen Liebe erfahrbar wird, nicht aber das Wesen, nicht das Sein Gottes. Dieses muss wesensmässig verborgen bleiben, und zwar, wie Rosenzweig mit einem für diese Spekulationen typischen Oxymoron festhält, „gerade indem es sich offenbart" (SE 424). Die Offenbarung zeigt dem menschlichen Bewusstsein also nicht das Wesen Gottes. Der denkende Mensch erfährt in der Offenbarung bloss die Präsenz eines sich selbst absolut übersteigenden Anderen. Gott ist diskursiv und bewusstseinsmässig nicht zu fassen. Er ist deshalb auch nicht einfach kongruent mit der Wahrheit an sich. Zwar ist es das Wesen Gottes, wahr zu sein, Gott *ist* zwar in gewissem Sinn die Wahrheit, doch ist er immer auch *mehr*. Hermann Cohen, auf den sich Rosenzweig hier implizit bezieht, spricht von der Wahrheit als einzigem „Geltungswert, der dem Wesen Gottes entspricht"[285]. Die Wahrheit ist bei Cohen das einzige „adäquate Attribut" Gottes, ohne ihn vollständig beschreiben zu können. Wahrheit steht aber „schon innerhalb der Korrelation zum Menschen, daher kann sie für Gott allein nicht ausdrücklich als Attribut namhaft gemacht werden"[286]. Gott besitzt demnach auch bei Rosenzweig immer eine Art „Überschuss über sein Wesen" (SE 429). Das bedeutet, dass jegliche Aussagen vom Typus „Gott ist das und das" nicht gänzlich zutreffend sein können. Rosenzweig fragt aber nicht nur: Was ist Gott? Er fragt auch: Was ist Wahrheit?

B) Tatsächlichkeit der Wahrheit. Rosenzweig verweist zuerst auf die von ihm verworfene idealistische Tradition, nach der die Wahrheit sich selbst verbürgt. Dass es gar keine Wahrheit gebe, könne man aber logisch nicht sagen, denn „mindestens dass es keine Wahrheit gebe, müsste dann – wahr sein" (SE 430). Die Frage, welches „das allgemeine und sichere Kriterium der Wahrheit einer jeden Erkenntnis sei", stellt Kant in der *Kritik der reinen Vernunft*. Er differenziert dort zwischen der Wahrheit logischer Urteile, für die das allgemeingültige Kriterium die Übereinstimmung des Urteils mit den Gesetzen des Denkens ist, und der Wahrheit so genannter materialer Urteile, für die es keine allgemeingültigen Kriterien geben kann.[287] Rosenzweig interessiert sich – und das ist symptomatisch für sein Denken – nicht für diese die Philosophie bis heute prägende Unterscheidung Kants. Für Rosenzweig im Zentrum steht die Beschaffenheit einer transzendentalen Wahrheit, wie sie sich als Faktizität im Leben darstellt. Wahrheit muss gewissermassen zur unbezweifelbaren Tatsache werden. Wie die Offenbarung auch etwas individuell Erfahrenes darstellt, so muss die Gewissheit, dass etwas wahr ist, *tatsächlich* erfahren werden. Damit

---

[285] Hermann Cohen, Religion der Vernunft aus den Quellen des Judentums, 2. Aufl. Frankfurt a.M. 1929, 480.
[286] Ebd.
[287] Immanuel Kant, Kritik der reinen Vernunft, nach der ersten und zweiten Originalausgabe hg. von Jens Timmermann, Hamburg 1998, 136.

setzt er sich vom idealistischen Wahrheitsbegriff ab und tendiert in Richtung eines Existentialismus. So geht es ihm auch nicht um ein Wissen von Wahrheit, sondern um ein Vertrauen darauf: „Auf einem letzten Vertrauen also darauf, dass der Boden, auf den sich die Wahrheit mit ihren eigenen Füssen stellt, tragfähig ist, beruht alles Vertrauen auf die Wahrheit. Die Wahrheit ist selbst der Wahrheit letzte Voraussetzung und ist es nicht als Wahrheit, die auf ihren eigenen Füssen stünde, sondern als Tatsache, der man vertraut. Die Wahrheit selber ist Tatsache noch vor der Tatsache ihrer Unleugbarkeit" (SE 431). Dass die Wahrheit an sich eine Tatsache ist, besagt auch, dass die Wahrheit nicht identisch mit Gott ist, aber „Wahrheit ist von Gott, Gott ist ihr Ursprung" (SE 432).

Die Erfahrung dieser Tatsächlichkeit sieht Rosenzweig im Gebet und im religiösen Ritus angelegt. Auch hier ist ein Bezug auf Hermann Cohen anzunehmen. Im Kontext seiner Überlegungen zum Gebet meint Cohen: „Gott ist der Gott der Wahrheit, und der Mensch soll der Mensch der Wahrhaftigkeit werden. Darum betet der Mensch zu Gott."[288] Für das Individuum wird die Erfahrung von Wahrheit als Wahrhaftigkeit konkret. Hier ist auch der Grund dafür gelegt, warum für Rosenzweig die Theorie der Wahrheit erst am Schluss seines Systems stehen kann. Wahrheit ist keine abstrakte Idee, keine dem blossen Denken zugängliche Korrelation von Urteil und rationalen Gesetzen. Sinnvoll kann von Wahrheit erst im ethischen Leben, in der Ausgestaltung des individuellen Lebens im religiösen Verband gesprochen werden. Wahrheit muss als Wahrhaftigkeit verbürgt werden, und zwar in der Zentrierung des Lebens auf die Erfahrung der Offenbarung hin. Mit kaum zu überbietendem Pathos schreibt Rosenzweig: „Unser Wahrlich, unser Ja und Amen, mit dem wir auf Gottes Offenbarung antworteten, – es enthüllt sich am Ziel als das klopfende Herz auch der ewigen Wahrheit. Wir finden uns wieder, uns selbst mitten im Brennen des fernsten Sterns der ewigen Wahrheit, nicht die Wahrheit in uns [...], sondern uns in der Wahrheit." (SE 436). Dieses „uns in der Wahrheit" bedeutet, dass die Wahrheit bei Rosenzweig letztlich nicht *erkannt* werden kann, sondern *bewährt* werden muss. Die Metapher des klopfenden Herzens besagt, dass Wahrheit nicht ideell gedacht wird, sondern als etwa Lebendiges. Wahrheit selbst ist also ein Prozess: Im aktiven, individuellen Nachvollzug wird Wahrheit erst zur Wahrheit gemacht, von jedem einzelnen immer wieder. Das Paradox ist nun, dass die absolute und einzigartige Wahrheit in verschiedener Weise und in verschiedenen Formen erlebt und bewährt wird. Es gibt in der menschlichen, pluralen Erlebniswirklichkeit kein objektives Kriterium, das die Entscheidung für eine der verschiedenen, immer absoluten Wahrheiten verbürgen würde.

C) Die menschliche Erfahrung von Wahrheit. Ganz entgegen etwa der hegelschen Rede von Wahrheit als dem Ganzen, ist es im *Stern* gerade die

---

[288] Cohen, Religion der Vernunft, 443.

Partikularität, das immer nur Teilhafte, das die Wahrheit ausmacht. Es ist das Wesen der Wahrheit, „zu teil zu sein". Eine Wahrheit, „die niemandes Teil ist", ist keine Wahrheit. Auch wenn man eine integrale, absolute Wahrheit annimmt, bildet diese paradoxerweise einen Teil, nämlich einen Teil Gottes, der immer mehr ist als jede Wahrheit (SE 462). Diese Theorie erinnert an die in der berühmten Ringparabel in Gotthold Ephraim Lessings Drama *Nathan der Weise* (1779) verbildlichte Idee der Toleranz aufgrund der unmöglichen Totalität eines Wahrheitsanspruchs menschlicher Religionen, die aber dennoch für sich selber gesehen wahr sind. Auch wenn Rosenzweig mit religiösen Kategorien und Begriffen operiert, geht es ihm in keiner Weise um die Verteidigung eines Dogmas oder einer einzig wahren Lehre, sondern gerade um eine Begründung des Pluralismus – oder vielleicht besser eines Dualismus von Wahrheitsanteilen, die gerade erst in gelebter Praxis als je meine Wahrheit auch zu Gottes Wahrheit wird. Denn mit seinem Wahrheitsschema deutet Rosenzweig nur die beiden monotheistischen Religionen Judentum und Christentum, die ja auch historisch klar mit einander verbunden sind. Als Zwischenbemerkung sei festgehalten, dass es eine interessante und komplexe Aufgabe für eine religionswissenschaftliche Rosenzweig-Lektüre darstellen würde, zu versuchen, ob sich auch unsere multikulturelle und längst nicht mehr auf die beiden abendländischen Monotheismen reduzierte Welt mit Rosenzweigs System deuten liesse. Rosenzweigs Denken besitzt gerade für die an Positionen der *post colonial studies* orientierten Kulturwissenschaften ein enormes, noch nicht ausgeschöpftes Inspirationspotential.

5. Judentum und Christentum

Dieses Potential wird jedoch dadurch eingeschränkt, dass Rosenzweig nur Juden und Christen als „Arbeiter am gleichen Werk" (SE 462) beschreibt, und dies gerade nicht im Sinn des aufklärerischen Toleranzgedankens, sondern als Theologie einer notwendigen, wechselseitig sich ergänzenden und komplettierenden Konstellation. Er spricht vom „Sternbild der Wahrheit" (SE 454), eine präzise Metapher für die Mechanik, die er zwischen Judentum und Christentum am Werk sieht. Es ist eben das *gleiche* „Werk", eine Art Uhrwerk, dessen *eine* Zeit für beide Teilnehmer unterschiedlich abläuft. Seit Einsteins spezieller Relativitätstheorie, die nur einige Jahre vor dem *Stern der Erlösung* formuliert wurde, und deren erstem Grundsatz, nämlich dem Prinzip der Zeitdilatation bewegter Uhren, weiss man, dass eine solche auf den ersten Blick paradoxe Konstruktion durchaus realistisch sein kann. Um im stellaren Bild zu bleiben, besetzen Judentum und Christentum sich unterschiedlich bewegende Positionen in einem gemeinsamen Raum, zu denen sich die jeweilige Zeit relativ verhält. Rosenzweigs Thesen zu Judentum und Christentum, die er bereits im ersten Buch des dritten Teils des *Sterns* sehr ausführlich referiert und hier nochmals bespricht, lassen sich auf den Gegensatz von Statik im Judentum und Dynamik im Christentum verkürzen. Jude ist man immer schon. Man wird als Jude geboren, Jude-Sein ist dem Juden ein „inneres Zuhause" (SE 440). Aus dieser Zugehörigkeit qua Geburt folgt auch eine grundsätzliche Bedeutung des Kollektivs im Judentum. Das, was den Juden zum Juden macht, liegt vor dem Einzelleben, es ist die Offenbarung an das Volk, es ist das Volk Israel, dem jeder einzelne immer schon durch seine Geburt von einer jüdischen Mutter angehört. Für den Christen ist es nach Rosenzweig gerade umgekehrt. Das Christentum muss in jedem Menschen immer neu plausibilisiert werden. Man ringt sich sein Christentum ab, Man *wird* also zum Christen, man *ist* es nicht,[289] während man Jude eben immer schon *ist*. Aus diesem Gegensatz erklärt Rosenzweig auch, dass das Christentum gleichsam nach Aussen gehen und missionieren muss. Die Offenbarung muss in die Welt getragen und damit die Christenheit ausgedehnt werden, während das Judentum immer bei sich bleibt und eigentlich raumlos und atemporal ist. Die Offenbarung des Judentums bedarf keiner Verbreitung, weder zeitlich noch räumlich. Die jüdische Zeit ist die zirkulare Zeit des Sterns selbst, während die christliche Zeit die lineare Zeit derjenigen ist, die im Raumschiff auf den Stern zurasen.

Dieses Bild passt zu einer anderen Metapher, die Rosenzweig im letzten Kapitel des *Stern* benutzt. Die „Rechnung des Christentums" sei die Addition, die des Judentums die Subtraktion. Damit ist auch eine gewisse defensive Haltung und eine Selbstbezüglichkeit des Judentums gemeint. Das Judentum „wird durch Subtraktion bestimmt, durch Verengung, durch Bildung immer neuer Reste" (SE 450). Dieses Beharren auf dem Inneren, eigenen, zeigt sich an der zentralen Stellung des jüdischen Gesetzes. Dieses ist nicht auf religiöse oder rituelle Gebote und Verbote oder eine Aufzählung von Vorschiften beschränkt. Der Talmud ist eine Sammlung von Diskussionen zu unterschiedlichen alltäglichen, religiösen, ökonomischen, ethischen oder sozialen Fragen, die rabbinische Literatur umfasst das gesamte Spektrum menschlichen Lebens. Da das Judentum jedoch nach dem Jahr 70 n.u.Z. (als die Römer Jerusalem erobern und den Zweiten Tempel zerstören) keine Staatsreligion mehr ist, keine Eigenstaatlichkeit hat und auch keinen Tempel mehr besitzt, wird die Anwendung des Gesetzes in vielerlei Hinsicht zu einer Textpraktik. Das Gesetz ist „fertig und unveränderlich" (SE 451). Es geht aber nicht ausschliesslich darum, das Gesetz anzuwenden, sondern es möglichst umfassend zu lesen und zu deuten – es zu „lernen", wie es im Judentum heisst. Und obwohl natürlich Vorschriften etwa zur rituellen Reinheit, zu den Gebeten etc. im observanten Alltag eine wichtige Rolle spielen, sind sie dennoch immer Gegenstand von

---

[289] Mit diesem Gedanken bezieht sich Rosenzweig auf den von ihm viel gelesenen frühchristlichen Autor und so genannten Kirchenvater Tertullian, der festhielt: „[...] fiunt, non nascuntur Christiani." (=Man wird, ist nicht von Geburt an Christ.), Tertullian, Apologeticum. Verteidigung des Christentums, Lateinisch und Deutsch, München 1952, 122 (Kapitel 18,2).

gelehrten Auslegungsdebatten. Dieses selbstbezügliche Studium spielt eine konstitutive Rolle für das orthodoxe Judentum. Denn die absolute Einlösung und Einhaltung des Gesetzes ist das virtuelle Ziel, das diese Welt von der kommenden, erlösten unterscheidet. Nach Rosenzweig ist es der „gott-, welt- und menschumfassende Vorgang der Erlösung" (SE 457), der sich zwischen jüdischem Mensch und jüdischem Gesetz abspielt.

Im Christentum dagegen fehlt nach Rosenzweig die Einheit von Glauben und Gefühl. Auch die Theologie des Sohn Gottes, also dass Gott in Jesus Christus wirklich Mensch geworden, gestorben und auferstanden ist, stiftet diese Einheit nicht. Denn es ist schwierig, an die Geschichte von Menschwerdung und Auferstehung und damit verbunden an das Versprechen künftiger Erlösung jedes einzelnen in der Gemeinschaft mit Christus *ganz* zu glauben. „Ob Christus mehr ist als eine Idee – kein Christ kann es wissen" (SE 461). Diese christliche Skepsis bildet auch den Ursprung des christlichen Antisemitismus. Die Christen sehen am Juden, dass dieser (durch seine Gebürtlichkeit an das Gesetz gebunden) immer schon die potentielle Erlösung mit sich trägt. Der Christ muss ist aber immer erst unterwegs zu dieser Erlösung, er muss für sie arbeiten. Dennoch stellt das Judentum für das Christentum nicht nur eine Provokation oder Beunruhigung dar, sondern auch eine Versicherung, eine Garantie seiner eigenen tatsächliche Wahrheit. Während die christliche Erlösung nicht konkret zu vergegenwärtigen ist, stellen die vor dem Christen stehenden, lebendigen Juden das nicht zu bezweifelnde Faktum der Durchdringung von Leben und Erlösung dar. Im Judentum kann die Erlösung jederzeit, in jedem Augenblick hereinbrechen. Aus christlicher Perspektive liegt dieser Zeitpunkt der Erlösung jedoch am Ende der Zeit. Juden *bleiben* Juden bis zu diesem eschatologischen Ende der christlichen Heilsgeschichte, nämlich bis alle Völker das Evangelium angenommen haben.

Diese theologischen Thesen zum Verhältnis von Judentum und Christentum sind hier nur sehr verkürzt dargestellt worden. Im hier zur Diskussion stehenden Teil des *Sterns* bilden sie filmisch gesprochen eine Rückblende auf das erste Buch des dritten Teils, wo sie religionsgeschichtlich sehr ausführlich hergeleitet werde. Im dritten Buch des dritten Teils möchte Rosenzweig damit lediglich seine Theorie von der Teilhaftigkeit und Tatsächlichkeit der Wahrheit belegen.

6. Schau und Antlitz, Anfang und Ende

Die menschliche Erfahrung von Wahrheit ist immer eine teilhafte. Doch Rosenzweig gibt sich nicht mit dieser Beschränkung auf das Partikulare zufrieden. Die *ganze* Wahrheit gibt sich nämlich im mystisch konnotierten Modus der Schau. Die ganze Wahrheit, die auch Gottes Wahrheit ist, kann geschaut werden, und eine solche Schau findet „jenseits des Lebens" statt (SE 462). Was ist mit diesem „Jenseits des Lebens" gemeint? In einem alltäglichen Verständnis würde man wohl sagen, dass jenseits des Lebens eben der Tod ist, und ein

Schauen der ganzen Wahrheit also nur dem möglich ist, der sich in einer Art Himmel befindet, in einem Leben nach dem Tod, das dem wahren und wirklichen Leben gleichkommt, gegen das das irdische Leben nur ein armseliges Vorspiel darstellt. Dieses landläufige Verständnis scheint aber im *Stern der Erlösung* nicht zuzutreffen.

Im *Tor* spricht Rosenzweig davon, dass „in der Welt selber ein Stück Überwelt" (SE 471) vorhanden sei und dass die Schau dort „verstattet" sei. Die Sprache dieses letzten Teils ist teilweise dunkel und führt bewusst an die Grenze zur Unverständlichkeit, sie ist mit Archaismen und an mystische Formeln erinnernden Wendungen aufgeladen. So ist denn auch das Partizip „verstattet" ein merkwürdiges Wort. Sowohl das *Grammatisch-kritische Wörterbuch* von Adelung als auch das *Deutsche Wörterbuch* von Jacob und Wilhelm Grimm (die klassischen philologischen Nachschlagewerke des Deutschen) sehen im Verb „verstatten" ein veraltetes Synonym von „gestatten": „Statt oder Raum zu etwas geben, doch nur im figürlichen Verstande, Freyheit geben, etwas zu thun, gestatten [...]."[290] Doch bei Rosenzweig ist dieses „Statt oder Raum" geben wohl ausdrücklich *nicht* im figürlichen, d.h. übertragenen Sinn gemeint. Ganz real geht es ihm um eine *Stätte*, einen Ort in dieser Welt. Die „umgelautete Form" „verstattet" kommt gemäss Grimm nur „vereinzelt" vor,[291] aber es ist gerade sie, die Rosenzweig benutzt. Die Bedeutung changiert zwischen der *Erlaubnis* zur Schau und ihrer *Verortung*. Tatsächlich scheint Rosenzweig mit dieser räumlichen Begrifflichkeit also eine Einfaltung des Transzendentalen in den Innenraum der Welt zu beschreiben. Es gibt gleichsam eine Art Enklave des Jenseits im Diesseits, ein extraterritorialer Punkt, der sich aber innerhalb unseres Raumes befindet. Von diesem Punkt geht die Schau der ganzen Wahrheit aus – es ist der Ort der Wahrheit.

Diese Stätte der Wahrheit wird als Antlitz beschrieben, und zwar als „ein Antlitz gleich dem eigenen" (SE 471). Dem Wort Antlitz für Gesicht eignet schon zu Rosenzweigs Zeiten ein archaisierender und biblischer Ton. Das Grimmsche *Wörterbuch* hält fest: „Luther verwendet das wort in der bibel sehr oft [...]." Und: „Heute klingt uns antlitz feierlicher und poetischer als angesicht oder gesicht."[292] Man würde nicht vom Gesicht Gottes sprechen, sondern von seinem Antlitz. Das sakrale Pathos des Wortes Antlitz ist bei Rosenzweig gewollt. Denn dieses Antlitz Gottes ist für Rosenzweig die Wahrheit, die uns anblickt und die wir anblicken. Aber wie ist es möglich, Gottes Antlitz zu sehen, physisch wahrzunehmen? Rosenzweig geht davon aus, dass die Erscheinung der göttlichen Gegenwart analog zur Wahrnehmung des menschlichen Gesichts ist. Antlitz heisst das menschliche Gesicht, insofern es als Gottes Prä-

---

[290] Lemma „verstatten", in: Johann Christoph Adelung, Grammatisch-kritisches Wörterbuch der hochdeutschen Mundart, München 1811.
[291] Lemma „verstatten", in: Deutsches Wörterbuch von Jacob und Wilhelm Grimm, 16 Bände in 32 Teilbänden, Leipzig 1854–1961.
[292] Lemma „antlitz", in: Deutsches Wörterbuch.

senz sinnlich wahrgenommen wird, was für jedes Gesicht potentiell möglich ist.[293] In jeder zwischenmenschlichen Begegnung ist also der transzendentale Punkt der Schau möglich. Ihr Ort ist das Antlitz. Es gibt eine Unsicherheit, ob dieser Schluss nun als Mystik gelesen werden muss, das heisst als Beschwörung einer jegliche diskursive Logik sprengenden Fülle intersubjektiver Erfahrung oder als philosophischer Versuch, einen Begriff für die Erfahrung tatsächlicher Wahrheit zu finden. Als Indiz für ein mystisches Verständnis der Rede vom Antlitz könnte dienen, dass Rosenzweig versucht, die Struktur der Gottesschau anhand von Kategorien des menschlichen Körpers, des Gesichts, zu beschreiben. Diese Analogie hat eine Tradition in der jüdischen Mystik, der Kabbala.[294] Die Verortung des *Sterns* in einen weitgespannten Zusammenhang von Spekulationen über die „Gestalt der Gottheit" ist aber letztlich ein Versuch zur Authentifizierung der vorgelegten Wahrheitskonzeption anhand der Tradition.

Das philosophische Verständnis von „Antlitz" würde besagen, dass Wahrheit nur aus einem intersubjektiven Prozess zu gewinnen, also kommunikativ verfasst wäre. Wahrheit ist – das würde dieses zweite Verständnis von Antlitz aussagen – nur intersubjektiv „verstattet". Das Antlitz ist ein Begriff des Denkens, der zwar der unmittelbaren Anschauung entstammt, aber nicht weniger als andere philosophische Termini abstrakte Bedeutung besitzt. Rosenzweig erklärt, dass er „in Bildern" spricht: „Aber die Bilder sind nicht willkürlich. Es gibt notwendige und zufällige Bilder" (SE 469). Die Metapher des Antlitzes ist deshalb für ihn notwendig, weil es den Teil des menschlichen Körpers darstellt, mit dem der Mensch „mit der Umwelt in Verbindung tritt" (SE 470) und, so kann man hinzufügen, die Leiblichkeit, die existentielle Tatsächlichkeit des Menschen mit einer sakralen Konnotation auflädt. Im Antlitz wird Wahrheit authentisch, sie bekommt im menschlichen Gesicht einen lebendigen Ort.

Die Authentizität der Wahrheit muss sich in einer alltäglichen Moral bewähren. Du sollst nun „von Herzen gut sein und einfältig wandeln mit deinem Gott". Diese simple Kinderregel bezeichnet Rosenzweig als „Letztes" (SE 471). Die Schlussrhetorik des *Stern* ist entschieden einer romantischen Ästhetik des Anfangs im Ende geschuldet: Wie Gott selbst der Erste und der Letzte ist, sich jeder Unterscheidung von Anfang und Schluss entzieht, so muss auch *Der Stern der Erlösung* auf diese romantische Struktur verweisen. Das Ende des Buches muss Anfang bedeuten. Doch: „Und dies Letzte ist nichts Letztes, sondern ein allzeit Nahes, das Nächste; nicht das letzte also, sondern das Erste. Wie schwer ist solch Erstes! Wie schwer ist aller Anfang!" (SE 471). Das Ende des *Stern*

---

[293] Vgl. Martin Brasser, „... nur das rechte blitzt". Das Motiv des Angesichts und des Antlitzes im *Stern der Erlösung* von Franz Rosenzweig, in: Yehoyoda Amir/Yossi Turner/Martin Brasser (Hg.), Faith, Truth, and Reason. New Perspectives on Franz Rosenzweig's Star of Redemption, Freiburg i.B./München, 125–136.

[294] Vgl. Gershom Scholem, Von der mystischen Gestalt der Gottheit. Studien zu Grundbegriffen der Kabbala, Frankfurt a.M. 1991.

der Erlösung, sein Letztes, ist also die Erkenntnis, das dieses Letzte ein Anfang sein muss, nämlich ein Anfang, die Wahrheit zu bewähren, und dass dieser Anfang schwer ist. Aus dieser Perspektive betrachtet wird die Differenz zwischen Anfang und Ende aufgehoben. Es ist eine Aufhebung, die sich letztlich auch der Form des Buches mit seiner linearen Struktur entzieht und die vielleicht eine ganz neue Art des Lesens und Schreibens erfordern würde. „Aller Anfang ist schwer!" heisst es in *Wilhelm Meisters Lehrjahren* von Goethe. Doch: „Das mag in gewissem Sinne wahr sein; allgemeiner aber kann man sagen: aller Anfang ist leicht, und die letzten Stufen werden am schwersten und seltensten erstiegen."[295]

Weiterführende Lektüre

Hufnagel, C., (1994), *Die kultische Gebärde. Kunst, Politik, Religion im Denken Franz Rosenzweigs*, Freiburg, Alber.

Wolfson, E. R., (2021), *Nomadism, Homelessness and the Homecoming of the Poet*, in: "Into Life", Franz Rosenzweig on Knowledge, Aesthetics, and Politics. Supplements to the Journal of Jewish Thought and Philosophy 31 (2021) 281–342; [https://doi.org./10.1163/9789004468559_013]

---

[295] Johann Wolfgang Goethe, Goethes Werke. Band 8, Hamburg 1950, 36–37.

Autoren / Contributors

Prof. **Rabbi Yehoyada Amir** is a professor of Jewish Thought at Hebrew Union College in Jerusalem, a former president of MARAM (The Israel Council of Reform Rabbis) and an honorary member of the Franz Rosenzweig Gesellschat. Author of: *Reason out Faith: The Philosophy of Franz Rosenzweig* (Hebrew – 2004; English – to be published soon); *The Renewal of Jewish Life in the Philosophy of Nachman Krochmal* (Hebrew 2018); co-editor (with Martin Brasser and Yossi Turner) of Faith, Truth, and Reason: New Perspectives on Fran'z Rosenzweig's "Star of Redemption" (2012); editor of Nachman Krochmal, *More Nebukhe ha-Zeman* (Hebrew, 2010); c0-editor (with Yossi Turner) 0f *The Philosophy of Eliezer Schweid: Jewish Culture and Universal Perspectives* (2020).

Caspar Battegay teaches modern German literature at the University of Basel (Privatdozent) and is a lecturer at the University of Applied Sciences of Northwestern Switzerland. He received his Dr. phil. from Hochschule für Jüdische Studien/University of Heidelberg in 2009. Since then he has taught at the universities of Graz, Basel, Bern and at the ETH Zürich. Between 2014 and 2017 he has been an "Ambizione"-Research Fellow of the Swiss National Foundation for Scientific Research (SNF) at the German Department of the University of Lausanne. From 2015 until 2020 he has been a member of "Die Junge Akademie der Berlin Brandenburgischen Akademie der Wissenschaften". He is the author and editor of several books on German and Jewish literature and cultural history, including *Geschichte der Möglichkeit. Utopie, Diaspora und die* 'jüdische Frage' (Wallstein 2018), *European-Jewish Utopias* (De Gruyter 2016), *Judentum und Popkultur. Ein Essay* (Transcript Verlag 2012) and *Das andere Blut. Gemeinschaft im deutsch-jüdischen Schreiben 1830–1930* (Böhlau 2011). Recent publication in English: "The Empire of Taste. Food and Remembrance in Joseph Roth's Radetzkymarsch", in: *Austrian Studies* 28 (2020).

Gérard Bensussan est philosophe et professeur émérite à l'Université de Sttrasbourg. Chercheur aux Archives Husserl de Paris (ENS rue d'Ulm), il a enseigné dans le monde entier et il est l'auteur de plus d'une vingtaine d'ouvrages dont Être *heureux? Ce qui dépend de nous et ce qui n'en dépend pas* (Mimesis, 2019), *Les deux morales* (Vrin, 2019), *L'Ecriture de l'involontaire. Philosophie de Proust* (Classiques Garnier, 2020). Un important ouvrage collectif vient de lui être consacré, *Contre toute attente. Autour de Gérard Bensussan* (Classiques Garnier, 2021)

Petar Bojanić (1964, Belgrade) is Principal Research Fellow of the Institute for Philosophy and Social Theory, University of Belgrade (IFDT), and Director of the Center for Advanced Studies – Southeast Europe, University of Rijeka (CAS SEE). The author of numerous studies on the XX century Jewish political tradition. With Sona Goldblum, Bojanić edited a special issue of *Les Cahiers philosophiques de Strasbourg* "Franz Rosenzweig: politique, histoire, religion" (29/2011). His book *Violence and Messianism* has been translated into six languages.

Martin Brasser (geb. 1961), Dr. phil., Studium der Philosophie und der Theologie in München und Tübingen; seit 2008 Dozent für Ethik an der Hochschule Luzern Wirtschaft und Geschäftsführer der Philosophie+Management GmbH; Mitbegründer der Internationalen Rosenzweig-Gesellschaft e.V. (IRG) im 2002; von 2002 bis 2012 Mitglied des Vorstands der IRG; Hauptherausgeber der Rosenzweig-Jahrbücher 1 (2006) – 7 (2013) und der Reihe Rosenzweigiana Bände 1 – 6. Publikationen in Auswahl: (Hg.), Rosenzweig als Leser. Kontextuelle Kommentare zum *Stern der Erlösung*, Conditio Judaica Bd. 44, Tübingen 2004, reprint 2014; Dialogue and System in Rosenzweig's *Star of Redemption*, in: ders., (Hg.), Rosenzweig Jahrbuch 7 (2013) 27–41; „… nur das rechte blitzt". Das Motiv des Angesichts und des Antlitzes im *Stern der Erlösung* von Franz Rosenzweig, in: Y. Amir, Y. Turner, M. Brasser (Hrsg.), Faith, Truth and Reason , Rosenzweigiana Bd. 6, S. 125–135, Freiburg i.Br. 2012.

Gabriella Caponigro (Rome, 1985) holds a PhD in Humanistic Studies from the "Gabriele d'Annunzio" University of Chieti-Pescara. Her scientific research focuses on contemporary Jewish philosophy, particularly on F. Rosenzweig, E. Levinas e W. Benjamin. She published several scientific papers and the monography *Unde Malum? Libertà e tirannia nel pensiero di Franz Rosenzweig* (preface by Bernhard Casper, Ets, Pisa 2015). The scope of her current work also includes interreligious dialogue. In this domain she has edited the collective volume *Figli di Abramo. Il dialogo fra religioni cinquant'anni dopo Nostra Aetate* (preface by Francesco Paolo Ciglia, Ets, Pisa 2017).

Prof. **Francesco Paolo Ciglia** is full professor of Moral Philosophy at the *Università «Gabriele d'Annunzio»* of Chieti-Pescara. He is a member, at times with an executive role, of numerous Societies, Istitutions, Scientific Commitees, and Redactional Boards of national and international reviews (among which: Internationale Rosenzweig Gesellschaft, Istituto di Studi Filosofici «Enrico Castelli», European Society for Moral Philosophy; Reviews: «Archivio di Filosofia / Archives of Philosophy, «Nuovo Giornale di Filosofia della Religione», Redazione Romana «Filosofia e teologia»), and author of 160 publications, of which seven are monographies, in different languages (Italian, French, English, German, Spanish and Portuguese). He is a specialist in figures and themes of philosophy of existence (L. Pareyson) and of 20th century Jewish thought (F. Rosenzweig; E. Levinas). Selective Bibliography: *Un passo fuori dall'uomo. La genesi del pensiero di Levinas*, Padova 1988; *Fenomenologie dell'umano. Sondaggi eccentrici sul pensiero di Levinas*, Roma 1996; *Scrutando la "Stella". Cinque studi su Rosenzweig*, Padova 1999; *Fra Atene e Gerusalemme. Il «nuovo pensiero» di Franz Rosenzweig*, Genova-Milano, 2009; *Voce di silenzio sottile. Sei studi su Levinas*, Pisa 2012; *Il filo di Arianna*, Pisa 2020; *Du néant à l'autre. Sur la mort dans la pensée d'Emmanuel Lévinas*, in: *Emmanuel Lévinas*, Textes rassemblés par J. Rolland, Lagrasse, 1984, S. 146–163; *Der gordische Knoten der Zeit. Aspekte des Dialogs zwischen Rosenzweig und Augustinus*, in: *Franz Rosenzweigs "neues Denken"* Internationaler Kongress Kassel 2004, 1. Band: *Selbstbegrenzendes Denken – in philosophos*, hg. Von Wolfdietrich Schmied-Kowarzik, Freiburg-München 2006, S. 323–345.

Ephraim Meir is Professor emeritus of Modern Jewish Philosophy at Bar-Ilan University and President of the Internationale Rosenzweig-Gesellschaft. From 2009 until 2017, he was the Levinas guest Professor for Jewish Dialogue Studies and Interreligious Theology at the Academy of World Religions, University of Hamburg. From August until December 2018 he was a research fellow at the Center of Theological Inquiry in Princeton. From January until June 2021 he was a research fellow at the Stellenbosch Institute for Advanced Study, South Africa. Among his latest works: *Dialogical Thought and Identity. Trans-Different Religiosity in Present Day Societies* (2013), *Interreligious Theology. Its Value and Mooring in Modern Jewish Philosophy* (2015), *Old-New Jewish Humanism* (2018), *Faith in the Plural* (2019) and *The Marvel of Relatedness* (2021). For more information, see https://www.ephraimmeir.com

Gesine Palmer, Dr. phil. (FU Berlin 1996), nach Studium Ev. Theologie, Judaistik, Allgemeine Religionsgeschichte in Hamburg, Berlin und Jerusalem. 1995–2001 Wiss. Mitarbeiterin FU Berlin, 2003–2006 Wiss. Mitarbeiterin FEST Heidelberg, seit 2007 Inhaberin *Büro für besondere Texte*, Berlin, seit 2021 zusätzlich Projektassistentin für christlich-jüdischen Dialog an der Katholischen Akademie Berlin. Gründungsmitglied u. Mitglied des Wiss. Beirats der IRG, Mitherausgeberin des Rosenzweig-Jahrbuches gemeinsam mit Martin Brasser, diverse weitere Mitgliedschaften, diverse Publikationen zu verschiedenen Themen in verschiedenen Medien, zuletzt: *Tausend Tode. Über Trauer reden*, Berlin 2020; zahlreiche Veröffentlichungen zu Hermann Cohen und Franz Rosenzweig, zuletzt: *Redeeming Liturgy: A Eulogist's Perspective on Rosenzweig's Concept of Liturgy*, in: Jahrbuch 12, *Gebet, Praxis, Erlösung*, (hg. Irene Kajon/Luca Bertolino), Freiburg i.Br., 2021, 46–59 und *From Jena to Jerusalem – Judaism as a Method 100 Years Later*, in: *Into Life. Franz Rosenzweig on Knowledge, Aesthetic, and Politics*, (hg. Antonios Kalatzis/ Enrico Lucca), Leiden 2021. Mehr unter https://gesine-palmer.de.

Emanuele Pompetti (geboren 1985 in Atri (TE), Italien) studierte Philosophie unter der Leitung von Prof. Dr. F. P. Ciglia an der Universität Chieti-Pescara und verfasste seine Bachelor- und Masterarbeit über den *Stern der Erlösung* von Franz Rosenzweig. Nach einem weiteren Abschluss in Querflöte am Konservatorium *Luisa D'Annunzio* in Pescara absolvierte er den Europäischen Anpassungslehrgang am Studienseminar Frankfurt. Seit 2012 ist er Studienrat im Kirchendienst an einer katholischen Schule des Bistums Mainz (Edith-Stein-Schule in Darmstadt) mit den Fächern Philosophie, Geschichte und Musik. Zu seiner wissenschaftlichen Tätigkeit zählen u. a. ein Forschungsaufenthalt (2008) an der Universität Freiburg i. B. zur Arbeit über Franz Rosenzweig unter der Beratung von Prof. Dr. Dr. Bernhard Casper, ein Vortrag am *Institut Catholique de Paris* (mit dem Titel: *Le problème du langage dans la philosophie de Franz Rosenzweig*) beim internationalen Kongress der Internationalen Rosenzweig-Gesellschaft *Nous et les autres* sowie der Aufsatz *Le problème du langage dans la Philosophie de Franz Rosenzweig* veröffentlicht in *Rosenzweig Jahrbuch / Rosenzweig Yearbook 7 – Dialogphilosophie / Philosophy of Dialogue*, Karl Alber Verlag, München, 2013.

Norbert Samuelson is professor emeritus at Arizona State University, having held the Grossman Chair of Jewish Studies there.[1] He has written 13 books and over 200 articles, with research interests in Jewish philosophy, philosophy and religion, philosophy and science, 20th-century philosophy (with an emphasis on Alfred North Whitehead and Franz Rosenzweig), history of Western philosophy, and Jewish Aristotelians (with an emphasis on Gersonides). He also lectures at university-level conferences around the world. Samuelson is a founding member of the International Society for Science and Religion and honory president of the International Rosenzweig Society and a member of the Editorial Board of The Journal of Jewish Thought and Philosophy.

---

[1] https://en.wikipedia.org/wiki/Norbert_M._Samuelson#cite_note-bio-1.

Renate Schindler, Dr. phil., studies in ancient philology, philosophy and Roman languages in Heidelberg, Paris, Berlin, Potsdam und Kassel. She submitted her Dissertation thesis (PhD) about *Zeit Geschichte Ewigkeit in Franz Rosenzweigs Stern der Erlösung* at the University of Kassel (2004, published at Parerga / Berlin 2007). It was funded by researcher's grants of the Heinrich-Böll-Foundation (1999–2002) and of the Istituto per gli Studi Filosofici Napoli (2002–2004). Since 2004 research-member of the Franz-Rosenzweig-Gesellschaft (Kassel) and the Hermann Cohen-Gesellschaft (Zürich). Since 1988 she teaches Philosophy and Ethics in two Berlin secondary schools. From 2006 to 2011 lecturer in collaboration with the Aristoteles-University, the Goethe Institute and the German General Consulate of Thessaloniki; organization of Conferences about German-Jewish and medieval philosophy and history in Greece. Since 2013 assistant professor of Leuphana-University Lüneburg in the field of seminars about moral and economy. She published numerous articles on German idealism and Jewish philosophy, above all on Cohen and Rosenzweig. Selective Bibliography: *Zur Zukunftsvision des ewigen Friedens. Denkimpulse in Hermann Cohens Schrift Deutschtum und Judentum*, forthcoming october 2021, in Luca Bertolino (Hg.): „*Facciamo l'uomo*": *Proposte filosofiche per un umanesimo critico. Studi in onore di Andrea Poma*. Mimesis Edizioni (Milano, Udine); *Das neue Denken – ein System der Philosophie? Zur Dialektik von Zeit und Ewigkeit in Franz Rosenzweigs Stern der Erlösung*, forthcoming in: „Filosofia". Rivista fondata nel 1950 da Augusto Guzzo, Quarta serie 2018, *Franz Rosenzweig, storia e redenzione*, Mimesis Edizioni: Milano, Udine, S.23–39; *Morte e critica dell'Idealismo in Franz Rosenzweig e Martin Heidegger*, in: V. Cesarone, F.P. Ciglia, O. Talone: *Filosofia e religione: nemiche mortali?*,Edizioni ETS, Pisa 2012, S. 307–317.

Jules Simon is Professor of Philosophy in the Department of Philosophy at the University of Texas at El Paso in El Paso, Texas. He writes, teaches, and lectures in the areas of phenomenology, ethical theory, aesthetics, and Jewish philosophy. He published a single-authored work, *Art and Responsibility: A Phenomenology of the Diverging Paths of Rosenzweig and Heidegger* (2011) and edited two books focusing on ethics and genocide—*The Double Binds of Ethics after the Holocaust: Salvaging the Fragments* (2009) and *History, Religion, and Meaning: American Reflections on the Holocaust and Israel*. He has published dozens of articles, book chapters, encyclopedia entries, and book reviews and has been invited to present lectures in India, Italy, Mexico, Spain, France, Germany, Israel, England, Wales, Canada, Norway, Finland, and at several universities in the United States. Most recently, he published: "Rosenzweig's *Midrashic* Speech-Acts: From Hegel and German Nationalism to a Modern-Day *ba'al teshuvah*" a chapter in the *Cambridge Companion to Jewish Theology* (2020) and "Rosenzweig and Benjamin, "Aesthetics and Politics: Reflections on Love and the Origins of Fascism" in *Filosofia: 2018 issue*. During Spring 2017, he has been a Research Fellow at the Jawaharlal Nehru Institute for Advanced

Study. He was also an invited Guest Professor at the Universidad Autónoma de Querétaro in Mexico (Summer 2010) and Guest Professor at the University of Tübingen in Germany (Summer 2005). He is Scientific Director for the Center for Science, Technology, Ethics and Policy (CSTEP), a center of ethical inquiry that explores the ethical and political implications of existing and newly emerging phenomena in science and technology.

Der Peer Review Prozess / The Peer Review Process

Most of the following contributions originated from lectures given at the 2012 International Rosenzweig Conference in Belgrade. There, all contributions were intensively discussed by all colleagues present. Following the meeting, the authors from each "neighboring" chapter gave their feedback to their "neighbors" (for example, whoever wrote the fourth introduction received feedback from the authors of the third and fifth introductions). And finally, the whole book was sent for review to an internationally recognized Rosenzweig scholar who is not part of the authorship. After incorporating his suggestions for improvement, this published version of the Belgrade Lectures is now available.

Danksagung / Acknowledgments

The editors would like to thank Prof. Dr. Luca Bertolino and Prof. Hanoch Ben-Pazi for their helpful reviews of this book and the Posen Foundation (Lucerne) for the generous financial support for publishing this book as an open access publication.

Index

A

All   47, 173
Angesicht   154
Angst   17
Antlitz   181
Augenblick   175

B

Bewährung   20, 135
Beziehung   65

C

Chor   120
Christentum   161, 178

D

das All   12

E

Elemente   26, 66
Endfrieden   155
Ereignis   35
Erfahrung   76
Erlösung   136
Ewigkeit   126, 161

F

Friede   154

G

Gebet   109, 134, 142
Gegenwart   126, 151
Gesetz   116, 180
Goethe   138
Gott   26, 35, 175

H

Heidentum 165
Held 64
Herzbuch 100
Heute 124, 151

I

Individuum 50

J

Judentum 162, 178

K

Kernfeuer 146
Kirche 139
Kunst 123
Kunstwerk 93

L

Leben 148, 168
Liebe 105, 116
Lüge 12

M

Mahl 153
Messias 128, 150
Metaphysik 26

N

Nichts 28, 46, 59, 72, 106

O

Offenbarung 100

P

pazifistischer Zug 156

R

Reich Gottes 119

S

Schweigen 152
Selbst 58
Spinoza 6
Sprachdenken 86, 103, 120
Standpunkt 78
Strahlen 159

T

Tat 35
Tatsächlichkeit 30, 176, 182
Tod 16, 42, 170
Trotz 61

U

Umkehr 107
Urheber 93

W

Wahrheit 20, 168
Weltuhr 115
Wir 149
Wirklichkeit 52, 92
Wunder 73, 110, 130

Z

Zeichen 52

www.ingramcontent.com/pod-product-compliance
Lightning Source LLC
Chambersburg PA
CBHW061246230426
43662CB00021B/2449